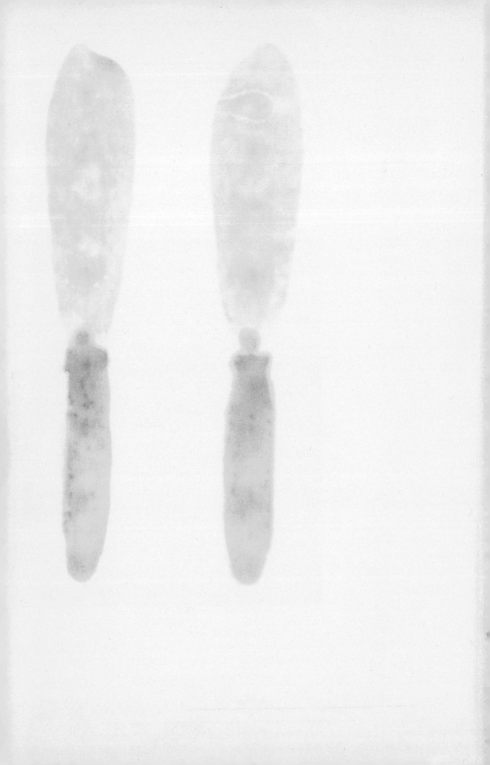

TWAYNE'S WORLD LEADERS SERIES

EDITORS OF THIS VOLUME

Arthur W. Brown
Baruch College, The City University
of New York
and
Thomas S. Knight
Adelphi University

Leon Trotsky

TWLS 72

Leon Trotsky

LEON TROTSKY

By ROBERT D. WARTH
University of Kentucky

TWAYNE PUBLISHERS
A DIVISION OF G. K. HALL & CO., BOSTON

Library of Congress Cataloging in Publication Data

Warth, Robert D
    Leon Trotsky.

    (Twayne's world leaders series ; TWLS 63)
    Bibliography: p. 201–206
    Includes index.
    1. Trotskii, Lev, 1879–1940.   2. Statesmen—
Russia—Biography.   3. Revolutionists—Russia—
Biography.   I. Title.
DK254.T6W37   947.084′092′4 [B]   77-8944
ISBN 0-8057-7720-2

Contents

About the Author

Robert D. Warth is professor of history at the University of Kentucky and specializes in twentieth century Russia and the history of Marxism. He received his graduate training at the University of Chicago, where he was awarded the Ph.D. degree in 1949. Dr. Warth is the author of *The Allies and the Russian Revolution* (1954), *Soviet Russia in World Politics* (1963), and two companion volumes in Twayne's World Leaders series, *Joseph Stalin* (1969) and *Lenin* (1973). He has also contributed articles and reviews to a wide variety of publications, including scholarly journals, encyclopedias, and literary quarterlies. He has traveled extensively in the Soviet Union.

Preface

Compared to his famous colleagues, Lenin and Stalin, Trotsky has been sorely neglected by historians and other scholars. Nearly forty years after his death fewer than half a dozen volumes that can be classified as works of enduring value have been devoted to his career (or some phase of it). Why? The obvious answer—that Trotsky never held supreme power as did Lenin and Stalin—is accurate but not entirely satisfactory. Whatever his rank order among the political luminaries of the modern world, Trotsky was by any standard a revolutionary leader of extraordinary talent whose achievements have not been obliterated by half a century of Soviet misrepresentation.

Without probing more deeply into additional reasons for the dearth of Trotsky studies, it could be said that the existence of a "big work" on the subject—Isaac Deutscher's massive three-volume biography—has discouraged others from undertaking a task that might seem redundant. However, as my comments in the Bibliography suggest, I believe a more critical approach toward Trotsky than Deutscher's relatively benign view is warranted, and within the confines of a short biography I have presented an alternative interpretation. It tends to stress Trotsky's personal failings and political mistakes, although I am fully aware that the traditional explanation for his political defeat—Stalin's control of the party "machine"—cannot be disregarded.

Since Trotsky spent much of his life abroad, I have sought to avoid possible confusion in dating events by using the Western calendar throughout (the Soviet regime adopted it in 1918).

Alexander Rabinowitch, the author of *The Bolsheviks Come to Power* (New York, 1976), and Constance A. Myer, the author of *The Prophet's Army* (Chicago, 1977), kindly permitted me to read copies of their work prior to publication. Travel funds provided by the University of Kentucky Research Foundation made it possible to use Trotsky manuscripts at Harvard, Stanford, and Indiana universities and to visit other research libraries. Anna M. Borguina, curator of the Nicolaevsky Collection at the Hoover Institution, assisted me in locating unpublished Trotsky materials. My wife (with some assistance from Mrs. Natalie Schick) cheerfully assumed the burden of transforming a handwritten manuscript into legible typewritten copy.

ROBERT D. WARTH

University of Kentucky

Chronology

1879   Born in the village of Yanovka in the southern Ukraine.

1888   Attends school in Odessa.

1896   Completes his formal schooling in Nikolayev.

1897   Organizes, with others, the South Russian Workers' Union in Nikolayev.

1898   Arrested for revolutionary activity and imprisoned in Kherson and Odessa.

1900   Marries Alexandra Sokolovskaya, a fellow revolutionary, while in custody.

1902   Escapes from exile in eastern Siberia and settles in London.

1903   Attends Second Congress of the Russian Social Democratic Labor party in London and sides with the Mensheviks.

1904   Severs formal ties with the Mensheviks and settles in Munich.

1905   Returns to Russia and serves as chairman of the St. Petersburg Soviet of Workers' Deputies.

1906   Convicted of revolutionary activity and sentenced to exile in Siberia for life.

1907   Escapes from Siberia, attends Fifth Party Congress in London, and settles in Vienna.

1908   Publishes the Russian language newspaper *Pravda* in Vienna.

1910   Attends party conference in Paris which temporarily unifies Bolshevik and Menshevik factions.

1912   Organizes unity conference of Russian Marxists in Vienna.

1914   Moves to Paris and becomes an editor of *Golos*, a daily newspaper in the Russian language.

1915   Attends anti-war conference of European socialists in Zimmerwald, Switzerland.

1916   Expelled from France for his anti-war activity.

1917   Resides briefly in the United States and returns to Russia after the collapse of the monarchy.
Joins Bolshevik party and elected chairman of the Petrograd Soviet.

Organizes the Bolshevik insurrection against the Provisional Government.

Appointed commissar for foreign affairs in the new Soviet government.

1918 Heads the Russian delegation at the peace negotiations with Germany at Brest–Litovsk.

Appointed commissar of war and organizes the Red Army.

1919 Organizes the successful defense of Petrograd against White forces.

1920 Appointed commissar for transport.

1921 Organizes the suppression of the Kronstadt Revolt by the Red Army.

1922 Rejects appointment as deputy chairman of the Council of People's Commissars (vice premier).

1923 Declines to rally his supporters at the Twelfth Party Congress.

1924 Makes an indirect attack on the party leaders with his essay, "The Lessons of October."

1925 Forced to resign as commissar of war.

1926 Forms a political alliance with Zinoviev and Kamenev against Stalin.

1927 Expelled from the Communist party.

1928 Deported to Alma Ata in Soviet Central Asia.

1929 Exiled to Turkey.

1930 Publishes his autobiography, *My Life*.

1933 Completes his most famous work, *The History of the Russian Revolution*.

Emigrates to France.

1935 Emigrates to Norway.

1936 Accused of organizing a conspiracy against the Soviet government at the first Moscow trial.

1937 Emigrates to Mexico.

Publishes his major anti-Stalinist work, *The Revolution Betrayed*.

1938 Sponsors the founding congress of the Fourth (Trotskyist) International at a meeting near Paris.

1940 Dies in Mexico City after a successful assassination attempt by a Stalinist agent.

CHAPTER 1

Young Bronstein: The Road to Marxism

EARLY on an October morning in 1902 a cab pulled up at the London address of Mr. and Mrs. Richter—better known by their Russian names as Vladimir Ilyich Ulyanov—Lenin—and Nadezhda Krupskaya. The caller knocked three times, as he had been instructed, and was admitted by Krupskaya who greeted him: "The Pero [Pen] has arrived!" Ordinarily an early riser, Lenin was still in bed and the "kindly expression of his face was tinged with justifiable amazement." Krupskaya paid for the cab.[1]

The unexpected visitor was a fugitive from Siberian exile and carried a false passport in the name of one of his former prison guards—Trotsky. "Pero"—or Trotsky—was then just short of his twenty-third birthday, a slender, handsome youth with bushy black hair, pale blue eyes, and a sense of his own importance that never deserted him during the trials and tribulations of his subsequent career as a professional revolutionary, a leader of the Soviet state, somewhat exotic importation in Russia. Like Lenin and most of the 1923, "Trotsky treasures his historical role and would probably be ready to make any personal sacrifice, not excluding the greatest sacrifice of all—that of his life—in order to go down in human memory surrounded by the aureole of a genuine revolutionary leader."[2]

Although History had been supremely generous to Trotsky at the time this judgment was made, it perversely concealed the pitfalls that lay ahead. In 1902 Trotsky was only vaguely known to the leaders of Russian socialism, and his meeting with Lenin was to mark his emergence upon the European scene as one of the revolutionary elite. He had only recently been converted to Marxism. While this doctrine had become thoroughly institutionalized though not yet respectable in western Europe, it was still a novel and somewhat exotic importation in Russia. Like Lenin and most of the radical intelligentsia, Trotsky had been an adherent of Populism, an

11

agrarian brand of socialism that overemphasized the revolutionary ardor of the peasant. The Populists dreamed of bypassing the evils of industrial capitalism by building upon the village commune as the nucleus of a socialist society.

Trotsky's childhood milieu had been that of the countryside, but neither he nor his parents were typical of the Russian peasantry. In the first place, they were kulaks, that is, well-to-do peasants, a status that had been won by shrewdness, frugality, and hard work. Secondly, they were Jews, an unenviable distinction in a land where popular and government-inspired anti-Semitism occasionally flared into violence.

Trotsky's immediate forebears—the family name was Bronstein—had escaped the circumscribed existence of most Jews in the Russian empire when Tsar Alexander I had opened state lands in the southern Ukraine to Jewish settlement early in the nineteenth century. In the spring of 1879 David Leontievich Bronstein, with his wife and two children, moved to a farm of some six-hundred-fifty acres in the province of Kherson not far from the Black Sea. He had purchased over one third of the land and leased the rest from a Colonel Yanovsky—a man whose energy and perseverance had proved inadequate to maintain a much larger estate. The Bronsteins lived in a humble thatched cottage that the colonel had built himself. They raised wheat, barley, and oats as well as an assortment of livestock. To prosperous city dwellers it would have seemed an isolated and spartan existence. But the Bronsteins were used to privation and hardship, and the new farm represented an opportunity to rise above their previous station in life.

On November 7, 1879, a baby boy was born, Lev (or Lyov) Davidovich, the future Leon Trotsky. He was the fifth child, two others having died in infancy. Although his mother and father were preoccupied with running the farm and were by nature unaffectionate, they were able to provide creature comforts and other amenities rare among peasant families. The tender ministrations of a devoted nurse, as well as the solicitous regard of his two sisters, furnished a measure of solace for what must have been a lonely childhood. This deprivation of parental love—if such was indeed the case—may have been responsible for the lack of emotional depth in the personality of the mature Trotsky.

The young boy was bright, energetic, and even-tempered. Although not physically underdeveloped, he took little or no interest in outdoor games and sports. His world was centered around the household, the adjoining workshop, and other farm buildings. The family, like the surrounding village of Yanovka, was culturally impoverished, but such was the normal pattern of life in rural Russia. No newspapers or magazines, still less a library or a school, were readily accessible. But the elder Bronstein, while illiterate, had respect for book learning; and his wife, who could read only with difficulty, obtained an occasional novel from the lending library in the nearest town. Neither seems to have been conventionally religious, and the family spoke a Russian-Ukrainian dialect instead of Yiddish, the customary language of Russian Jews. Mrs. Bronstein, however, retained enough piety to observe the Sabbath and a few rites of orthodox Judaism.

At the age of seven, young Lyova—his affectionate diminutive—was sent to a private Jewish school in the nearby settlement of Gromokla. Since instruction was chiefly in Yiddish, of which he claimed to know nothing, the experience was not a happy one. But he did learn the Russian alphabet, and when he was allowed to return home after a few months, he began to improve his reading and writing skills. Thus began a love affair with words that progressed into a lifelong infatuation. He became a precocious versifier, and although he was an abnormally shy lad, his parents forced him to read his poems aloud before guests. "With a pounding heart, with tears in my eyes, I would read my verses, ashamed of my borrowed lines and limping rhymes," he recollected many years later. "Be that as it may, I had tasted of the tree of knowledge."[3] If he had not yet grasped instinctively the trite formula that "knowledge is power," he dimly perceived that intellectual prowess was the key to personal fulfillment and expanding self-esteem. "In my eyes," he wrote, recalling his feelings a few years later, "authors, journalists, and artists always stood for a world which was more attractive than any other, one open only to the elect."[4]

Perhaps at the time he first became literate—or it may have been as an adolescent—Trotsky acquired the glimmerings of a social conscience. It is also possible that professional revolutionaries have a propensity in adult life to project their political views backward into childhood. At any rate, it seemed to the mature Trotsky that he had sensed as a boy the personal bitterness and grinding poverty imbedded in the structure of the rural economy. But these feelings were the product of a sensitive nature, not those of an incipent rebel, for he had no intuitive understanding of social problems. Although Trotsky was endowed with the wisdom of hindsight, he generously refrained from depicting his father as a grasping kulak in his autobiography.

During the summer of 1888, well over a year from the time Lyova left the Jewish school, a guest from Odessa, who was to have a decisive influence on the young boy, was received in the Bronstein home. His name was Moisei Spentser. He was a nephew of Mrs. Bronstein in his late twenties who suffered from tubercular symptoms and sought a cure in the country air. "A bit of a journalist and a bit of a statistician," he had been barred from seeking a higher education because of a minor political offense. He took a liking to Lyova, tutored him in arithmetic and grammar, and by kindly example smoothed some of the rough edges on the rustic lad. Lyova was enchanted with his new mentor, but was also disquieted: he sensed in him an urban life style radically different from his own.

Spentser left at the end of the summer and not long afterward took as his bride the principal of a state school for Jewish girls in Odessa. They invited Lyova to come and live with them while he attended school. His parents consented, with the understanding that they would pay his expenses, and in the spring of 1889 he set out for Odessa, the busy and cosmopolitan seaport on the Black Sea. It was his first real break with his rural environment. Never again would he be able to adjust to village life, though he was to spend his summer vacations at the Bronstein farm.

Odessa was not simply a large Russian city, but a major melting pot of the Middle East where many nationalities mingled together in relative harmony. Jews were the largest single minority and comprised about thirty per cent of the population. Tsar Alexander III's decree—issued only the year before—had limited Jewish enrollment in secondary schools to a maximum of ten per cent. Lyova took the entrance examinations to enter the St. Paul *Realschule*—a relatively progressive institution founded under German Lutheran auspices—but, because of his inferior educational background, he failed to qualify under the Jewish quota. He then entered the preparatory class attached to the school.

The Spentsers lived in modest circumstances, and their small apartment could barely accommodate the newcomer. He was as-

signed a corner of the dining room, with a curtain to insure a mod-
icum of privacy. It was to remain his bedroom for the first four years
of his schooling. The discipline of his new home he found rather
exacting at first: he was suddenly expected to acquire the civility and
social graces of the urban middle class. But the transition was fairly
smooth despite occasional bouts of homesickness, and he came to
relish the atmosphere of culture and intellectual sophistication that
initially had been somewhat bewildering. The theater proved a
novel and exciting experience, as did the Russian literary classics,
some of which the Spentsers read to him in the evenings. As for his
schoolwork, he quickly distinguished himself as a model student in
both deportment and scholarship. He probably struck many of his
classmates as excessively bookish and inordinately vain: he enjoyed
displaying his superior knowledge and would dredge up little-
known facts to confound his teachers. As in his home village of
Yanovka, he took no interest in sports and games. Nor did he express an interest in the sea, the most striking feature in the area.
Not once during his seven years in Odessa did he go boating, learn
to swim, or try his hand at fishing. It was a curiously circumscribed
existence, yet it obviously suited the precocious youngster. It was
not learning for its own sake that he valued as much as inflating his
own ego by engaging in an intellectual competition that he felt
confident of winning.

When Lyova was in the second grade—his third year in
Odessa—the even tenor of his life was rudely interrupted by a
traumatic episode. He was expelled from St. Paul's for helping to
organize a protest against an unpopular teacher. Without informing
his parents, he stayed on with his guardians until the end of the
school year and then went home, sorely troubled, for his usual
summer vacation. His elder sister was commissioned to break the
news while Lyova departed to visit a friend. His father took it in
good part, apparently rather proud that his son had the courage to
defy the academic establishment.

Restless and moody, Lyova temporarily lost interest in study but
returned to Odessa late in the summer to take a special oral examination permitting his readmission. He passed satisfactorily and was
allowed to enter the third grade. His relations with his classmates
were thereafter regulated by their conduct at the time of the original
incident. The informers he cut completely; his defenders he rewarded with friendship. "Such, one might say, was the first political

test I underwent," he wrote, obviously thinking of his ill-fortune in the 1920's. "The talebearers and the envious at one pole, the frank, courageous boys at the other, and the neutral, vacillating mass in the middle."[5] One doubts that human beings, whether boys or grown men, can be so neatly categorized. At the age of fourteen, Lyova was forced to drop out of school. He suffered from an ailment which the doctors, ignorant of psychosomatic medicine, diagnosed as "chronic catarrh of the digestive tract." It was, in fact, a nervous stomach and was to trouble him for the rest of his life. He returned to the country, and a tutor was engaged for the balance of the school year. But the two did not get along well—the tutor, according to Trotsky, had serious defects of personality and character—and their relationship ended after a violent quarrel.

Lyova returned to St. Paul's for two more years of study. In 1894, shortly after he began the fifth grade, Tsar Alexander III died. Classes were cancelled and memorial services, "trying and dull," were held; but the political implications of the Tsar's death apparently made no impression on any of the students. Alexander's reign had been brief and reactionary, and liberals hoped, as they always did with each succession to the throne, that the new ruler would be susceptible to moderate reform. Again, they were disappointed. Nicholas II, who did not envisage a break with his father's legacy, sharply rebuked those who would allow themselves to be carried away by "senseless dreams." A weak but stubborn man, Nicholas proved even less competent than his predecessors to govern his realm with any consistent policy or with any sense of purpose beyond the dubious mystique provided by the Romanov dynasty.

The Spentsers and their protégé shared the vague liberalism that prevailed in intellectual circles. But active opposition to the tsarist regime, either by word or deed, would not have occurred to them. Nevertheless, Trotsky indicates that his seven years at St. Paul's, including the preparatory class, challenged his political indifference. The school sowed in him, "contrary to its direct purpose, the seeds of enmity for the existing order." Possibly so, for revolutionaries, like everyone else, are a product of their environment, and formal schooling is an indispensable part of it. More convincing is his somewhat grudging admission that however mediocre his teachers seemed in retrospect, they instilled in him certain fundamentals: "elementary knowledge, the habit of methodical work, and outward discipline."[6]

St. Paul's did not offer a seventh year, as did most Russian schools, and young Bronstein completed his last year at Nikolayev, a smaller city near the Black Sea and closer to home than Odessa. The decision was presumably the elder Bronstein's: He could not be unaware that his son was drifting away from the rural ties of his childhood, and that their own relationship had become strained. The generation gap was only partly responsible. Lyova had gradually succumbed to an urban life style and was increasingly disturbed by the bleak realities of peasant existence. As if suffering from a guilty conscience because his father had now become a prosperous landowner, his behavior was "more unbalanced and quarrelsome" at Yanovka. During vacations he helped with the bookkeeping, and there were "sudden, brief flashes of temper" between father and son when wages were paid. The farm workers sensed that the boy sympathized with them—not that they were ever cheated—and the elder Bronstein naturally resented the implication that he was a hard and unfeeling employer.

Lyova's year in Nikolayev—he was then seventeen—was critical to his political development and emotional maturity. He roomed with a family whose children were somewhat older and already committed, at least in theory, to the revolutionary cause. Unwilling to expose his own political innocence, he adopted an attitude of ironic superiority, posing as a conservative sophisticate who had gone beyond the stage of indulging in "socialist utopias". For several months he maintained this role, too proud to admit that his judgment had been faulty. He then reversed his politics so abruptly and with such passionate assurance that some of his radical friends backed away in alarm. His conversion to an ill-defined socialism was based less upon rational conviction than upon a subconscious protest; Lyova was perhaps reverting to his childhood disdain of social injustice. He was still abysmally ignorant of politics and the rival ideologies of Populism and Marxism. Every new conversation forced him to this "bitter, painful and desperate conclusion."[7]

Young Bronstein began to cut classes and to neglect his studies. However, his natural brilliance and considerable store of knowledge maintained his reputation as an outstanding student. He began, impatiently and unsystematically, to pore over political pamphlets and serious works in history and the social sciences. Lacking proper guidance and a secure intellectual anchorage, he remained adrift in a sea of competing ideas and fashionable doctrines. His enthusiasms were intense but short-lived. For several months he became a staunch disciple of Jeremy Bentham, whose utilitarian ethic of pleasure and pain he would later denounce as social cookbook recipes. He then embraced the "realistic aesthetics" of Nikolai Chernyshevsky, whose novel *What Is To Be Done?* had such a profound impact on Lenin and other members of the radical intelligentsia. Karl Marx was the one notable author who repelled him. Although it is doubtful whether he read Marx firsthand, he was skeptical of Marxism because it appeared to be a completed system.

Trotsky (as we may, somewhat prematurely, begin to call him) found a friend and mentor in a self-educated gardener of Czech birth, Franz Shvigovsky, whose cottage became a meeting place for radical students and a few veterans of revolutionary Populism. The elder Bronstein, in Nikolayev to market grain, learned of his son's dangerous proclivities and sought to wield his paternal authority. He concluded that a course in civil engineering—a sensible and practical subject—would be the right measure for weaning his errant son from revolutionary nonsense. Furthermore, a trained engineer would certainly be a useful asset around the farm, where several buildings were in the planning stage. A more tactful man might have persuaded the headstrong boy, who was sorely troubled about a future career, to accept his viewpoint. But he adopted a tone of ultimatum, and the two had several stormy scenes that culminated in a threat by the senior Bronstein to cut off his son's financial support. To the young rebel this was insufferable parental tyranny: "His revolt against his father and his revolt against the social system now became united."[8]

Trotsky moved in with Shvigovsky, and with others they lived a communal life, meager in material rewards but heady with youthful idealism. He earned a little money as a private tutor and joined his fellow "communards" in a variety of good works. They sought to organize a society for the distribution of "useful books," but their contacts with "the people" were limited. Another project, a "university" for mutual instruction, foundered when their intellectual resources proved inadequate. Trotsky himself became a "sociologist" and delivered two lectures before running out of things to say.

He even attempted, with one of his friends, to write a play with "social tendencies"; this too expired from intellectual malnutrition. The commune became so notorious as a potential hotbed of sedition that the police planted an informer in their midst, ostensibly a common laborer. Efforts to convert him to socialism were naturally unavailing, though he feigned great interest to draw out the conspirators. Since no arrests followed, the local authorities must have concluded that these young busybodies were essentially harmless—talkers but not doers.

The commune and its circle of sympathizers were overwhelmingly Populist in sentiment. Alexandra Sokolovskaya was one exception. She was an attractive girl in her early twenties who had become a Marxist. She and Trotsky became formidable rivals; their mutual attraction was concealed by sarcastic outbursts. "You still think you're a Marxist?" Trotsky taunted her on one occasion. "I can't imagine how a young girl so full of life can stand that dry, narrow, impractical stuff!" "I can't imagine," was her rejoinder, "how a person who thinks he is logical can be contented with a headful of vague, idealistic emotions!" Later, at a New Year's eve party, Trotsky pretended that he had been won over to Marxism and then proposed a toast: "A curse upon all Marxists and upon those who want to bring dryness and hardness into all the relations of life."[9] Sokolovskaya, hurt and angry, abruptly left the party, vowing never to speak to her tormenter again.

Perhaps ashamed of his boorishness, Trotsky omitted any reference to his quarrelsome relationship with Sokolovskaya from his autobiography. Her arguments had eroded his brash certitude; but, as in his earlier conversion to revolutionary socialism, he refused to admit to himself that the Marxist doctrine was rational and "scientific," whereas the Populists' ideas were "romantic" and utopian.

Trotsky made a final gesture toward respectability before plunging into a revolutionary career. Having completed his secondary education in the late spring of 1896, he accepted his father's invitation to visit Yanovka "as a guest." Their antagonism flared anew, and one of Trotsky's uncles, an engineer from Odessa and a witness to their "daily scenes of battle," offered some sensible advice: "Get the boy out of the house and stop arguing with him. The more you insist, the more determined he is."[10] He proposed that his nephew come and live with him and attend some classes in mathematics at the University of Odessa. The offer seemed a reasonable compromise: the young firebrand, not yet eighteen, was less cocksure about his future plans than he pretended.

Apparently, Trotsky did not officially enroll at the university during the fall term, but he did attend several lectures, and his natural gift for mathematics tempted him momentarily into pursuing the subject professionally. The balance of his time he spent in rather amateurish "revolutionary" activity—obtaining illegal literature, arguing with local Marxists, and agitating workers. In December, aboard the last steamer before winter set in, he returned to Nikolayev and to the familiar haunts of the Shvigovsky circle.

Although Trotsky was somewhat vague about it in later years—perhaps deliberately so—he became more sympathetic to the Marxist position in the months that followed, yet he was not prepared to sever his ties with Populism. He was the key figure in founding a revolutionary organization called the South Russian Workers' Union, a name chosen to represent expectations rather than reality, as its members—students and workers—were recruited locally. He drafted a constitution along social democratic lines, but there were no hard and fast ideological requirements, and Populists were welcomed along with Marxists. Most of the workers were concerned with economic issues, hardly aware of the finer points of doctrine that separated the two strands of socialism in Russia. By midsummer the Union claimed two hundred dues-paying members, an impressive number considering the feeble response that similar groups received in far larger cities than Nikolayev.

A soiled and mutilated copy of the *Communist Manifesto*, obtained in Odessa, served as a basic instructional text. Eventually the group was able to provide its own literature, chiefly proclamations that Trotsky wrote in longhand for the hectograph, a crude substitute for a regular printing press. It took him about two hours to transcribe a page for duplication—back-breaking work, both literally and figuratively. In the fall he also took over the task of publishing and distributing a little magazine entitled *Nashe Dyelo* ("Our Cause"). His dedication was awesome. There had been "a little of the young rooster in his radicalism," but it was now replaced by a more mature and disciplined commitment.

Part of this transformation may have been wrought by Sokolovskaya. Trotsky and she became reconciled: he now loved her with a passion akin to his revolutionary fervor. Poised, practical, and compassionate, she was not only older and in some ways wiser than her fiancé (they probably became lovers in 1897), but she also possessed greater emotional maturity and a less demanding ego. She spoke of him in later years, long after their romantic ties had been severed, with friendly detachment: "He can be very tender and sympathetic, and he can be very assertive and arrogant; but in one thing he never changes—that is his devotion to the revolution. In all my revolutionary experience I have never met any other person so completely consecrated."[11]

The local police, seemingly no more experienced than the Union members, were disinclined to believe that the assortment of young misfits congregating in Shvigovsky's garden could instigate so much mischief among the factory and dock workers. Surely, they reasoned, there must be older and wiser heads guiding these troublemakers. Surveillance increased, informers penetrated the organization, and finally, in February, 1898, there were mass arrests. Trotsky was among more than two hundred suspects incarcerated in the old prison in Nikolayev. After three weeks in a roomy but unheated cell, he was transferred to the nearby city of Kherson. There his accommodations were even more depressing, though he suffered less from the winter cold. With inadequate food, no change of his lice-ridden clothing, no soap or washing facilities, and no recreation or reading material, he endured three months of solitude worse than any he was to encounter in the future. At last a large parcel sent by his mother, expedited by a bribe to the assistant warden, provided such luxuries as fresh linen, blankets, soap, canned goods, and fresh fruit.

Not long afterward Trotsky was escorted via steamboat to a modern prison in Odessa. Once again he was placed in solitary confinement; yet this time he was able to communicate with his fellow prisoners in various ways, including the traditional method of tapping on the walls. The regimen was more enlightened here than in Nikolayev and Kherson, and he spent a good deal of time reading conservative historical and religious periodicals—about all that the meager prison library had to offer. He "studied them insatiably," learning the "sects and heresies of ancient and modern times," Russian orthodoxy, and "the best arguments against Catholicism, Protestantism, Tolstoyism, and Darwinism."[12] He indulged in theological disputation with one of the guards, a pious neurotic "well read in the holy books," and teased him by pointing out that the jailers played the same role toward their prisoners as the Roman soldiers did toward the Christian saints. Through his sister he obtained copies of the New Testament in Russian, English, French, German, and Italian, thereby improving his language skills as well as his knowledge of the scriptures, though his linguistic aptitude was to remain mediocre. He never did master a foreign language despite his long residence abroad.

Eventually Trotsky had access to secular books sent in from the outside and read a wide range of theoretical and historical works. Darwin's *Origin of Species*, apparently the only scientific treatise available, made a profound impression on him. "Darwin stood for me like a mighty doorkeeper at the entrance to the temple of the universe. I was intoxicated with his minute, precise, conscientious, and at the same time powerful, thought." He had now become a confirmed Marxist and credited Darwin with destroying the last of his ideological prejudices: "Through obstinacy I [had] still defended, against the Marxian epidemic that was spreading among the intelligentsia, my 'individuality,' a sufficiently ignorant one."[13] Marx's own writings were unobtainable.

The history of Freemasonry, a subject he chanced across, held a special fascination for him. He acquired a notebook of a thousand numbered pages and for months copied excerpts from his voluminous reading, interspersed with his own reflections on Freemasonry and his other pet topic—the materialist philosophy of history. The notebook was temporarily preserved but was eventually lost in Switzerland, much to his regret.

The inquiry into the "Nikolayev affair" took place toward the close of Trotsky's first year in prison. The evidence was sufficiently damning to convict him, but the procedure was administrative rather than judicial. Political prisoners were supposedly protected by certain legal safeguards; actually the few that they did have could be easily ignored by the government. Another year passed before a verdict was pronounced: four years of exile for Trotsky and three other principal defendants in eastern Siberia. They spent the winter and spring of 1900 in a transfer prison in Moscow, where Trotsky and Sokolovskaya (arrested later) were married by a Jewish chaplain. A previous attempt to marry had been thwarted by the elder Bronstein, who regarded his son's fiancée as a corrupting influence and took the trouble to telegraph the minister of interior in St.

Petersburg. Marriages of convenience were common among revolutionaries sent into exile, and Trotsky's reticent account of their romance reinforces this wholly misleading impression.

The Moscow prison was a relatively lenient institution. No longer in solitary confinement, Trotsky shared a large tower room with a number of other male "politicals." He was impudent and defiant of authority. On one occasion he was dragged off to an isolated cell and placed on a bread-and-water diet for a breach of discipline. Always eager for self-expression, he wrote incessantly and managed to smuggle out a manuscript on the labor movement in Nikolayev and Odessa that was published later in Geneva. He studied with great care Lenin's *Development of Capitalism in Russia* which had appeared in a legal edition the previous year. Reflecting upon the bitter controversy aroused by the revisionist critique of Marxism written by Eduard Bernstein, a German Social Democrat, he sided with the apostles of orthodoxy.

During the early summer the exiles began their long and tedious journey. They traveled by rail to Irkutsk in eastern Siberia, and there the party split up according to ultimate destination. Trotsky and his wife were barged down the Lena River—that is, northward toward the Arctic Ocean. At intervals one or two exiles would be put ashore at the tiny villages along the bank. The former gold mining settlement of Ust-Kut, with perhaps a hundred peasant huts, became the couple's new home just as the Siberian winter set in. The scenic beauty of the place made little impression on Trotsky, who was wholly involved with his books and his wife. Cockroaches were a major problem, and in the summer gnats and mosquitoes made outdoor activity an ordeal. Transfers were readily obtained from the provincial governor at Irkutsk, and for a time they lived at a village farther east. Since their government allowance of nineteen rubles a month was barely adequate, Trotsky found a job working for a rich merchant. He was soon discharged, however, because of a billing error he made, and they returned to Ust-Kut in the dead of winter. A daughter, then ten months old, had increased both the size of the family and the burden of his responsibility.

A few months later they moved south to Verkholensk, where a large colony of exiles resided. Populists, many of whom had lived there for years, formed a local "aristocracy," while a smaller number of Marxists, mostly young people, composed a separate clique. Personal squabbles, alcoholism, and suicide were a part of the daily routine. "Hard intellectual work," as Trotsky observed, was the only way to preserve one's emotional stability under such conditions. He and several other Marxists were among the few who followed that prescription. Adopting the pen name "Antid Oto," he became a contributor to a liberal newspaper published in Irkutsk. The name was chosen at random: *Antidoto* happened to be the first word he came across when he opened an Italian dictionary. He jestingly told his friends that he wanted to inject the Marxist "antidote" into the bourgeois press. His specialty was the short essay, usually involving a literary theme or a sketch of Siberian peasant life. His style, somewhat immature and at times excessively florid, was neverthe-less vivid and forceful, conveying an emotional intensity characteris-tic of his later writings and speeches. Wary of the censorship, he criticized the government only by allusion and innuendo, and occa-sionally resorted to a semi-fictional technique. His Marxism was lightly applied and generally free of the doctrinaire spirit and sectar-ian cant that later came to disfigure party pronouncements and other examples of official dogma. The range of his knowledge was impressive, if sometimes ostentatious, for so young a man. As a self-taught journalist, he acquired useful skills that would serve him well in the future: He could express his views clearly and he had a reliable means of earning a living. During his two years as a literary correspondent, he earned a solid reputation among the Siberian exiles and even a kind of modest renown among radicals in Euro-pean Russia.

In the summer of 1902 Trotsky received a number of books whose bindings concealed literary contraband from abroad. For the first time he learned of *Iskra* ("The Spark"), the chief organ of Russian Marxism. He was also impressed with Lenin's seminal work on the problem of creating a party of professional revolutionaries entitled (in honor of Chernyshevsky's novel) *What Is To Be Done?* His own prowess as a journalist and as the author of proclamations for the fledgling Siberian Union—a Social Democratic organization of only regional appeal—suddenly seemed inconsequential in comparison with the mighty deeds of Lenin and his colleagues who were fighting tsarist absolutism from their European exile.

Trotsky, though he was romanticizing the "elder statesmen" of the movement—no centralized party of Russian Marxists yet existed—felt compelled to join the heroic struggle from a better vantage point than the Siberian wilderness. His resolve to escape was tempered by his status as a family man: he now had two daughters, the younger only four months old. Sokolovskaya, a dedicated revolutionary first and a wife and mother second, quelled his doubts with two words: "You must." Both of them scorned "bourgeois morality," and without further deliberation, preparations began for the long and presumably difficult journey to European Russia.

Escape from Verkholensk itself presented no great problem. Security was lax, but to increase the odds in Trotsky's favor they prepared a dummy which occupied his bed for several days and satisfied the local police inspector that his charge was indisposed. Meanwhile the fugitive, buried under a load of hay in a peasant's cart, reached Irkutsk and the Trans-Siberian Railroad. Friends provided him with clothes, a suitcase, and a false passport. The station police, with surprising indifference, let him pass without a close check on his credentials. The journey by train was slow and monotonous—"quite without romantic glamour"—but also without incident, and he read a Russian translation of the *Iliad*, drank endless cups of tea, and "dreamed of the life abroad."[14]

At the Volga city of Samara, Trotsky broke his journey. The Russian headquarters of the *Iskra* organization was located there under the leadership of Gleb Krzhizhanovsky, a friend of Lenin's and later head of the Soviet government's State Planning Commission. Trotsky carried a letter of introduction from his contacts in Irkutsk, and Krzhizhanovsky received him cordially, eventually sending him to Kharkov, Poltava, and Kiev to strengthen the *Iskra* group's influence in the Ukraine. The mission accomplished little, and he returned to Samara to find that Lenin had written urging that he be sent abroad.

Provided with money and a railway ticket, Trotsky (or Pero, as Krzhizhanovsky nicknamed him) made his way to the frontier. With the help of a revolutionary contact and professional smugglers he crossed into Austria. He had been overly generous with his money—a habit of profligacy that was to endure—and had only enough for a ticket to Vienna. There, with his customary self-assurance, he called on Victor Adler, the leading Austrian Social Democrat, and obtained money to continue his journey. After a stopover in Zurich, where he aroused Paul Axelrod, one of *Iskra*'s board of directors, in the middle of the night and replenished his funds, he went on to Paris. Finally, he arrived in London, and his long pilgrimage from Siberia to the intellectual center of Russian Marxism came to an end.

CHAPTER 2

The Iskra *Period and the "Majestic Prologue" of 1905*

L ENIN was impressed with the bright and energetic young man, and Trotsky promptly "fell in love" with *Iskra*. He studied the published issues with rapt attention and soon became a contributor, at first writing only short notes but later graduating to political articles and even editorials. Krupskaya found him a room nearby where two of Lenin's associates from *Iskra*—Julius Martov and Vera Zasulich—also had accommodations. He saw a good deal more of his fellow lodgers than he did of Lenin. A somewhat austere family man, Lenin was less given to the bohemian habits and endless debates of the Russian émigrés.

Trotsky did not make a special effort to improve his English, and during his relatively short stay in London he absorbed very little of what the great metropolis had to offer. Because of his "topographic cretinism," as he called it, he found his way around with difficulty. He thought the convolutions of British Marxism dull, and the existence of Christian Socialist churches—he attended services at one with Lenin and Krupskaya—was beyond his comprehension. The one institution he deemed highly praiseworthy was the great library of the British Museum, where he gorged himself as time permitted. In order to test his mettle as a public speaker, a lecture on historical materialism was arranged for him in the Whitechapel district. He acquitted himself admirably, and during the discussion period he jousted successfully with two distinguished émigrés, one a Populist, the other an anarchist. "I was honestly amazed," he recalled, "at the infantile arguments with which these worthy elders were trying to crush Marxism."[1]

Trotsky's natural talent as a speaker was now duly recognized, and he was dispatched on a lecture tour to Brussels, Liège, and Paris. During his trip, Lenin recalled Trotsky to London with the intention of sending him back to Russia. Apparently, Krzhizhanovsky had requested Trotsky's services. But Leon Deutsch, a Marxist of the older generation, interceded and succeeded in persuading Lenin that the "youngster" needed a bit of seasoning abroad before being cast adrift in the Russian underground. Lenin finally agreed, and Trotsky settled in Paris, where the Russian student colony, the largest in western Europe, was in a state of ferment over the different schools of revolutionary strategy. He had been assigned the task of converting these young intellectuals to orthodox Marxism. He spent many of his free hours with Natalia Sedova, a student at the Sorbonne and a member of the *Iskra* faction. In time she became his second wife and lifelong companion, though the legal tie with Sokolovskaya was never formally broken. His parents later helped to bring up his two daughters. His reticence in his autobiography on this aspect of his personal life betrays some embarrassment at the rather shabby treatment he accorded his wife and children, however lofty his motives for leaving Sokolovskaya in the first place.

Under Sedova's tutelage Trotsky's initial indifference to the artistic and cosmopolitan charms of Paris gave way to restrained admiration. It was in some degree, he confessed, "the case of a barbarian struggling for self-preservation." If his understanding of Western culture, especially its art, remained "pure dilettantism," his taste was nevertheless more highly cultivated than that of most Russian Marxists—Lenin included—whose contempt for bourgeois civilization concealed various degrees of nationalism and philistinism.

Trotsky's infatuation with *Iskra* became less like puppy love. He had innocently assumed that such a noble publication must of necessity be guided by men whose ideals and character were as pure and high-minded as the cause they served. But *Iskra* had been born in strife and bitterness, and a kind of armed truce allowed Lenin, as de facto managing editor, to run the newspaper in London with a relatively free hand. His latent rival, Georgi Plekhanov, the patriarch of Russian Marxism, resided in Geneva but exercised his formidable influence as a member of the editorial board by mail and by periodic trips to London. Lenin's relations with his other colleagues—he had been especially fond of Martov—were not as cordial as they had been. There were inevitable differences of temperament and working style, and in view of the sharp political disagreements that would soon disrupt the unity of the *Iskra* organization, it is tempting to read more into the situation than a sober appraisal might warrant. Trotsky, for example, later decided that Lenin was a "hard" and Martov a "soft" on the basis of such intangibles as "resoluteness and readiness to go on to the end." He embellishes this estimate with such colorful and probably irrelevant vignettes as Lenin glancing at Martov "with a critical and somewhat suspicious look," while Martov, "feeling his glance, would look down and move his thin shoulders nervously."[2]

Whatever the reasons for the incipient discord, Trotsky's own role in the affair was not without significance. Lenin proposed in March, 1903, that the brilliant newcomer be admitted to the editorial board as a "man of rare abilities" and of "conviction and energy." True, he was young and his literary style was a bit too ornate, but he would outgrow it. Martov, and all but one member of the board, enthusiastically seconded the idea. The dissenter was Plekhanov. Something of a haughty patrician, he had taken an instinctive dislike to the brash young prodigy and seized upon Lenin's comment about Trotsky's style as a sufficient disqualification. Plekhanov's veto could have been overridden, but to restore peace Trotsky was simply invited to editorial conferences in an advisory capacity. The whole question of membership on the editorial board was deferred to a forthcoming party congress that was expected to unite all Russian Marxists in a single organization.

Despite Lenin's objections, *Iskra* itself was moved to Geneva shortly after the controversy over Trotsky. Presumably the decision rested on practical grounds—living costs were lower and Russia was more accessible for distribution purposes. But the other editors, while recognizing Lenin's dedication and hard work, apparently resented his stranglehold on what was supposed to be a cooperative enterprise. Certainly Plekhanov and Axelrod did. Trotsky, though he had reason to be grateful to his benefactor, did not look upon himself as Lenin's disciple. He tended to share the "soft" views of his good friends Martov, Zasulich, and Axelrod, and he naturally resented Plekhanov's hostile attitude. This complex intermingling of motives, temperament, and ideology was soon to have a denouement—but in a manner that none of the principals anticipated.

On July 30, 1903, the long awaited congress of Russian Social Democrats convened in Brussels. It was called the "second" in deference to a stillborn conference of Russian Marxists held at Minsk in 1898. Lenin, with Krupskaya's secretarial assistance, maintained extensive contacts in Russia, and the *Iskra* faction easily controlled a majority of the fifty-seven delegates, who in theory represented twenty-six different Marxist organizations. Trotsky had qualms about this projected "dictatorship of the editorial board," but Lenin argued pragmatically that in the existing disarray of Russian Social Democracy there was no other choice.

Trotsky attended the congress as a delegate of the Siberian Union, though his mandate from that organization was tenuous at best. He carried a false Bulgarian passport, and as "Mr. Samokovliev" he received a polite invitation to visit the local police station. He wisely demurred, for those who complied with a similar request were summarily ordered to leave the country within twenty-four hours. In addition to the unwelcome attentions of the Belgian police and of tsarist agents, the warehouse where the proceedings opened was overrun with rats and infested with fleas. After a week the congress moved to London, where the political atmosphere was more benign and the meeting hall—a "socialist" church—was less attractive to vermin.

The only factions that seemed likely to contest the *Iskra* majority were the so-called Jewish Bund and an amorphous group known as the Economists. The five delegates representing the Bund argued for autonomy within the party and claimed the exclusive right to interpret Social Democracy to Jewish workers. Trotsky, whose natural eloquence had been seasoned on the lecture circuit, was among those of Jewish origin who condemned this approach as a form of separatism. He was willing to concede a minimal amount of cultural nationalism, such as the right to speak one's native tongue, but he firmly believed that Marxism was based on a theory of international working class solidarity that rendered superfluous the outmoded distinctions of race, religion, and nationality. By tacit agreement, only Trotsky and others of Jewish origin spoke about the issue, and the Bundists were overwhelmingly defeated.

Economism, the doctrine that bread-and-butter issues are more meaningful to the average worker than political activity, had languished in 1901 as strikes and demonstrations tended to undercut its major premise. But the Economists, using the nomenclature of the French Revolution, also objected to the "Jacobinism" of the orthodox majority, and their strength was undetermined until the

proceedings at the congress revealed that only two or three delegates could be tentatively identified with the original cause. Trotsky
distinguished himself as "Lenin's cudgel" by lambasting the
Economist speakers, and ironically, in view of his later stand, he
chose to defend the centralized party structure that appeared to be
replacing the democratic federalism of previous Russian Social
Democracy.

The *Iskra* steamroller, to the surprise of everyone concerned,
began to falter once these and other peripheral issues had been
settled. Policy differences, somewhat exaggerated in retrospect,
combined with human frailty to disrupt the party on the very eve of
its cohesion. Lenin's zeal, made more tactless by nervous fatigue,
proved self-defeating. His resolution to define party membership
lost by five votes to a formula proposed by Martov. Lenin envisaged
a small and disciplined band of revolutionary conspirators, whereas
Martov conceived of a broader (but still elitist) organization of like-
minded individuals. Trotsky voted with the majority, remaining
loyal to his "soft" friends. Lenin did not take this rebuff lightly and
contradicted his conciliatory remark that disagreement was not a
life-and-death matter to the party: "We shall not perish from a bad
clause in our bylaws!"[3]

There followed what can only be regarded as a disguised struggle
for power between Lenin and Martov, a fateful confrontation that
produced two parties instead of one. Lenin redoubled his efforts,
canvassing Trotsky, among others, with dogged determination but
little success. At one *Iskra* caucus, which Trotsky chaired, Lenin
lost his self-control and stalked out of the meeting, banging the door
behind him. It was good luck rather than diligence that enabled
Lenin to win a hollow victory in the end. The five Bundists and two
so-called Economists quit the congress, leaving him with a narrow
voting edge. Lenin took advantage of his slight majority by estab-
lishing a new editorial board for *Iskra*. He removed Zasulich, Axelrod, and Alexander Potresov (all "softs") and reappointed himself,
Plekhanov, and Martov. The latter spurned the gesture by refusing
to serve. Lenin also had his way by securing his men positions on
the Central Committee.

Exhausted and embittered, the delegates called a premature halt
to the congress on August 23, but not before passing a series of
innocuous resolutions that were designed to conceal the rupture in
the party by creating a false sense of solidarity. Lenin's followers

came to be called Bolsheviks (majoritarians), while Martov and his group passively accepted the Menshevik (minoritarian) label despite the short-lived predominance of the Leninists.

To Trotsky, who had offered a motion to uphold the old editorial board, Lenin's conduct was unpardonable, "both horrible and outrageous." He believed that he had taken a morally principled stand, whereas Lenin had become the "party's disorganizer," imposing his "iron fist" for the satisfaction of his own lust for power.[4] He made his opinion known with his usual vehemence, thus aggravating a breach that was to remain unrepaired for fourteen years. His estimate of Lenin, which he had cause to regret in later years (and for which he made handsome amends), was not entirely off the mark. Lenin may not have been fanatical; however, he was awesomely self-confident and had an implacable will, precisely those characteristics necessary for leading a revolutionary party in an assault upon the tsarist redoubt. His "power hunger" was less a thirst for personal glory and historical immortality—traits more in keeping with Trotsky's personality—than an impassioned drive to mold an underground party in his own ruthless image. That he had dictatorial ambitions in 1903, even over his own faction, seems far-fetched. Yet he remained stubbornly convinced that his policy was wholly correct, though he had the grace to admit that he had "behaved and acted in a state of frightful irritation."

Trotsky became a Menshevik, but his allegiance, never wholehearted, was brief. Like Plekhanov, he deplored the schism and favored measures to repair it despite the aggressiveness with which he attacked Lenin. Martov, deeply alienated, was more reluctant than his associates to reach a compromise. Preliminary negotiations, however, took place through intermediaries, and when they led nowhere a strategy conference of leading Mensheviks convened in Geneva early in the fall. It was agreed that a boycott of *Iskra* and the Central Committee should continue. Martov and Trotsky prepared a pompous and somewhat belligerent resolution giving notice that their faction would pursue the fight as a "literary group." A five-man committee, including Trotsky, became the cutting edge of the anti-Bolshevik campaign.

The weak link in Lenin's armor was Plekhanov. Astonishingly, considering their past differences, the father figure of Russian Marxism had emerged as something of a Leninist shield-bearer. But the pressure from his old comrades and his growing uneasiness at

Lenin's intransigence proved more decisive than his temporary commitment to Bolshevik policy. He proposed that the original editorial board be restored, and when Lenin refused he threatened to resign. For Lenin to become the sole editor of *Iskra* without Plekhanov's moral authority behind him was clearly untenable. He then made what turned out to be a serious tactical blunder in tendering his own resignation instead. The old editors were reappointed, and in their wake came Trotsky, still a precocious upstart in the jaundiced view of the veteran Plekhanov. As a staunch supporter of what had now emerged as the winning coalition, Trotsky could not be politely brushed aside. He resumed his contributions to *Iskra* but not without receiving complaints from Plekhanov, who, though now himself a critic of Lenin, resented Trotsky's impudent sallies at the expense of a former colleague.

The antagonism between the two came to a head in March, 1904, when Trotsky's article on the Russo-Japanese war, which had begun shortly before, aroused Plekhanov's ire for its alleged stylistic atrocities and fuzzy ideas. The charge, while not without merit, seems to have been a pretext for the virtual ultimatum that Plekhanov presented to his fellow editors: either accept his resignation or refuse Trotsky's further contributions. Martov and his associates were able to delay a decision for several week's. They accused Plekhanov of acting for personal motives—probably a correct assessment—and rejected Trotsky's offer to leave Geneva for underground work in Russia. But in April, when Plekhanov carried out his threat, they felt obliged to jettison their junior partner, who was already beginning to entertain doubts about the Menshevik program (or so he later maintained).

Trotsky was exasperated by the incident, and no doubt it played a major part in his decision to sever his connections with the Mensheviks five months later. He left Geneva for Munich, glad of an opportunity to rid himself, if only temporarily, of Russian émigré politics. His host was Alexander Helphand, a Russian of Jewish origin who had settled in Germany and made a reputation in Marxist circles with a series of books and articles written under his pen name—Parvus. The circumstances of their initial acquaintance are unknown, but the cosmopolitan Parvus, about a dozen years his senior, proved an excellent guide to the artistic treasures and bohemian haunts of his adopted city. The two became fast friends, and Parvus, then at the zenith of his intellectual powers, influenced

Trotsky's thinking in ways that are difficult if not impossible to unravel. The younger man was too conscious of his own talents to become a disciple, nor was he blind to Parvus's faults. "There was always something mad and unreliable about him," Trotsky later commented. A revolutionary socialist, he had bourgeois tastes combined with a libertine moral code, and among his more extravagant ambitions was a desire for unlimited wealth.

In Trotsky's absence the Mensheviks, using *Iskra* as a mouthpiece of considerable prestige among émigrés and underground workers, kept up their anti-Leninist barrage. The object of their scorn proved intractable and had counterattacked in the spring with a substantial polemic, *One Step Forward, Two Steps Back.* Trotsky joined the fray (though Lenin had all but ignored him since the split) with a pamphlet, *Our Political Tasks,* which was dedicated to his "dear teacher" Axelrod and published in Geneva in August, 1904. It was an odd mixture of intuitive political analysis and tasteless personal abuse. Added to previous stylistic indiscretions, it made a weighty contribution to his long estrangement from Lenin. Few Marxists— Lenin, though overly contentious, was not among them—ever descended to Trotsky's level in exchanging vulgar epithets. Maturity brought a mellower style, but he never quite overcame his jejune habit of confusing faulty ideology with personal malevolence.

Trotsky's attack bore down heavily on the Bolshevik-Jacobin and Lenin-Robespierre analogy, an argument he had used before and which Plekhanov, too, found attractive. Lenin's concept of an elite party, he charged, was derived from a profound distrust of the masses, a conviction that an "orthodox theocracy" of intellectuals should rule in the name of the working class. And his oft-quoted remark about where Lenin's methods would lead constituted an impressive feat of political fortune-telling: "The party organization 'replaces' the party itself, the central committee replaces the party organization, and finally a single 'dictator' replaces the central committee."[5]

However accurate as prognostication and however obnoxious its language, Trotsky's ambitious diatribe was already somewhat dated at the time of its appearance. His own political allegiance had already shifted, and the enemy therefore seemed less the epitome of evil than when he had personally manned the battlements of Menshevism. A Bolshevik rout, moreover, appeared to be well under way. A bit fearful that History had passed him by, Trotsky hedged his bets in a preface that took a rather lofty tone in declaring that the credibility of extremists in both factions had been destroyed. The task that lay ahead was now one of reconciliation, and he proposed that the Menshevik committee (of which he was still a member) be dissolved. But he had misjudged the situation completely. Both sides were preparing to renew the battle, and the mood of combat readiness was not conducive to arbitration. Nor were Trotsky's credentials as an "honest broker" impressive. The Bolsheviks loathed him for his vituperative pen, while many if not most of the Mensheviks regarded him as shifty and unreliable.

Lenin's personal view of Trotsky was now wholly scornful. When a colleague praised Trotsky's oratory, Lenin replied: "All Voroshilov-Balalaykins [characters in Russian fiction] are orators. The type includes half-educated seminarists with the gift of . . . gab, university lecturers who babble about Marxism, and pettifogging lawyers. There are elements of all these in Trotsky."[6]

Trotsky's formal break with Menshevism occurred a few weeks later when he sent *Iskra* an "Open Letter to Comrades." Martov, the managing editor, refused to publish it, presumably after consulting his colleagues. A "stormy correspondence" between the two followed that fell just short of personal estrangement. The letter was eventually discussed at a meeting with Trotsky in Geneva, and the Menshevik leaders, anxious to avoid an embarrassing public quarrel, offered him a few concessions. They abolished, at least *pro forma*, the Menshevik "central committee," thus releasing him from his last obligation to their faction. They also invited him to resume his association with *Iskra*—Plekhanov's objections were somehow overcome—and this indirect apology must have soothed his injured pride for the unceremonious manner of his original departure. He resumed his contributions on a more modest scale, and in so doing he again gave the appearance of embracing the Menshevik creed. But the divorce was final: he sought the path of independent, revolutionary Marxism. Ideologically, Trotsky was never very far from Bolshevism, but emotionally, he was drawn to Menshevism because of personal sentiment and his temperamental clash with Lenin.

During the final months of 1904, Trotsky wrote a long essay intended for separate publication. Its theme, the bankruptcy of bourgeois liberalism, was one well calculated to alienate his *Iskra* associates, for the Mensheviks regarded the liberal opponents of tsarism as allies in a common struggle. With a perversity that seemed irresponsible to Martov, Trotsky denounced the "banquet campaign" of the progressive bourgeoisie who, in imitation of the French revolutionaries of 1848, hoped to achieve constitutional reform. Not only the urban proletariat but also the peasantry ("a vast reservoir of potential revolutionary energy") would furnish the popular impetus to overthrow the monarchy. Perhaps the army, essentially an organization of peasants in uniform, would be the key to popular rebellion. But the major weapon must be the general strike, "a political strike of the proletariat which should be turned into a political demonstration of the entire population."[7] Of the émigré Marxists, Trotsky alone conveyed a sense of impending events, of the "majestic prologue" (as he later put it) that was to be the Revolution of 1905. He was also alone in suggesting an important role for the peasantry and the army, as well as emphasizing the enormous potential of the general strike—then unheard of in Russia—as a means of bringing the autocracy to its knees.

Trotsky had completed his manuscript, but his Menshevik publisher was reluctant to print such unorthodox material. Returning to Geneva on January 23, 1905, after a lecture tour and a sleepless night on the train, he called at the *Iskra* offices and found an excited Martov, who thrust the latest newspaper into his hands. It contained a telegraphic report of Bloody Sunday—a massacre of St. Petersburg workers attempting to present a petition to the Tsar. "A dull, burning sensation seemed to overpower me," Trotsky recalled, while his wife noted that he "turned pale" and "nearly fainted." The Trotskys set out for Munich, where Parvus offered the hospitality of his home. Trotsky's manuscript greatly impressed him. "The events have fully confirmed this analysis," he told his guest. "Now, no one can deny that the general strike is the most important means of fighting. The 22nd of January was the first political strike, even if it is disguised under a priest's cloak" (Father Georgi Gapon had led the procession).

Parvus wrote an introduction boldly predicting a "revolutionary provisional government" with a "Social Democratic majority," thus venturing for the first time into the theory eventually labeled "permanent revolution." Marxists of all persuasions, Trotsky among them, took it for granted that a revolution in Russia would be "bourgeois" in character. How could it be otherwise in a semi-feudal land where the proletariat, the Marxist locomotive of history, formed such a tiny minority? But Trotsky and Parvus both assumed that the workers would spearhead the revolution. If so, could they be expected to relinquish power to a socially advanced class—the bourgeoisie—in order to fulfill the Marxist dictum that industrial capitalism must ripen and mature before a socialist revolution could take place? To refuse would present an awkward situation: a working class government attempting to rule over the vast majority. And no one, not even Parvus, advocated forsaking democratic principle for the sake of socialism. Yet here, clearly adumbrated, was the dilemma that was to face the Bolsheviks in 1917.

The pamphlet was published in Geneva not long after the Bloody Sunday incident, and it created a stir among the Russian intellectuals abroad.[8] Trotsky turned out a number of articles on various aspects of the embryonic revolution in Russia while living in Munich. But anxious to get to the scene of the action, he soon went on to Vienna and called on Victor Adler, who had befriended him in 1902. Adler's home had become a center for aiding returning émigrés, and a hairdresser there altered Trotsky's appearance to fool the Russian police. He was still a fugitive from Siberia, not an ordinary political expatriate. His wife went ahead to make contacts and to arrange a place to live. Furnished with a false passport, Trotsky reached the city of Kiev in February, and as a security measure he changed his residence frequently. On one occasion he found refuge in a hospital where he knew one of the doctors and was greatly embarrassed and a little ashamed when an "amiable old nurse" persisted in giving him footbaths. His most intimate revolutionary associate in Kiev was Leonid Krasin, a gifted engineer and a Bolshevik member of the Central Committee. A specialist in weapons, explosives, and the more violent aspects of kindling a successful revolution, Krasin had an amazing range of contacts in Kiev and other Russian cities. He also had access to a first-rate printing press in the Caucasus. There Trotsky's longer writings were published; his proclamations and other ephemera he entrusted to the local underground press.

In the spring of 1905 Trotsky made his way to St. Petersburg. Krasin supplied him with secret addresses, and the most valuable proved to be the home of Alexander Litkins, the chief medical officer of an artillery school. Trotsky and other revolutionaries used it frequently during the turbulent days that followed, for the good doctor's residence was above suspicion. He carried the passport of a landowner named Vikentiev, but in revolutionary circles he was known as Peter Petrovich. Since the luminaries of Social Democracy were not on the scene—Lenin and Martov returned late in the year while Plekhanov never did get back—he became the most prominent Marxist in the Russian underground and quickly established a reputation for his lively broadsides and trenchant essays. A conciliationist in regard to the party quarrel, which most of the rank and file found incomprehensible, he tried to subordinate political differences to the common struggle. Still on excellent terms with Krasin, also a conciliator (much to Lenin's chagrin), he maintained close ties with the local Menshevik organization. A professional police informer, "Nikolai of the Gold Spectacles," brought disaster to the group. Trotsky's wife, among others, was arrested in May, and Trotsky fled to the relative safety of Finland (then a semi-autonomous part of the Russian empire), where he at last found ample leisure to pursue his theoretical work.

The wave of strikes and demonstrations in the wake of Bloody Sunday had now subsided. Organized leadership that would provide discipline and direction to the elemental popular protest was lacking. Neither the Social Democrats nor the Socialist Revolutionaries (the heirs of Populism) had the experience or the numbers to sustain an open attack on the monarchy, though Trotsky, Parvus, and Lenin all preached the necessity of an armed insurrection. Martov took a different tack. Edging closer to the liberals as Trotsky and Lenin backed away, he called on the "bourgeois democracy" to assume the same position in Russia that it had in western Europe. During the spring and early summer, as the government sought to appease its opponents with the promise of a consultative assembly, Russia's small but vocal middle class did indeed give the appearance of taking up the historic burden that Martov had assigned to it. But it was less interested in revolution than in wresting constitutional reform from the Tsar, as Trotsky was quick to point out.

The émigré leaders, poorly informed on the pace of events in their homeland, proceeded with their internecine struggle. In late April, Lenin convened a party congress of doubtful legality in London. The delegates—all Bolsheviks—were an uncommonly independent lot, more interested in restoring party harmony than in pursuing Lenin's vendetta against the Mensheviks. Some of them, such as Krasin, had learned at first hand that the Mensheviks in the underground were quite a different breed from the intellectuals who spoke for their faction abroad. Swayed by Trotsky's argument

that the proletariat was bound to play a decisive role in any revolutionary government, Krasin offered an amendment conveying
these sentiments to one of Lenin's political resolutions, and the
Bolshevik chieftain accepted it with good grace, apparently unaware
of its original source. Martov held to the theory, which he equated
with orthodox Marxism, that Social Democrats could not properly
enter a bourgeois government, revolutionary or not.

Trotsky spent a peaceful summer in Finland isolated from political activity but heavily engaged in literary projects—all of them, of
course, with a revolutionary purpose. His most memorable endeavor
during this period of self-imposed but involuntary exile was a ringing open letter to Paul Milyukov, an eminent historian and the
acknowledged leader of middle class liberalism. Milyukov, who
welcomed the so-called Bulygin Duma (the consultative assembly
announced in early March) as a progressive step toward representative government, became the symbolic target of Trotsky's scorn for
Russian liberalism and its willingness to accept the "constitutional
mirage" at face value. "If the revolution does not ebb away," the
letter warned, "the bureaucracy will cling to you as its support; and
if you really try to become its support . . . the victorious revolution
will throw you out."[9] His pungent sallies at the expense of the
liberals, though they could not be published in the legal press, won
an appreciative audience from the radical intelligentsia.

In September, Trotsky moved farther into the interior, finding a
nearly deserted resort hotel on the shore of a lake. His idyllic retreat
was interrupted in late October by the latest news from the capital: a
general strike with political overtones had broken out and spread
across the land like a raging epidemic. Sensing that his historic
moment had arrived, Trotsky rushed to St. Petersburg and that
same evening made his debut as a popular orator in the great hall of
the Technological Institute. His audience consisted chiefly of the
newly elected members to the Soviet of Workers' Deputies, a strike
committee that quickly took on quasi-governmental functions. The
Soviet was a non-party body, and the Bolsheviks regarded it suspi-
ciously at first, partly because Mensheviks had been prominent in
its formation. There Trotsky, just short of his twenty-sixth birthday,
found his natural sphere as a revolutionary tribune, indefatigable
journalist, and aspiring politician. Within days of his arrival he became, if not its dominant personality, a figure of great prestige and

substantial influence. But the elected chairman, a young lawyer named Georgi Nosar (alias Khrustalyov), held formal command until his arrest several weeks later. He was by no means a front man for his brilliant colleague. Like many of his former political associates, Trotsky was less than generous in his retrospective treatment of Nosar.

With the country in a state of semi-paralysis, the Tsar hesitated between repression and reform. General Dmitri Trepov, the governor-general of St. Petersburg, issued an order to his troops on October 27: "No blank volleys, and spare no bullets." Three days later, accepting the counsel of moderation offered by Sergei Witte, his premier designate, Nicholas II signed an imperial manifesto providing for an elected legislature—a national Duma. Trotsky, then residing at the home of his friend Dr. Litkens, was greeted by his host the next morning with a copy of the decree in the government newspaper and "a smile of happy excitement at odds with the customary skepticism on his intelligent face." Outside in the street Trotsky learned that troops had fired on the Technological Institute. The building was locked and guarded as he went past. Someone suggested walking to the university since it was inviolable from the police, and he joined a small procession that grew to major proportions as it neared the main courtyard. He squeezed in with difficulty. "The students' blue caps and the red banners were bright spots among the hundred-thousand-strong crowd." The silence was complete as Trotsky, invited to speak, faced the huge throng from a balcony:

Citizens! Now that we have got the ruling clique with its back to the wall, they promise us freedom. They promise us electoral rights and legislative power. Who promises these things? Nicholas the Second. . . . It is this tireless hangman on the throne whom we have forced to promise us freedom. What a great triumph! But do not be too quick to celebrate victory; victory is not yet complete. . . . Is the promise of liberty the same as liberty itself? . . . Look around, citizens; has anything changed since yesterday? Have the gates of our prisons been opened? . . .

"Amnesty! Amnesty! Amnesty!" comes the shout from below.

If the government had sincerely decided to make up its quarrel with the people, the first thing it would do would be to proclaim an amnesty. But, citizens, is an amnesty all? Today they will let out hundreds of political fighters, tomorrow they will seize thousands of others. Isn't the order to spare no bullets hanging by the side of the manifesto about our freedoms? . . . Isn't Trepov, the hangman, master of Petersburg?

"Down with Trepov!" came the answering shout.

Yes, down with Trepov! but is he the only one? Are there no villains in the bureaucracy's reserves to take his place? Trepov rules over us with the help of the army. . . . We cannot, we do not want to, we must not live at gunpoint. Citizens! Let our demand be the withdrawal of troops from Petersburg! . . .

"Out with the troops! All troops to leave Petersburg!"

Citizens! Our strength is in ourselves. With sword in hand we must stand guard over our freedom. As for the Tsar's manifesto, look, it's only a scrap of paper. Here it is before you—here it is crumpled in my fist. Today they have issued it, tomorrow they will take it away and tear it into pieces, just as I am now tearing up this paper freedom before your eyes![10]

Trotsky was a superb "rabble-rouser," a master of impromptu oratory that fascinated crowds at all educational levels. Once he had overcome his adolescent fear of public speaking, his ego thrived on the enthusiastic response of a mass audience. His voice, a gift that he never cultivated with formal training, had a natural vibrancy and a superior range—like his exceptional talent as a writer, it compensated for a curiously stunted personality. Trotsky lacked the emotional depth and self-awareness that would have allowed him to relate to people as individuals and not as objects to be manipulated. His brilliance of intellect, his polished manners, his somewhat foppish dress, and his charming conversation could never conceal this one glaring flaw—his genius, as a onetime admirer has put it, "for losing friends and alienating people."[11]

In the revolutionary situation of 1905—to be repeated on a grander scale in 1917—Trotsky for the first time found the fame and glory that he craved. His personal deficiencies seemed insignificant; he felt that he had earned a place in the front rank of the grandiose march of History. His speech at the university (which cannot be authenticated beyond his own reconstructed version of it) pointed up the choice that the public now had to make: Should the nation settle for a "scrap of paper" or should it persevere in the path of revolution? The answer, while not immediately forthcoming, soon became apparent. The more prosperous segments of society as well as the less militant members of the working class were willing to accept the Tsar's promise—whether it be paper or not. For the land-hungry peasants, whose sporadic revolts during the course of the year had conjured up the frightening spectacle of a vast jacquerie, the response was equivocal. The politically unsophisticated *muzhik* cared little for parliaments and constitutions, nor was he a revolutionary in the sense understood by the urban radicals. His passion for dispossessing landlords, temporarily at a low ebb during the general strike, flared anew toward the end of the year. But it was too late—the regime had regained its self-confidence and surface stability. "Local cretinism is history's curse on all peasant riots," Trotsky lamented. "The peasantry, however revolutionary it may be, is not capable of playing an independent, still less a leading, political role. . . . It would be unworthy of a Marxist to believe that a party of muzhiks can place itself at the head of a bourgeois revolution and, by its own initiative, liberate the nation's productive forces from their archaic shackles."[12]

Despite the Soviet Executive Committee's decision to call off the general strike early in November, Trotsky set a frantic pace. His wife, who had served six months in the provincial city of Tver under police supervision, joined him in the capital, and as Mr. and Mrs. Vikentiev they rented a room in the apartment of a stock exchange speculator. In the Soviet he was known as Yanovsky, a name derived from his native village, but in his capacity as a journalist he continued to sign himself Trotsky. He wrote for and edited three newspapers: *Izvestia* ("The News"), the official Soviet organ; *Russkaya Gazeta*, a small daily which he and Parvus took over; and *Nachalo* ("The Beginning"), an independent paper to which Martov and other Mensheviks contributed. Largely because of Trotsky's devoted labor and colorful style, the *Gazeta*'s original circulation of about thirty thousand more than tripled within a few days and reached half a million by the time a police raid closed it down. *Nachalo*, modeled on the *Neue Rheinische Zeitung* that the young Karl Marx had edited in 1848, also achieved remarkable success, far outstripping the rather drab Bolshevik newspaper.

For approximately six weeks the government and the Soviet played a waiting game; neither was anxious to test the other's strength. Revolutionaries, like Trotsky, preferred that the Soviet become a more daring agency of popular disaffection. Rather than confine its activities, for the most part, to enlarging the sphere of civic liberty promised in the Tsar's manifesto, the Executive Committee should make preparations for an armed rebellion. An important departure from its typical policies, however—the struggle for the eight hour day—ended badly with lockouts and layoffs. This issue gave way to others of a political nature, and a second general strike was called on November 15. The St. Petersburg workers responded with solidarity, but the middle class showed signs of serious disaffection. The Soviet wisely decided to conduct an orderly retreat and canceled the strike five days later.

In the three weeks that followed, despite instances of mutiny in the armed forces, the government regained the initiative. Nosar was arrested on December 9, and the Soviet chose a three-man presidium (with Trotsky first among equals) to replace him. While boldly calling for a continuation of preparations for an armed uprising, it had no real intention of provoking a clash, armed or otherwise. On December 16 the blow fell: police and soldiers surrounded the Soviet assembly hall. The deputies had been forewarned, and journalists, party representatives, and other guests were on hand to observe the formal arrest. Trotsky, then chairing a meeting of the Executive Committee, determined to submit with a show of peaceful bravado. He told the arresting officer, who stood respectfully outside the room, "I suggest you close the door and do not disturb our business." The meeting went on as the perplexed officer withdrew. Finally a police commander, pale with fright (he half expected a bullet in the head), cautiously ventured into the room, and his men placed themselves behind the deputies' chairs. Trotsky then ended the short life of the St. Petersburg Soviet of 1905: "I declare the meeting of the Executive Committee closed."[13]

Over two hundred members of the Soviet and an undetermined number of observers were imprisoned. The leaders expected a militant response by the workers, but a third general strike revealed only a creeping apathy. An unsuccessful revolt in Moscow represented the last gasp of the revolutionary movement, though minor disturbances continued into the new year.

Since Trotsky had become firmly identified as the principal Soviet leader, his zealous tactics and flamboyant style were questioned by other Social Democrats when the postmortems began. That he had consistently overestimated the revolutionary consciousness of the masses was undeniable, and his defense was typical of his impetuous nature. "If battles were engaged only in the certainty of victory," he argued, "there would be no battles fought in this world. A preliminary calculation of forces cannot determine in advance the outcome of revolutionary conflicts. If it could, the class struggle should have long since been replaced by bookkeeping."[14] Yet his belligerence had been carefully restrained by his colleagues, and the record of the Soviet was hardly one of reckless adventurism. Among the fleeting victories that the forces of rebellion enjoyed in 1905, the enduring mystique of the St. Petersburg Soviet was not the least of them. And it made Trotsky, if not a figure of national renown, an authentic revolutionary hero to many who were only dimly aware of such Marxist celebrities as Lenin, Martov, and Plekhanov.

Most of the prisoners were eventually taken to the fortress of Peter and Paul, the historic island redoubt on the Neva River where many "politicals" had languished in the nineteenth century. Some, including Trotsky, were later transferred to the House of Preliminary Detention. Their treatment was surprisingly lenient, initially because the regime had not yet regained full confidence in its own authority and thereafter because of the quasi-liberalism associated with the experiment in constitutional government. Although assigned to specific cells at the detention prison, they were not confined during the day and could wander about with relatively few restrictions. Many of the jailers were personally sympathetic to the prisoners, and one official requested (and received) Trotsky's photograph, suitably inscribed, and a copy of one of his publications. The authorities allowed liberal visiting and mail privileges, and an ample supply of reading material was readily available. Trotsky made good use of his enforced leisure, turning out a sizable number of manuscripts which his lawyers usually carried out in their briefcases. He also read incessantly, perusing the European literary classics (mostly French novels) for relaxation while analyzing more formidable works for his "scientific" (i.e., Marxist) investigations. He studied with particular care the theory of rent and the history of social relations in Russia. His "big work" on rent, incomplete and unpublished, was lost many years later and caused him almost as much distress as the previous loss of his manuscript on Freemasonry.

Disagreement in the higher reaches of the imperial administration over the proper course of government policy led to uncertainty as to whether the Soviet leaders would be formally charged with crimes against the state and brought to trial. Reports and rumors of amnesty alternated with insinuations that execution might be their ultimate fate. Nicholas II, resentful of his loss of authority implied in the October manifesto, found in his chief minister, Count Witte, a convenient scapegoat and finally accepted his resignation in the spring of 1906. But the promised Duma, elected on the restricted but not ungenerous suffrage right of male citizens, met shortly afterward with cautious optimism about its future role in the political life of the country. The Bolsheviks had boycotted the elections on principle, while the Mensheviks had belatedly decided to participate. Witte's successor, Peter Stolypin, presided over the arbitrary dissolution of the first Duma in July. The public failed to protest. Its silence was an encouraging sign to the apostles of reaction who were now in a position to urge a spirited prosecution of the Soviet "conspirators."

The trial, however, was delayed until early October, 1906, and was held before a special tribunal of seven judges. Trotsky was resolved to defy the regime, using the courtroom as an open forum for revolutionary propaganda. Martov, as the Menshevik spokesman, recommended a legal approach—that is, the defendants would argue that their conduct had been perfectly legitimate under the guidelines laid down by the October manifesto and that they had never contemplated an armed uprising. Such a defense struck Trotsky as unworthy of revolutionaries—not that his colleagues had all been militant "professionals." He informed Martov of his attitude, and his fellow defendants agreed to form a united front in defiance of their captors.

The fifty-one Soviet deputies formally indicted (another had been executed, the others released) were accused of preparing an insurrection, an act prohibited under two articles of the criminal code. The indictment, Trotsky commented later, was "a pathetic concoction cooked up between gendarmes and prosecutors" and reflected "the revolution in the same way as a dirty puddle in a police station yard reflects the sun." The proceedings, carried on with scrupulous equity, occupied a full month. Some four hundred witnesses—a cross section of Russian society—were called and more than half actually testified. Trotsky's parents, observing their son with a mixture of pride and apprehension, were among the small number of spectators. Hundreds of petitions and signed resolutions protested the trial, and flowers sent to the accused swamped the courtroom, an overly fragrant intrusion that the presiding judge obligingly allowed. In perverse contrast to such permissiveness, the courthouse was placed under martial law, with armed soldiers outside and gendarmes with drawn sabers inside. "Exaggerated severity and unbounded license," Trotsky remarked, "combined here into a bizarre whole, both illuminating, from different aspects, the extraordinary confusion which still reigned in governmental spheres as a legacy of the October strike."[15]

The case for the defense reached a rhetorical climax with Trotsky's ringing speech on October 17. Concentrating on the key issue, the government's contention that the Soviet had plotted an armed insurrection, he conceded that the state held a "monopoly of violence" which private individuals breached at their own peril. But he boldly asserted that although the Soviet had never "raised or discussed" the subject of an armed rising "throughout the fifty days of its existence," it considered itself "entitled through the agency of one or another of its organs to use force or repressive measures in certain cases." No Social Democrat supposed that "the old state apparatus" would "hand over power to the people or surrender a single one of its principal positions." Therefore, he argued, "Insurrection, armed insurrection, gentlemen of the court, was inevitable from our point of view. It was and remains a historical necessity in the process of the people's struggle against the military and police state." For two months this idea reigned at "all meetings and assemblies, dominated the entire revolutionary press, filled the entire political atmosphere and . . . crystallized in the consciousness of every member of the Soviet." That is why, he continued, it "formed part of the Soviet's resolutions, and why, too, there was never any need for us to discuss it." The criminal law "knows all about conspiratorial associations but cannot understand the concept of a mass organization"; it "knows about assassinations and mutinies but does not and cannot know revolution."

In conclusion, Trotsky passed over to the offensive with the kind of brazen insolence that had already become his trademark. "What we have is not a national government but an automaton for mass murder," he charged. "If you tell me that the pogroms, the murders, the burnings, the rapes . . . are the form of government of the Russian Empire—then I will agree with the prosecution that in October and November last we were arming ourselves, directly and immediately, against the form of government of the Russian Empire."[16]

When these pyrotechnics ended, the court recessed for a time at the request of one of the defense lawyers. By an odd coincidence he was to become Trotsky's persecutor in 1917 in his capacity as minister of justice under the Provisional Government. A dozen or so

attorneys for the defense congratulated Trotsky for his brilliant performance and shook his hand. Even the chief prosecutor was impressed. When court resumed, he paid tribute to the speaker for his
sincerity and frankness while pointing out that the government's
case had been proved by the leading defendant himself.

The trial came to an abrupt halt when a former police official who
had revealed the extent of the government's involvement in pogroms was denied an opportunity to testify on behalf of the defense
or to permit his evidence to be read into the record. Heretofore
judiciously impartial, the court felt constrained to avoid an embarrassing and politically dangerous subject. The accused, in protest,
refused to cooperate and asked to be returned to their cells. After
the defense attorneys had also withdrawn, the prosecutor summed
up, and the expected verdict was delivered before a nearly empty
coutroom. Fifteen defendants, including Trotsky, were sentenced
to exile in Siberia for life.

On January 16, 1907, the deportees were sent to a transit prison,
their ultimate destination still a secret. Trotsky had become used to
his routine at the House of Detention and was nervously apprehen-
sive about the change. But he had hardly made the adjustment
when, a week later, the group was escorted under heavy guard to a
railway station. The journey by train was uneventful, and they were
treated with every consideration within the limits of the situation.
The authorities took extraordinary precautions to prevent escapes
and to circumvent popular demonstrations. At Tyumen in eastern
Siberia they transferred to horse-drawn sleighs, and the procession
slowly made its way to Tobolsk. Here their destination was disclosed: Obdorsk, a village far to the north beyond the Arctic Circle.
After a day's rest the journey resumed at a faster pace along the Ob
River. "The convoy spreads over a tremendous distance," Trotsky
wrote of his experience. "From time to time one of the drivers gives
a high-pitched shout which sets the horses galloping, raising thick
clouds of snow-dust. The speed takes your breath away. The sleighs
almost pile up on top of one another, a horse's mouth suddenly
appears from behind your shoulder and breathes into your face.
Then one of the sleighs capsizes or some part of the harness breaks
or comes undone. The whole convoy stops. After many hours of
driving you feel as though hypnotized. The air is very still. The
drivers call to one another in their guttural voices. Then the horses
start up again and soon we are galloping once more."[17]

The farther into the wilderness they traveled the more dismayed Trotsky became at the growing distance from the railroad: the railroad was both the symbol of civilization and the chief means of transportation should he contrive to escape. A passport and gold pieces were concealed in his boots in case an opportunity presented itself. On February 25 the party reached Berezov, with about three hundred miles yet to go, and a two-day halt was announced. Trotsky feigned illness—a physician and fellow deportee taught him how to fake the symptoms of sciatica—and was admitted to the hospital. His "recovery" was delayed beyond the departure date, and he remained behind, free to roam around the town. No one suspected an escape attempt at that season of the year. He located a shrewd peasant who was able to find a guide, a native of the region. For a suitable price the guide obtained three reindeer and a sleigh, and Trotsky, heavily bundled in furs, slipped away with him in the dead of night. Avoiding the main road back to Tobolsk, they followed a little-used route westward to the Urals, where a narrow gauge railway at one of the mining camps connected with the main line to Perm. Trotsky described his week-long trip as a "magnificent ride through a desert of virgin snow," but there were perils in the frozen tundra of which he was well aware. A major snowstorm, for example, would have immobilized him. Luckily the weather remained good, though the temperature was usually well below zero.

As they neared the Urals, the danger of discovery grew in proportion to population density, and Trotsky posed as an engineer and a member of a recent polar expedition. The reindeer were exchanged for horses, and he reached the local Ural railway without trouble. But not until he was seated in a comfortable coach on the line to Perm did he relax. He risked a telegram to his wife, who met him at a junction point, and they returned to St. Petersburg together. Dr. Litkens again served as a faithful host, but they soon decided that Finland would be a safer refuge.

Trotsky visited both Lenin and Martov, who were living in neighboring Finnish villages. Lenin praised his work but taunted him for not drawing the necessary conclusions, that is, for not going over to the Bolsheviks. Trotsky settled down near Helsinki for several weeks with his wife and infant son, born while he was in prison. There he wrote an account of his exile and escape, and with the publisher's advance he set out for western Europe via Stockholm, once more an émigré.[18]

CHAPTER 3

The Independent Marxist

TROTSKY arrived in London in time for the Fifth Party Congress which was held from May 13 to June 1, 1907. The delegates still hoped for a revolutionary upsurge in Russia, and the events of the past two years encouraged the conciliationists to believe that a united party might still be achieved. The Bolsheviks commanded a slight majority over the Mensheviks, but Lenin failed to acquire the decisive victory that he anticipated. Trotsky, still cultivating his role as an independent, formed a bloc of his own with several sympathizers. His flamboyant and arrogant personality, flushed by his triumph in 1905, grated harshly on many of the delegates (Lenin called him a "poseur"). Furthermore, his style of oratory was better suited to a mass audience than to the pedantic acrimony of a party congress.

In his speeches Trotsky adhered to the talisman of "permanent revolution," finding an ideological ally in Rosa Luxemburg, a Polish Social Democrat. Lenin, referring to Luxemburg in a jocular vein, remarked, "It is all because she does not speak Russian too well." Trotsky's riposte, "But then, she speaks excellent Marxian," received the appreciative laughter of a circle of delegates in the lobby.[1] Lenin had not abandoned hope of winning him over to Bolshevism, and they shared a distaste for the Mensheviks's tendency to cohabit with the liberals. They also agreed that the workers and peasants should form the vanguard of the revolutionary movement. But Trotsky, conscious of his new status, did not relish the thought of working in Lenin's shadow, and he retained an emotional antipathy toward the Bolshevik chieftain because of past quarrels. If genuine party unity could not be realized—and there is no reason to doubt his sincerity in working toward it—why should he abstain from organizing his own followers, beholden to neither of the old factions?

For the next decade Trotsky made a half-hearted effort to rally around him a loyal group of supporters. But his intellectual precocity and his gift for mass persuasion was ill-suited to the grubby and demeaning task of political recruitment. Nor did he relish (as Lenin seemed to) the post of ideological watchdog, for heresy and apostasy were endemic to revolutionary politics. His spirits (and seemingly his talents) soared in a revolutionary crisis and flagged just as rapidly when the tide of reaction swept in. Those drawn to "Trotskyism" (if the term may be used anachronistically) tended to be cast in the same mold as their leader: temperamental members of the intelligentsia whose Marxism was more romantic than pragmatic. Lenin, in the lean years of discouragement and retreat, attracted a different breed. These "hards," men such as Gregory Zinoviev, Leo Kamenev, and Joseph Stalin, may have lacked the urbanity and polish of the Westernized Marxists who followed in Trotsky's wake, but they were professionals who seldom flinched at the difficult and sometimes sordid tasks that Lenin assigned.

During his second exile abroad Trotsky concentrated on journalism and belletristic essays, belying his self-appraisal that he was chiefly concerned with interpreting the experience of 1905 and "paving the way for the next revolution by theoretical research." He did publish a fascinating series of vignettes and other material on 1905 that concluded with a more comprehensive statement of his and Parvus's theory of permanent revolution.[2] This updated version expounded the daring thesis that the Russian proletariat was capable of not only seizing power in place of the weak and spineless bourgeoisie, but also of setting off a socialist chain reaction throughout Europe—and perhaps beyond. Socialism could not be built in backward Russia, however, without the aid of the European workers. But Trotsky's prophetic judgment remained little known, partly because the edition was confiscated shortly after its appearance in 1906. Only when the Bolshevik Revolution cast a new and favorable light on his prediction did the doctrine receive a respectful hearing.

As an émigré, Trotsky apparently lost interest in serious research on political and social questions and declined to elaborate the idea of permanent revolution or even to make the original version accessible to European readers. Nor did his record as a politician, divorced from his native land, inspire confidence in his qualities as a leader. Yet, he remained the most cosmopolitan of the Russian Marxists. He eagerly absorbed the cultural advantages of Western civilization but carefully refrained from dictating the path that Russian socialism should take. His flexibility, a source of suspicion to Bolsheviks and Mensheviks alike, was a commendable trait to the elder statesmen of European Social Democracy who found the factional disputes and doctrinal bickering of their Russian brethren all but incomprehensible.

Trotsky settled in Berlin after the Fifth Congress. His wife joined him there, as did Parvus, who had also escaped from Siberian exile. During the summer the three enjoyed a hike through the mountains of Saxony, though the Trotskys nearly lost their lives when making a perilous descent down a steep precipice. Later they spent a few weeks at a resort in Bohemia. Parvus attempted unsuccessfully to get Luxemburg to join them. In August they went their separate ways: Trotsky to Stuttgart to attend a congress of the Second (Socialist) International, his wife back to Russia to retrieve their infant son, and Parvus to Berlin. At Stuttgart, and later in the German capital, Trotsky met all the famous German Social Democrats. Despite his "disturbing theoretical premonitions" about the state of their party, it still functioned as "mother, teacher, and living example" for him and the Russian Marxists. Parvus introduced him to Karl Kautsky, the most eminent European socialist, and at the time Trotsky was suitably impressed. But his final judgment, colored by Kautsky's later heresies, was not flattering: "His mind was too angular and dry, too lacking in nimbleness and psychological insight. His evaluations were schematic, his jokes trite. For the same reason he was a poor speaker."[3]

In October, 1907, to avoid the unwelcome attentions of the Berlin police, Trotsky moved to Vienna. His wife and son returned from Russia not long afterward. Until the outbreak of war in 1914 he lived in modest and sometimes straitened circumstances in the suburbs, apparently changing his residence only once. Most of the Russian émigrés preferred to reside in Paris or Switzerland, but Trotsky wanted to be near his German political contacts. It is quite likely that he also desired a period of respite from the incessant squabbles of his countrymen. He was already writing frequently for the socialist press in Germany, and under his old pen name Antid Oto he became a regular contributor to a Leftist but "bourgeois" daily in Russia, *Kievskaya Mysl* ("Kievan Thought"). For this latter assignment he took the trouble of obtaining the formal consent of the party's Central Committee, which then had a Leninist majority. He rejected an offer to contribute to the Bolshevik organ published in Geneva, claiming that he was too busy, and the offended Lenin put his refusal down to "mere posturing."[4] Trotsky's relations with Parvus gradually cooled, largely because of their divergent views on the theory of permanent revolution, but no open break occurred until 1915 when he denounced his former friend as a "political Falstaff" and chauvinist, "fit only to help the dead bury his corpse."[5]

Trotsky plunged into the life of his adopted city with a certain zest, though his memoirs speak rather disparagingly of the Austrian milieu as too much like a "squirrel in a cage." He renewed his acquaintance with Victor Adler, for whom he held an affectionate regard, and came to know all the prominent Austrian socialists. "They were well-educated people whose knowledge of various subjects was superior to mine," he conceded, but they "were not revolutionaries." Karl Renner, the future leader of the Austrian republic, was, for example, "as far from revolutionary dialectics as the most conservative Egyptian pharaoh."[6] His contemporary opinion of these men was a good deal less abrasive, and if he was as disillusioned with the Vienna Marxists as he later maintained, it is puzzling that he joined the Austrian Social Democratic party, contributed to its press, and engaged in its activities with no discernible repugnance at its reformist tendencies. His explanation that he found its leaders "alien" but its followers less philistine is not wholly convincing. Like all the Russian Marxists—even Lenin—he did not fully realize until the debacle of European socialism during World War I that its revolutionary militancy had been eroded by parliamentary democracy, trade union respectability, and rising living standards.

In October, 1908, Trotsky began to publish his own newspaper, *Pravda* ("The Truth"), which aimed at a mass audience rather than at political sophisticates. It was either smuggled into Russia across Austria's Galician frontier or by ship to ports on the Black Sea. Because of slender resources and the burden of responsibility that Trotsky personally assumed, it appeared infrequently—never more than half a dozen issues a year. His chief contributor, both literary and financial, was Adolf Yoffe, a gifted but neurasthenic intellectual who later became a well-known Soviet diplomat. Through Yoffe, a patient of the distinguished psychoanalyst Alfred Adler, Trotsky became interested in the Freudian school and its various offshoots and was probably the only Marxist of reputation who understood

and appreciated these new currents in psychology. Other contributors included David Ryazanov, a learned authority on Marx and
Engels, and Mikhail Skobelev, a Menshevik who became minister
of labor in the Provisional Government in 1917.

Pravda, as an underground paper, never attained a large circulation, nor did it wield as much influence toward party unity as
Trotsky would have liked and as his editorials urged. His memoirs
do not hint of personal unhappiness, but his obscurity compared to
the heady days of 1905 must have been a source of bitter disap-
pointment, if not more serious emotional problems, for one so
confident of his historical destiny. But "émigré neurosis" was the
common lot of the Russian expatriates, especially in the years from
1907 to 1914 when the tsarist regime seemed unassailable.

Trotsky's financial situation was not the best since his work on
Pravda sometimes left him no leisure to earn the modest fees paid
by the Kiev newspaper and other less dependable sources. Occasionally he had to resell books purchased in more affluent times or to
pawn household items. And more than once the family possessions
were seized when the rent fell too far behind. His parents, by now
reconciled to his revolutionary career, visited him several times and
most probably "lent" him money. His mother, who suffered from
actinomycosis, a parasitical disease, died in 1910 at Yanovka. In
1912, after recovering from an undisclosed illness, Trotsky was again
financially embarrassed, and his old "mentor" Axelrod came to his
rescue. "If only I were firmly convinced that this money did not
come from your own more than modest budget," he wrote with
profound gratitude.[7]

Russian Social Democracy, if not quite moribund by 1909,
showed distressing symptoms of infirmity. The underground apparatus suffered from pernicious anemia, its cadres decimated by
police vigilance and, more seriously, by the pervasive lethargy that
infected the entire revolutionary movement. Under these conditions the rancorous strife of the émigré leaders appeared pointless,
indeed suicidal. Lenin, the most intransigent, found himself surrounded by Bolshevik "conciliators" and reluctantly took part in a
party conference in Paris early in 1910. Trotsky also attended, and
as an apostle of moderation he was pleased that *Pravda* received the
formal commendation of the Central Committee for its neutral
stand. Judging by outward results, the conference achieved what

previous party congresses had failed to do—the unification of the warring factions. Among other gestures of good will, the Bolsheviks and Mensheviks agreed to suspend their own newspapers in favor of the nonpartisan *Sotsial-Demokrat* and to pay a regular subsidy to "that windbag Trotsky" (as Lenin called him) for the continuation of *Pravda*.

Once more the armistice proved illusory. Delighted with the compromise and the vote of confidence in his own publication, Trotsky was obliged to admit only a few months later that his optimism had been premature. The rights and wrongs of the renewed dispute were, as usual, difficult to unravel, and he refused to render a firm judgment. Kamenev, a Bolshevik conciliator chosen as the Central Committee's representative on *Pravda*, objected to this lenient treatment of the obdurate Mensheviks and quarreled with Trotsky. He resigned during the summer, and the funds for *Pravda* were cut off. This in turn embittered Trotsky, who discerned Lenin's hand behind the affair, and a new round of anti-Bolshevik invective from his accomplished pen served to place him alongside the Mensheviks. He did attempt to preserve amenities by refraining from a personal attack on Lenin, commenting in one editorial, for example, that "the circle which seeks to place itself above the party will find itself outside it."[8] In private he continued to be critical of Martov and Axelrod, but his public pronouncements jeopardized his self-appointed role as a peacemaker. That a rapprochement between Lenin and Plekhanov, long at odds with one another, could be temporarily revived was due in part to their mutual distaste for Trotsky, whom they regarded as an unprincipled meddler and a conniving intriguer.

Not content with chastising the Bolsheviks in *Pravda*, Trotsky pursued the controversy in the pages of the German socialist press. In August, 1910, he met Lenin by chance as the two changed trains en route to a socialist congress in Copenhagen. They conversed amicably at first, but Lenin became incensed when Trotsky described his latest contribution to *Vorwärts*, the German Social Democratic organ, which had touched in very uncomplimentary terms on the vexed question of Bolshevik "expropriations." Never scrupulous about the source of his funds, Lenin had condoned if not encouraged the robbery of state banks and similar crimes committed in the name of the revolutionary cause. The Fifth Congress in London and the more recent Paris conference had condemned these unsavory methods, but Lenin inquired if the offending article might be stopped by telegraph. "No," said Trotsky. "The article was to appear this morning—and what's the use of holding it up? It is perfectly right."[9]

At the congress itself, Plekhanov, backed by Lenin, tried in vain to get the Russian delegation to censure Trotsky for his uncomplimentary remarks about the Russian émigré socialists and for his effrontery in spreading the party feud before the German Social Democrats. On the specific matter of expropriations, however, Plekhanov shared the Menshevik view that such tactics were deplorable.

During the winter of 1910–11 Trotsky lectured for about three weeks at a Marxist school in Bologna, Italy, sponsored by a group of dissident Bolsheviks and financed by the novelist Maxim Gorky. His chief subject was the history of the Austrian socialist and labor movement, but he also taught a class on newspaper editing, using *Vorwärts* as a model, and gave one lecture on the novelist Leo Tolstoy. Lenin, though invited, declined to participate in such a suspect enterprise. Unable to discredit it, he began a school of his own near Paris the following spring.

In January, 1912, Lenin attempted another coup in the name of the party. A conference met in Prague with only fourteen voting delegates (including two police agents), ostensibly representing ten party committees. The Mensheviks had been pointedly ignored, though Plekhanov and "Judas Trotsky" (Lenin's favorite epithet for him at the time) received invitations and promptly refused them. The delegates elected a Central Committee of Bolsheviks, a usurpation that outraged Lenin's opponents and confused many rank-and-file Social Democrats in Russia. Trotsky poured out his indignation in the columns of *Pravda*. Neither did he spare the Mensheviks, whose concentration on legal party work and neglect of the underground apparatus struck him as improper behavior. But he still preserved his integrity, as he saw it, by acting as a force for reconciliation.

Trotsky's renewed attempt to serve as the party's better conscience was made no easier by the Bolshevik decision in the spring to publish a legal newspaper in St. Petersburg under the name *Pravda*. This insolent appropriation of the title, the good will, and the reputation of his newspaper was a provocation that he protested with righteous indignation. He complained of a "swindle" in a letter to Axelrod and denounced the "Leninist circle" as the "incarnation of factional reaction and highhanded sectarianism" in an editorial.[10] But his grievance, which he registered directly with the Bolshevik editors, was coolly ignored. Lenin advised them to reply: "It's a useless waste of time sending quarrelsome and complaining letters. They will not be answered."[11] The Vienna *Pravda* ceased publication in May—only twenty-five issues had been published since 1908—while the Bolshevik *Pravda* flourished, though its name changed eight times within the next two years as it sought with temporary success to evade a governmental ban. In 1914, just before war broke out, it was suppressed outright.

A revived strike movement in 1912 brought new hope to the revolutionaries who were desperate for encouraging signs and portents. Trotsky, ever faithful to the ideal of a united party, organized a peace conference in Vienna in August. As on prior occasions, it merely succeeded in widening the breach. Lenin had gone his own way and declined to attend. The assortment of Mensheviks, Jewish Bundists, Bolshevik dissenters, and Trotskyists did little more than denounce his obnoxious tactics and bicker with one another. The lone "regular" Bolshevik turned out to be a police agent whose orders were to disrupt the proceedings. In the end the delegates curbed their obstreperous tendencies and under Trotsky's chairmanship passed several tactful resolutions, seeking to avoid further controversy. They chose an Organization Committee to perpetuate the August Bloc (as it became known), but Lenin continued to hold the "company name"—that is, the Central Committee—a psychological advantage that was intangible but certainly substantial.

The August Bloc, contrary to Trotsky's avowed intentions, never became anything more than an anti-Leninist movement. Ryazanov exaggerated only slightly when he maintained that "personal hatred for the scoundrel Lenin [kept] together most of the Mensheviks, Bundists, and Trotsky."[12] It had disintegrated long before Trotsky formally repudiated his own handiwork in 1915. But until then he frequently repeated his previous mistake of appearing as a Menshevik stalking horse, loudly berating the Bolsheviks for their schismatic misdeeds while admonishing Martov and his associates, hardly less committed to the feud than Lenin, in subdued and less public tones.

The threat of war in the Balkans presented Trotsky with a welcome respite after his futile labors at the Vienna conference. Tired of émigré politics, he accepted an offer to become the Balkan correspondent for the *Kievskaya Mysl*. War broke out in October, 1912, shortly after he arrived in Belgrade. Serbia and its partners sought to scourge their once powerful enemy, the Ottoman Turks. Vaguely sympathetic toward the Slavs, whose long struggle for independence had enlisted support from European liberals throughout the nineteenth century, Trotsky changed his mind when he observed the primitive chauvinism and barbaric cruelty that had been unleashed by the war. He ran afoul of the Bulgarian censorship by insisting on reporting atrocities committed against the Turks. When his old target in 1905, Professor Milyukov, appeared in Sofia as a Pan-Slavist and apologist for Bulgaria, he produced another scathing open letter that the legal Menshevik daily in St. Petersburg published. The attack set off a prolonged controversy in the Russian press, and some of the pro-monarchist papers hinted that "Antid Oto" (he used his old pen name) was an Austrian agent.

The war ended with Turkey's defeat, but the victors fell out over the spoils, and a second round in the conflict—Serbia and Greece vs. Bulgaria—brought Trotsky back to the Balkans. His dispatches surveyed a variety of topics, many of them not directly related to the war, and constituted some of the finest journalism of his career. In Romania he saw a good deal of an old acquaintance, Christian Rakovsky, and their renewed friendship was probably the closest to affectionate camaraderie that he was ever to know. Rakovsky, a Bulgarian by birth, acquired Romanian citizenship through the fortunes of Balkan politics and cartography. A talented linguist, a physician by training, and a landlord by inheritance, he became the founder and leader of the Romanian Socialist party and was to die a Trotskyist martyr in Stalinist Russia.

The Balkan wars were but preliminary tremors leading to the main event. The chauvinist frenzy that Trotsky had observed with such foreboding in Belgrade, Sofia, and Bucharest spread to Vienna in the summer of 1914. In reconstructing those days, he speculated in a curiously un-Marxian vein about the motives of "porters, laundresses, shoemakers, apprentices and youngsters from the suburbs" who composed the patriotic crowds. "Those who are oppressed and deceived by life," he concluded, "feel that they are on an equal footing with the rich and powerful." And he drew a parallel, quite unusual for a revolutionary, to the Viennese "demonstrating the glory of Hapsburg arms" with the Russian masses in the general strike of 1905: "No wonder that in history war has often been the mother of revolution."[13]

On August 3, in anticipation of hostilities between Austria and Russia, Trotsky was escorted to police headquarters by his friend Victor Adler. Advised that Russian and Serbian citizens might be arrested the next day, he and his family left for neutral Switzerland within a few hours. He settled in Zurich for several months and while there wrote *The War and the International,* an anti-war tract that set the tone for the minority European socialists who continued to struggle against the "social patriotism" of the majority. Although forewarned, he was shocked (as was Lenin) by the capitulation of the German Social Democrats to the war hysteria. His pamphlet, first published serially in the Parisian *Golos* ("The Voice"), was later translated and distributed in Germany, where, he eventually learned, a court sentenced him to prison *in absentia.* "For the slanderers and spies of the Entente," he observed, "this German court-sentence was always a stumbling-block in their noble efforts to prove that I was nothing more than an agent of the German general staff."

On November 19, 1914, with the German army occupying part of northeastern France, Trotsky moved to Paris as a correspondent for *Kievskaya Mysl.* His family remained in Zurich until the spring of 1915. He joined Martov and others on the staff of the daily *Golos,* which militantly opposed the war and therefore fought a running battle with the censorship. Pleased that his old associate had not succumbed to social patriotism, as some of the Mensheviks (e.g., Plekhanov) had, he nevertheless found Martov less than resolute and even something of a pacifist. Rejecting Trotsky's stern formula of "permanent war or proletarian revolution" and Lenin's incendiary slogan, "Turn the imperialist war into a civil war," Martov pulled back from a decisive break with the majority socialists of the Second International and with the patriotic wing of Menshevism. "Martov's first reaction to events was nearly always revolutionary," Trotsky conceded, "but before he could put his ideas on paper, his mind would be besieged by doubts from all sides. His rich, pliant, and multiform intelligence lacked the support of will."[14]

In January, 1915, *Golos* closed down at the demand of the authorities and reemerged approximately two weeks later as *Nashe Slovo* ("Our Word"). The new paper led a precarious existence since it was in constant financial difficulty, and the deletions imposed by the censors gave it a somewhat ragged appearance. But it survived these misfortunes, only to perish when most of the staff returned to Russia in 1917. Its editors and contributors included a distinguished array of socialist literati, both Russian and West European. Trotsky became its mainstay, though originally he had been suspicious of its Menshevik sponsorship. Ryazanov, who had written for the Vienna *Pravda*, assisted him, and Vladimir Antonov-Ovseyenko, a former Russian army officer, served as a kind of general manager. Martov clashed with his colleagues repeatedly, but Trotsky tried to maintain a personal relationship with him despite continued disagreement on editorial policy. From his Swiss exile Lenin observed the ambivalence of *Nashe Slovo* with mounting irritation. By trying to "run with the hare and hunt with the hounds," he protested in the spring of 1915, it had admitted its "ideological and political bankruptcy."[15]

While not a great distance from Lenin in his attitude toward the war, Trotsky held out against any alignment with the Bolsheviks. He still retained his emotional ties with the Mensheviks, and did not agree with Lenin that Russia's military defeat was desirable as a means of expediting revolution. He argued, in effect, that the proper duty of revolutionaries was to ply their trade with impartiality—that is, to ignore as irrelevant the question of who the victors and vanquished might be, although it was to be hoped that the war would end before there were decisive results on the battlefield.

These differences were spelled out on a more personal basis in September, 1915, when the two met again at a gathering of anti-war socialists in Zimmerwald, Switzerland, a tiny village near Berne. Thirty-eight delegates representing eleven countries attended, and while the proceedings were hardly momentous, they acquired significance in retrospect because of the Bolshevik Revolution and the disintegration of the Second International. The majority, typified by Martov and Axelrod, hesitated to denounce their "chauvinist" comrades, and a minority, of whom Lenin was the most vociferous, advocated "revolutionary defeatism." Trotsky, with four or five others, sought a middle position. Three draft manifestoes were submitted, and a committee of seven, including Lenin and Trotsky, worked on a suitable compromise. No one seems to have been wholly pleased with the result—unless it was Trotsky, who wrote the final text with some help from the Swiss socialist Robert Grimm.

But in the interest of solidarity it was accepted as a stirring condemnation of the war, of the "ruling forces of capitalist society," and—less vigorously—of the patriotic socialists. As to the proper remedies for this deplorable state of affairs, the manifesto fell strangely silent. It mentioned neither revolution nor civil war and closed with a highly charged exhortation to end the suffering caused by this "bloody barbarity." To a large extent it relied on the rhetoric of pacifism—or at least war weariness—rather than that of revolutionary socialism, but Lenin recorded only a mild protest in the name of the Zimmerwald Left.

The censorship prevented *Nashe Slovo* from any detailed comment on the conference, but Trotsky ingeniously reported on it nonetheless by publishing a "diary" without reference to the time or circumstances of the meeting. "It has been held," he boasted. "And this is the big fact, Mr. Censor! . . . The conference has saved Europe itself, covering the blood and dishonor of fratricide."[16] He declined the subsequent overtures of the Zimmerwald Left, which sought to maintain itself as an organizational entity and was ultimately to become the nucleus of the Third (Communist) International. Yet *Nashe Slovo*, with his reluctant consent, edged closer to the Bolsheviks, and finally Martov, after a series of semi-ultimatums, resigned in the spring of 1916. Shortly thereafter, the so-called second Zimmerwald conference, actually held at the Swiss village of Kienthal, drew up a bolder manifesto than the one Trotsky had drafted in 1915, though it still fell short of Lenin's extreme position. Unable to attend the Kienthal meeting because the French authorities denied him permission to enter Switzerland, Trotsky publicly endorsed the conference results.

The Trotsky of *Nashe Slovo* was of a different breed than the Antid Oto of *Kievskaya Mysl*. Although receptive to "advanced" social opinions, the Kiev paper was a patriotic organ, and its French correspondent found it expedient to conceal his anti-war opinions for fear of losing his meager but indispensable source of income. For a revolutionary socialist, particularly one with Trotsky's haughty pride, it must have been a humiliating experience. His failure to allude to the peculiar schizophrenia of his wartime journalism in his autobiography reinforces this impression. Confined largely to descriptive and factual reporting, he wrote with his customary verve and passion, and his best pieces compare favorably with his reports during the Balkan wars.

The French censorship, subject to indirect pressure from the Russian embassy, continued its war of attrition against *Nashe Slovo*. In September, 1916, the newspaper was suppressed and again succeeded in resurrecting itself under a new name. But Trotsky was expelled from France and ordered to go to a country of his own choosing. Since England and Italy declined to receive him, a return to Switzerland seemed the obvious solution. The necessary visa was refused, apparently because of Allied intervention in Berne. After fending off the French police for about six weeks, he was escorted to the Spanish border and made his way to Madrid. Ignorant of the language and without contacts, he visited the art treasures of the Prado and tried to read the local newspapers with the aid of a dictionary. The police arrested him in a week's time—they had been warned in a telegram from Paris about a "dangerous anarchist" in their midst. Escorted to Cadiz on the south Atlantic coast, he balked at being placed aboard a ship bound for Cuba and was allowed to remain until a passage to the United States could be arranged. He stayed several weeks in Cadiz under mild police observation and then won permission to meet his family in Barcelona.

The Trotskys sailed for New York on December 25 aboard the *Monserrat*, an old Spanish vessel ill-suited to ocean voyages in the dead of winter. But it carried a neutral flag, a conspicuous advantage for avoiding German submarines, which to some extent compensated for the "high fares," "bad accommodations," and "even worse food." On January 13, 1917, a raw and wet Sunday, they landed in New York City, "its streets a triumph of cubism, its moral philosophy that of the dollar."

Trotsky and his family rented an inexpensive apartment in the Bronx containing such unaccustomed luxuries as electric lights, a bath, a stove, a telephone, and an elevator. He joined the editorial staff of a small daily, *Novy Mir* ("New World"), whose most prominent member was Nikolai Bukharin, a staunch Bolshevik despite ideological differences with Lenin. He also found the time to speak (in Russian or German, for his English was poor) to various socialist groups in New York and other eastern cities. His stay in the United States was so brief—about ten weeks—and his fame so sudden after his departure that a number of fanciful tales about his obscurity and poverty gained currency. One story claimed that he was a codfish cleaner, another that he was a dishwasher, a third that he eked out a living as a tailor. But his sole occupation was that of a revolutionary socialist. As such, he took a dim view of the philistine American brand, although he found Eugene Debs an attractive figure.[17]

Disgusted with the "innocuous pacifist neutrality" of the Socialist party organ, Trotsky and his colleagues were planning a competing Marxist weekly when in mid-March the first confused reports arrived of an uprising in Petrograd (St. Petersburg had been renamed for patriotic reasons in 1914). The revolutionaries, both in Russia and abroad, were caught by surprise. The Tsar and his government were swept aside by the anonymous crowds of the capital with such ridiculous ease that the event itself seemed to mock the heroic but futile efforts of previous generations. A Provisional Government, with Trotsky's old adversary Milyukov as minister of foreign affairs, stepped into the political vacuum, and the Petrograd Soviet revived on the strength of the legend it had created in 1905. Journalists flocked to the offices of *Novy Mir* as if its editors, being Russian expatriates, had special knowledge denied to foreigners. Trotsky's prediction that the "proletariat party" (meaning, apparently, the anti-war Social Democrats) would inevitably assume power during the second stage of the Russian Revolution was treated with polite skepticism when not ridiculed as absurd nonsense.

On March 27 Trotsky, his family, and a number of other Russian émigrés sailed on the Norwegian ship *Christianiafjord*. He left with some regret that he "only managed to catch the general life-rhythm of the monster known as New York. . . . a peep into the foundry in which the fate of man is to be forged."[18] Well equipped with passports and visas, he anticipated no difficulty. But when the ship arrived in Halifax, Nova Scotia, Canadian officials cross-examined the Russian passengers about their political plans and convictions. Trotsky refused to cooperate and was later carried off bodily and taken by train to a camp for German war prisoners at Amherst. His wife and two boys (a second son had been born in Paris) were allowed to stay in Halifax under police surveillance. The authorities presented no formal charges: the camp commandant offered only the general comment—certainly accurate enough—that he was "dangerous to the Allies."

Trotsky's cables to London and Petrograd were held up, and he was confined to the camp for nearly a month. But once the news that he had been interned in Canada leaked out in Russia, his release was only a matter of time. In Petrograd the British ambassador's lame excuse that he had been detained for traveling "under a subsidy from the German embassy, to overthrow the Provisional Russian government," invited derision and fresh protests. *Pravda*, the revived Bolshevik organ, denounced the accusation as "malicious slander."[19] The real culprit, however, was Milyukov, who requested on April 10 that Trotsky (and several others) be held until further notice despite a sweeping amnesty granted to political victims of the tsarist regime. Under pressure from the Petrograd Soviet the Provisional Government, in the person of its foreign minister, finally relented, and the prisoners were released. Trotsky had spent his confinement as a minor celebrity among the eight hundred or more German prisoners. He harangued them on the imperialist war and other favorite topics until the camp commander, receiving a protest from outraged German officers, forbade any more public speeches.

Trotsky left Amherst on April 29 and rejoined his family in Halifax. They sailed on a slow Danish vessel—the voyage took over two weeks—and traveled by train across Sweden. In Finland, on the journey to Petrograd, Trotsky encountered two acquaintances, Emile Vandervelde and Henri de Man, prominent Belgian socialists on a patriotic mission to spur the Russian war effort. An unfriendly discussion ensued, though Trotsky later claimed that he had snubbed them because of their doctrinal apostasy. On May 17, more than ten years since he had left his homeland, he arrived at Finland Station in the Russian capital.

CHAPTER 4

Convert to Bolshevism

TROTSKY received a tumultuous welcome in Petrograd, though it was smaller and less ostentatious than the reception accorded Lenin, who had arrived from Switzerland via Germany at the same station a little more than a month before. As a latecomer on the revolutionary scene, he had to acclimate himself to the "new" Petrograd, with its competing ideologies, popular demonstrations, and precarious balance of power between the "legal" government and the Petrograd Soviet. The Provisional Government had survived its first crisis, a controversy over foreign policy. Milyukov, insisting on the sanctity of the secret treaties that the tsarist regime had signed with its allies, aroused the suspicion of the unruly workers and soldiers of the capital. Their mass protest, hovering on the edge of prolonged and bloody rioting, forced a reorganization of the cabinet that was consummated the day after Trotsky's arrival. Milyukov resigned under pressure, and five moderate socialists active in the Petrograd Soviet accepted ministerial portfolios. A sixth, Alexander Kerensky, shifted from Justice to War and soon became a promising candidate for the premiership. The socialism of these new government leaders—and their stand on the war—was of a kind to arouse Trotsky's contempt, and he described Kerensky in retrospect with searing ridicule: "A provincial lawyer . . . [with] no theoretical preparation, no political schooling, no ability to think, no political will. The place of these qualities was occupied by a nimble susceptibility, an inflammable temperament, and that kind of eloquence which operates neither upon mind or will, but upon the nerves. . . . His best speeches were merely a sumptuous pounding of water in a mortar. In 1917, the water boiled and sent up steam, and the clouds of steam provided a halo."[1]

Trotsky and his family found humble quarters in the Kiev Hostelry but soon moved to the lavish apartment of a wealthy acquain-

63

tance named Serebrovsky who had been a militant revolutionary in 1905. Political differences quickly emerged, however, as Serebrovsky was a patriot, and they moved back to the hostelry. As de facto chairman of the previous Soviet, Trotsky was assured of a polite if not cordial reception in its reincarnation, though its new chairman, Nikolai Chkheidze, a Menshevik "defensist," greeted him with little enthusiasm. The small Bolshevik contingent on the Executive Committee proposed that he be admitted to that body on the strength of his position in 1905, and the Socialist Revolutionary and Menshevik majority, after some hesitation, invited him to participate in an advisory capacity. He thus found a platform for his oratory, and when his opinion was solicited as to the viability of the new cabinet he responded by questioning the wisdom of socialist participation. "Our next move," he declared, should be the "transfer [of] the whole power into the hands of the Soviets"—a revolutionary formula that the moderate socialists considered obnoxious but which coincided with Lenin's slogan, "All power to the Soviets!"

Not yet disposed to join the Bolsheviks, Trotsky found a congenial political home with a small group of independent Left socialists known as the *Mezhrayonka* (Inter-District Committee). Its membership constituted an intellectual elite, and the more distinguished among them—men such as Ryazanov, Yoffe, and Anatole Lunacharsky—had been associated with some of Trotsky's journalistic endeavors. The organization lacked a basis for mass support and considered merging with the Bolsheviks. On May 23 Lenin and his principal lieutenants met Trotsky and several of his new associates in an attempt to reach a working agreement. The negotiations were never reported in any detail, but Lenin offered the *Mezhrayontsi* key positions in the party, and Trotsky an editorial post on *Pravda*. The old antagonism still festered, however, at least on Trotsky's part, and he haughtily insisted on a refurbished party with a new name. "I cannot call myself a Bolshevik," he declared. "Old factional labels are undesirable."[2] Such a position was wholly unrealistic. Lenin had nurtured his party in the lean years of emigration and did not propose to dismantle it, even semantically, now that it was beginning to enjoy political success. His distaste for Trotsky's temperamental personality could only have been reinforced by this new confrontation.

The *Mezhrayontsi*, going their own way for the time being,

founded a journal, *Vperyod* ("Forward"), under Trotsky's editorship. Intended as a weekly, it appeared only at irregular intervals and never mustered proper financial support or gained a mass readership. Seeking a more prestigious outlet for his literary talent, Trotsky approached the editorial staff of Maxim Gorky's *Novaya Zhizn* ("New Life")—"a small political reconnoiter," as he condescendingly put it later. But its editors were unwilling to jettison their ties with Menshevism, and he allegedly concluded the discussion by remarking: "Now I see there is nothing left for me to do but found a newspaper together with Lenin."[3]

Frustrated as a journalist, Trotsky had ample opportunity to exercise his skills as an orator. He spoke at a variety of public meetings, and the wooden amphitheater known as the Modern Circus became his favorite rostrum. There an enthusiastic audience, filling every nook and cranny, listened with rapt attention and explosive appreciation as he discussed current events and the course of the revolution with impassioned eloquence. England, because of his experience in Canada, was his favorite whipping boy among the great powers, and he denounced the evils of British imperialism with special relish. The mood of the crowd sometimes set the tone and content of his speech, and on those occasions he would discard his prepared remarks and allow his subconscious the freedom of improvisation. He also became a favorite with the sailors of Kronstadt, the naval base near Petrograd. Perhaps the most militant of all the revolutionary groups, they were prone to mutinous violence and semi-anarchistic outbursts. Trotsky, though declining to endorse their unruly behavior, defended them before the Soviet and won a measure of devotion far exceeding that of any other revolutionary leader, including Lenin.

By the early summer of 1917, the spirit of good will and revolutionary camaraderie that followed the fall of the monarchy had almost entirely dissipated. Inflation continued to erode the living standards of the urban masses, and the workers as well as the soldiers of the Petrograd garrison displayed a growing resentment of the counsels of moderation emanating from the Menshevik-Socialist Revolutionary leadership in the Soviet. Passive since 1906, the peasants began to demonstrate their immemorial hunger for land by performing acts of sabotage against the gentry. The outright seizure of the land, endemic later in the year, awaited the self-demobilization of the army, for the common soldier was almost invariably a peasant in uniform. The harassed Provisional Government could contrive no more imaginative a response than to promise that a future Constituent Assembly would consider the agrarian problem after the war. But as a stopgap solution to the government's decaying moral authority and a scheme to refurbish the image of a patriotic Russia defending its "revolutionary honor," preparations began for a new military offensive. Kerensky, as "Persuader-in-Chief," toured the front in a vain attempt to infuse the troops with a fighting spirit.

The Soviet, imbued with a "defensist" philosophy in regard to the war, gave at best only lukewarm support. Its idealistic formula of ending the carnage in a general peace "without annexations and indemnities" found expression in a proposal made originally by moderate socialists in neutral Holland and Scandinavia to convene an international socialist conference in Stockholm. Toward the end of May, Angelica Balabanoff, an independent Marxist, called a meeting of Zimmerwaldists and other interested parties to discuss the matter of participation. The majority decided to boycott the projected conference, and no one rivaled Trotsky's vehemence in denouncing its socialist sponsors. His extremism irritated Lenin, and Balabanoff inquired as they left the meeting together: "Can you explain to me, Vladimir Ilyich, why Trotsky does not join your party? What is it that separates him from you? Why does he publish his own paper? He seems more Bolshevik than the Bolsheviks." Lenin seemed surprised and annoyed by the question. "Don't you know?" he responded curtly. "Ambition, ambition, and more ambition." The tone of his voice conveyed his disgust for what he regarded as another manifestation of Trotsky's vanity.[4]

Whatever his personal feelings toward Trotsky—and there is no evidence that they ever became intimate or went beyond the amenities of a political partnership—Lenin respected his extraordinary gifts and welcomed his cooperation. Both attended the First Congress of Soviets which opened in Petrograd on June 16, but neither played a prominent role. Lenin, "surrounded by a hostile crowd that looked upon him as a wild beast," aroused the delegates to laughter when he asserted that his party was ready to assume the responsibilities of political power at any time. Trotsky's major address, delivered on June 22, centered on the familiar theme of the imperialist war, and he predicted that the coming offensive would end in failure. "Every thinking soldier," he declared, "asks himself: for every five drops of blood that I shed today will not one drop alone be shed in the interest of the Russian Revolution and four for the French stock exchange and for English imperialism?"[5] For the first time he established a working relationship with Lenin by revising a Bolshevik resolution attacking the military offensive. Trotsky's services were used more frequently thereafter, and he began to think of himself as a Bolshevik despite his lingering uneasiness at the party label. His formal admission was delayed until August, apparently to allow time to bring in the whole *Mezhrayonka* organization. Unfortunately, none of the principals, including Trotsky himself, saw fit to relate the details of his decision to cast his lot with Bolshevism.

The "Kerensky offensive," launched on July 1, became a disastrous rout, a debacle that even Trotsky and the Bolshevik doomsayers had not foreseen. Nor did they anticipate the massive semi-insurrection that erupted in the capital in mid-July. The most volatile and "Bolshevized" unit of the garrison, the First Machine Gun Regiment, became the catalyst for the seething frustration of the local workers and soldiers. Trotsky and Lunacharsky addressed the machine gunners on the fifteenth but with no premonition of what was to follow. The next morning the regiment held a mass meeting and decided to conduct an armed demonstration. Lenin was out of town for a brief respite, and his adjutants were caught by surprise, though many of the lesser Bolsheviks welcomed a show of strength as a salutary lesson for the government and its Soviet supporters. But the pent-up anger flared into sporadic violence on the seventeenth as Kronstadt sailors, factory workers, and other regiments marched to the Tauride Palace, where the Soviet Executive Committee held forth. By assuming leadership of the trigger-happy demonstrators the Bolsheviks could have toppled the government with ease. Lenin, however, was wary of premature action before the revolutionary crisis had matured. Hastily recalled to Petrograd, he counseled restraint and vigilance in a brief speech to a huge crowd that had gathered at Bolshevik headquarters.

In the afternoon the mob outside the Tauride Palace grew ugly. When Victor Chernov, the Socialist Revolutionary minister of agriculture, tried to speak he was seized by a group of sailors as a "hostage." Fearing a lynching, Trotsky, Kamenev, Lunacharsky, and Martov rushed to his rescue. Although well known to the

Kronstadters, Trotsky could hardly make himself heard. "You've come to declare your will and show the Soviet that the working class no longer wants to see the bourgeoisie in power," he announced, intending to tame the crowd with flattery. "But why hurt your own cause by petty acts of violence against casual individuals? Individuals are not worthy of your attention." And he ended his short speech with an adroit psychological ploy: "Those here in favor of violence raise their hands." No one did so, and the shaken Chernov was released. Trotsky later maintained that Chernov's captors were *agents provocateurs*, but his evidence is not persuasive.[6]

By late evening, as "loyal" regiments arrived at the Tauride Palace, the street crowds dwindled and finally dispersed. The popular mood suddenly shifted, and within hours military and civilian "patriots" roamed the city seeking vengeance on the Bolsheviks. Documents of doubtful authenticity, hastily released by the Ministry of Justice, sought to prove that Lenin and his cohorts were German agents. "The month of the great slander," as Trotsky labeled it, set in. That German money had indeed found its way into Bolshevik coffers seems likely, but the government's case, though outwardly impressive, was insubstantial. Lenin and Zinoviev, wary of a "legal lynching," went underground. Kamenev and a number of lesser Bolsheviks were arrested. Trotsky spent several days hiding in the apartment of a Menshevik friend before "surfacing" at the Tauride Palace to defend Lenin from the German agent calumny. He recalled running a gauntlet of "furious glances, venomous whispers, grinding of teeth, and a demonstrative elbowing. . . . The route to the canteen of the [Soviet] Executive Committee was a little Golgotha in those days."

On July 23, in a demonstration of his solidarity with the Bolsheviks, he addressed an open letter to the Provisional Government declaring that though he was not a party member he fully shared the views of Lenin, Zinoviev, and Kamenev, and that there were no logical grounds for exempting him from arrest. Gorky's *Novaya Zhizn* published his statement since the Bolshevik papers had been suppressed. The government had been prepared to ignore him, but his insolent bravado invited retaliation, and on August 5 he and Lunacharsky were arrested and sent to one of the prisons that Trotsky had become familiar with in 1905. The relative leniency of tsarist times had given way to a sterner regimen in which "politicals" were no longer separated from common criminals. The food was inadequate, probably because of inflation and a supply and distribution problem rather than a deliberate attempt to punish the prisoners. But conditions improved when the anti-Bolshevik political climate had run its course.

Trotsky put his pen to work and apparently had no difficulty sending his articles to the Bolshevik press, which had now revived under different labels. Perhaps his most telling pronouncement was another open letter to the government (Kerensky had now become premier) deriding its slovenly indictment: the prosecution charged him with returning to Russia via Germany and with becoming a member of the Bolshevik Central Committee. Events were shortly to confirm this latter charge. A party congress, held semi-clandestinely and without Lenin or Zinoviev, absorbed the *Mezhrayontsi* and named Trotsky and twenty-one others to the new Central Committee. It became apparent that some of the Old Bolsheviks harbored a lingering resentment toward their eminent new recruit when they failed by a single vote to appoint him to the editorial staff of the leading party organ. Under the circumstances, however, it could only be an honorary post, and he was duly elected after his release from custody.

While Trotsky languished in prison, the Bolsheviks licked their wounds, and Right wing opinion enjoyed a brief resurgence, a "man on horseback" emerged in the public spotlight. This potential savior of the propertied class was Lavr Kornilov, a professional soldier whom Kerensky had appointed commander-in-chief after the ill-fated July offensive. Bolshevik propaganda had rung the tocsin of "counterrevolution" so loudly and so frequently that the concept had been debased by the time a genuine menace to the Revolution appeared. Lenin had applied the Napoleonic label to Kerensky with reckless abandon, and Trotsky, never at a loss for a rhetorical flourish, had spoken of the future premier as "the mathematical center of Russian Bonapartism" more than two months before. But Kerensky's qualities, however demagogic, were ill-suited to dictatorship, and he awoke rather late to the realization that his appointee made little distinction among the various brands of socialism and that he himself might suffer the same fate as his "colleagues" of the extreme Left.

Although unwilling to take power in its own right, the Petrograd Soviet seized the initiative in defending the capital when Kornilov's troops threatened to bring down the Provisional Government in the

second week of September. The Bolshevik Red Guard, a workers'
militia all but disbanded after the July Days, was allowed to rearm,
and Bolshevik agitators were sent out to sap the morale of the attacking force. Trotsky's fate and that of his fellow prisoners hung in the
balance. During the height of the emergency a group of sailors
visited the prison and asked him if the time was ripe to overthrow
the government. "No, not yet," was his alleged reply. "Use
Kerensky as a gun-rest to shoot Kornilov. Afterward we will settle
with Kerensky."[7]

The paradox of some Bolsheviks defending the government while
others were being prosecuted by it came to an end when most of the
political prisoners were released. Trotsky, after a lengthy interrogation, had finally refused to give further testimony, and on September 17 he was freed on bail of three thousand rubles. By this
time the Kornilov adventure had collapsed without a shot being
fired. Armed support for counterrevolution proved as evanescent as
that for the tsarist regime the previous March. Trotsky resumed his
prominent role in the Petrograd Soviet, now as a Bolshevik tribune,
and he also reappeared on a regular basis at the Modern Circus. He
and his family found new quarters in a rather well-to-do neighbor-
hood. Some of the residents indicated displeasure at the proximity
of so notorious a radical, but the protests ceased abruptly when a
Bolshevik sailor made some "friendly" visits.

Public opinion, traumatized by the attempted Kornilov *Putsch*,
veered sharply to the Left. The Bolsheviks flourished, not simply
because they had formed the advance guard against a threatened
military dictatorship, but because the "bourgeoisie" and its lackeys
had been badly compromised in the eyes of the masses. On September 13 a Bolshevik resolution secured a majority vote in the
Petrograd Soviet, and five days later a similar victory was recorded
in the Moscow Soviet. The Provisional Government, which had
depended on Soviet support for its very existence, began to flounder
badly, and Kerensky attempted to shore up his waning authority by
ruling temporarily through a five-man "Directory" instead of a coalition cabinet.

The Mensheviks and Socialist Revolutionaries, in an effort to restore their sagging prestige, organized with Kerensky's support a
popular assembly known as the Democratic Conference. Lenin,
who had sought sanctuary in Finland, condemned it as a fake parliament representing "only the compromising upper strata of the

petty bourgeoisie" and demanded a boycott. But his general staff in Petrograd overruled him, and a delegation of sixty-six, most of them workers and soldiers, attended under Trotsky's leadership. The rude behavior of the Bolsheviks contrasted sharply with the polite loquaciousness of the intelligentsia who dominated the proceedings. Trotsky spoke at the opening session on September 27, and the Left Menshevik, Nikolai Sukhanov, noted that his usual "metallic clarity of speech and the polished phrase" were absent. Nonetheless, it was a "magnificent oration" in which the audience, though unresponsive to Bolshevik ideas, listened with appreciation if not admiration to his sallies against Kerensky and his indictment of the Kadets (Constitutional Democrats) for their involvement in the Kornilov revolt. After upbraiding the organizers of the conference for its unrepresentative character, he escorted his followers from the assembly hall. "Whereas the [Moscow] State Conference gave an impetus to the insurrection of Kornilov," he argued, "the Democratic Conference finally cleared the road for the Bolshevik insurrection."[8] His verdict inflates the significance of the latter conference out of all proportion to its modest role in the steady deterioration of the Provisional Government.

As Kerensky proceeded to ignore the will of his moderate socialist allies by forming a new cabinet with Kadet participation, the Petrograd Soviet elected Trotsky as its chairman on October 8. His acceptance speech contained a promise of democratic procedure that later events (and Trotsky himself) were to repudiate: "We shall conduct the work of the Petersburg Soviet in a spirit of justice and of complete freedom for all factions; the hand of the presidium will never lend itself to the repression of a minority."[9] The Soviet passed his resolution, which denounced Kerensky's new government as counterrevolutionary and expressed the hope that the forthcoming Second Congress of Soviets would establish a "truly revolutionary government."

Out of the Democratic Conference another interim assembly emerged—the Council of the Republic or Pre-Parliament. Again Lenin called for a boycott, and in the Bolshevik Central Committee Trotsky became the leading spokesman for the boycotters, emerging with a nine to eight majority. The narrowness of the decision led to a Bolshevik conference at which the Central Committee was overruled by a vote of seventy-seven to fifty (Lenin commented in his "diary": "Trotsky was for the boycott. Bravo, Comrade Trotsky!")[10]

The question involved more than a matter of political tactics, for the boycotters, by abandoning the parliamentary game, demonstrated their willingness to consider a Bolshevik seizure of power. The "conciliators," on the other hand, recoiled from the idea of a test of strength, regarding it as premature and dangerous.

Abiding by the party decision, Trotsky led the Bolshevik delegation (again sixty-six members) at the opening session of the Pre-Parliament on October 20. A sensational rumor made the rounds that the Bolsheviks ("bandits, idlers, and hooligans" to most of the bourgeois deputies) were prepared to disrupt the assembly with a demonstration. Trotsky, when queried, replied: "A mere nothing, a little shot from a pistol." His cryptic response was not reassuring, and a tense silence gripped the hall as he prepared to speak, having been allotted ten minutes to make a special announcement in the name of his party. He again attacked the government, emphasizing its dependence on the "propertied elements" and its reluctance to convene the long promised Constituent Assembly. The bourgeoisie was "openly steering a course for the bony hand of hunger" and favored the idea of "surrendering the revolutionary capital to German troops." This latter charge (which seems to have had little or no basis in fact) caused an uproar, recalling the "barroom atmosphere of the bourgeois State Duma." The chairman finally restored order as Trotsky feigned complete indifference. Resuming his speech, he referred to "this government of national treachery," again triggering an explosion of protest that spurred most of the conservative delegates to their feet. He began to lose his poise and concluded amid the noisy commotion: "We have nothing in common with that murderous intrigue against the people conducted behind the official scenes. In withdrawing from the provisional council we call upon the workers, soldiers, and peasants of all Russia to be stalwart and courageous. Petrograd is in danger! The revolution is in danger! The nation is in danger! The government is intensifying that danger. . . . All power to the Soviets! All land to the people! Long live an immediate, honorable, democratic peace! Long live the Constituent Assembly!"[11]

Trotsky then led the Bolshevik delegation out of the chamber, just as he had at the Democratic Conference. This ostentatious exit had an air of spontaneity, but it had been predetermined two days before by the Central Committee, with Kamenev the lone dissenter. Most of the remaining delegates were delighted to be rid of the troublemakers, who were, after all, only "specimens of a peculiar breed of wild beast who were leaving the society of mankind." In Trotsky's view, "The withdrawal from the Pre-Parliament in the eyes of the people burned the last bridges uniting the party of insurrection with official society."[12]

But were the Bolsheviks, in Trotsky's confident assumption, the "party of insurrection"? Lenin did not think so and had been bombarding his lieutenants with urgent messages pleading for action. Trotsky himself, though more resolute than his colleagues, was less optimistic about an armed seizure of power by the Bolsheviks alone than his comments after the fact strongly imply. He preferred a quasi-legal approach under the authority of the Petrograd Soviet and wanted the timing of the rising to coincide, if possible, with the next Congress of Soviets. But Lenin, frantic with impatience lest the party let slip its historic opportunity, protested against further delay. The congress had been postponed to November 2, and the "tempo of Russian life," he argued, "is such that this almost means postponing it to the Greek calends" (i.e., it would never meet). Hoping to incite the party by his personal presence, he returned to Petrograd about the same time the Bolsheviks walked out of the Pre-Parliament. The warrant for his arrest was still outstanding, and he found refuge in the apartment of a friend of Krupskaya's.

The Petrograd Soviet endorsed Trotsky's conduct in the Pre-Parliament and passed a resolution of censure in which the assembly was labeled "counterrevolutionary." At the same session (on October 22) the delegates voted to establish a "revolutionary committee of defense" which would protect the capital from an attack by "military and civilian Kornilovites." The supposed menace from the Right was one of Trotsky's favorite refrains; although his concern may have been largely rhetorical, Lenin's appears to have been genuine. From this "defense committee" an organization emerged a few days later that was formally designated the Military Revolutionary Committee, but its reputation as the tactical command post for the Bolshevik Revolution is more legendary than factual. Trotsky, as chairman of the Petrograd Soviet, became its ex officio leader (or so he maintained). Curiously, his claim has not been corroborated by other sources, though there is no reason to doubt that he was the key figure in the agitational as well as the technical preparations for the armed uprising.

On October 23 Trotsky attended a secret meeting of the Bolshevik Central Committee at which Lenin presented his case for an immediate seizure of power. It was held in the apartment of Nikolai Sukhanov, the most famous chronicler of the revolutionary year, but unfortunately for future historians, in his absence. Although the twelve participants argued all night, little more than the substance of their decision is known: Lenin's impassioned pleas for insurrection gained the necessary support by a vote of ten to two (Zinoviev and Kamenev were the dissenters). But no date was set, nor was there an attempt to flesh out a battle plan. Moreover, the easy margin of Lenin's victory in the Central Committee concealed serious misgivings at all levels of the party as to the wisdom of an immediate confrontation with the Provisional Government. Since Lenin's strategy was to prove correct, the recollections of his assistants tend to underplay their fear and hesitation. As Trotsky put it, "The doubts are painted in with water colors and the confidence in heavy oil."[13]

Trotsky's visibility in the two weeks preceding the Bolshevik Revolution was greater than that of any other party member. "Tearing himself from his work at revolutionary headquarters," Sukhanov reported, he "rushed from the Obukhovsky [factory] to the Trubochny, from the Putilov to the Baltic [shipyards], from the riding school to the barracks, and it seemed that he spoke everywhere simultaneously. Every Petrograd worker and soldier knew him and heard him. His influence on the masses and at headquarters was overwhelming. He was the central figure of those days and the principal hero of this remarkable page of history."[14] In contrast to this ample testimony of Trotsky's ubiquitousness in the capital—and Sukhanov could have added to his list Trotsky's appearances at the Modern Circus and the Petrograd Soviet—there is a dearth of evidence as to his tactical command decisions and to his political relations with Lenin and the Central Committee. As opposed to the great epic celebrated by the party historians (including Trotsky), a strange air of improvisation and equivocation surrounds the Bolshevik triumph. The leaders apparently never agreed on a specific date to launch a coup d'état, nor is there any indication that they drew up a master plan or even tentative guidelines on the military aspects of the takeover. Lenin's two closest associates, Zinoviev and Kamenev, remained firm opponents of the enterprise, infuriating their chief by voicing their objections in Gorky's newspaper. As for Lenin himself, he remained in seclusion until the insurrection had actually begun. Almost by default, it would seem, History thrust Trotsky into the role of chief conspirator against the Provisional Government.

The Bolsheviks had as their striking force a reactivated Red Guard, the Kronstadt sailors, and several units of the garrison. While this was hardly a formidable army, the government's military support, as future events soon demonstrated, was unreliable to the point of uselessness. The Bolshevik Military Organization commanded this puny but, under the circumstances, quite adequate body of troops, and maintained a kind of interlocking directorate with the Soviet's Military Revolutionary Committee. The latter met infrequently, and its effective leader, Nikolai Podvoisky, was a veteran party worker of energy and dedication but lacked professional military training.

One of Trotsky's greatest services to his adopted party as it cautiously and rather fearfully tested the government's strength was his campaign to neutralize the garrison. On any and all occasions he denounced Kerensky's plan to transfer various regiments from Petrograd to the front as a counterrevolutionary step and a plot to deliver the capital to the Germans. The theme had first been developed at the Pre-Parliament, and the government did use the potential German threat as a pretext to order the removal of disaffected units of the garrison. With the memory of Kornilov still fresh, Trotsky and the Bolshevik press had only to conjure up the general's image to arouse distrust of Kerensky's intentions. The slogan "Petrograd in danger" rallied the soldiers and workers to the Soviet—and indirectly to the Bolshevik cause—as no forthright summons to insurrection could have done. A decisive but undramatic shift of power occurred on October 28 when, at a meeting of regimental committees, a resolution openly defied the government's authority by forbidding any units to leave the city without Soviet permission.

Trotsky recognized that the Red Guard was a more reliable Bolshevik weapon than the soldiers of the garrison, few of whom were spoiling for a fight. If more highly motivated, it was poorly armed. A partial solution was found in late October when a workers' delegation complained to Trotsky about a shortage of weapons. He explained that the Bolsheviks had no access to the arsenals, but they countered his assertion by relating their visit to the Sestroretsk arms factory, where they had been told that weapons were available if the

Soviet would authorize their distribution. He promptly wrote out an order for five thousand rifles, and it was just as promptly honored.

By this time rumors had spread throughout the city that a Bolshevik rising was imminent. But they were based on the false assumption that the aimless mass violence of the July Days would be repeated on a larger scale. "We are told that we are preparing a staff for the seizure of power," Trotsky boldly announced at a meeting of the Petrograd Soviet on October 29. "We make no secret of it." Two days later, before the same body, he shifted his emphasis to the alleged conspiracy of the bourgeoisie. "We have not set a date for the attack. But the opposing side has, evidently, already set it. We will . . . repel it . . . and we will declare that at the first counterrevolutionary attempt to hamper the work of the Congress of Soviets we will answer with a counteroffensive which will be ruthless and which we will carry out to the end."[15]

In the midst of these turbulent events—the celebrated "ten days that shook the world"—Trotsky found time for a "cause" that, in contrast to his revolutionary duties, seems superfluous and almost comic. He worked himself into a state of righteous indignation because the city government had decided to levy a five kopeck streetcar fare on the soldiers of the garrison, who had formerly ridden free of charge (civilians paid twenty kopecks). Seemingly a sensible solution to a mounting financial burden, it struck him as an outrageous imposition which he proceeded to denounce in a ringing speech to the Petrograd Soviet. To Sukhanov, who witnessed the "rather miserable scene," it was an example of Trotsky's demagogy—a yielding to "primitive capriciousness and anarchy."[16]

Trotsky put his "demagogy" to better use on November 4 at a mass meeting at the People's House. He "promptly began to heat up the atmosphere with his skill and brilliance," recalled Sukhanov. Trotsky painted a vivid picture of the suffering in the trenches and the duty of the bourgeoisie to share its good fortune with the freezing soldiers and the working poor. The notion "could not but excite the enthusiasm of a crowd which had been reared on the tsarist whip. . . . [It] was a mood close to ecstacy . . . as if the crowd, spontaneously and of its own accord, would break into some religious hymn." After obtaining an enthusiastic show of hands to one of his rhetorical propositions, Trotsky drew to a close: "Let this vote of yours be your oath—with all your strength and at any sacrifice to support the Soviet, which has taken on itself the great burden of bringing to a conclusion the victory of the revolution and of giving land, bread, and peace!"[17]

If Trotsky was as confident of victory as his public statements profess, his optimism must have been based on considerations other than a resolute and united front against the enemy. For the party—at least its leadership—was in disarray. Lenin, still in hiding, took no part in the final preparations. He seems to have been almost exclusively occupied with berating Zinoviev and Kamenev for their "strikebreaking" activities and with urging their expulsion from the party. The Central Committee was reluctant to take such a drastic step. Zinoviev had become politically inactive and gone back into hiding. Kamenev, who had offered to resign from the Central Committee, was finally released by a vote of five to three (Trotsky sided with the majority). Stalin, who was sympathetic to the "strikebreakers" despite his support for Lenin, submitted his resignation from the editorial board of the chief Bolshevik organ. It was rejected, according to Trotsky, "in order not to complicate an already difficult situation."

Although Kerensky maintained a confident attitude, the government had no reliable troops to command. The garrison had acknowledged the authority of the Petrograd Soviet on November 3, and the Bolshevik Military Organization occupied itself with assigning party workers to various regiments as political commissars and other measures to secure the loyalty or neutrality of both officers and men. One potential trouble spot was the Peter and Paul fortress, whose commandant refused to recognize the Bolshevik representative. Trotsky, when consulted about the problem, rejected a forceful solution for the agitational strategy that had worked so well at the time of Kornilov's abortive revolt. On the afternoon of November 6 he and other speakers harangued the fortress garrison and peacefully secured its allegiance to the Soviet. The weapons in the arsenal, which is said to have contained one hundred thousand rifles, were distributed to the Red Guard.

With every prospect of success, the Bolshevik high command still hesitated to give the signal to attack. As Trotsky wrote later, the word "insurrection" was not used: "This was not wholly a formal measure of caution, for the term did not fit the actual situation. It was being left to the government of Kerensky, as you might say, to insurrect . . . the talk was still not about insurrection, but about the 'defense' of the coming Congress of Soviets—with armed forces if necessary."[18]

Whether the Bolsheviks timed their rising for November 7 (as the party historians unanimously claim) or whether, as Trotsky broadly hinted, they hung back waiting for the government to make the first move, is not definitely known. But the sequence of events tends to support his diffident and almost inadvertent account. In the early morning of November 6, military cadets seized the Bolshevik printing plant and sealed the premises, which was the initial skirmish in Kerensky's halfhearted attempt to carry the fight to the enemy. Two workers rushed to the nearby Smolny Institute, a former school for young ladies that served as Bolshevik headquarters, and spread the alarm to Trotsky and Podvoisky. "A piece of official sealing-wax on the door of the Bolshevik editorial-rooms—as a military measure that is not much," Trotsky observed afterward. "But what a superb signal for battle!"[19] A company of the Litovsky Regiment and a battalion of engineers were called out; they brushed aside the token police guard, broke the government seals, and within a short time the presses were rolling again. The cruiser *Aurora*, ordered to sea, remained in the harbor when the crew, after consulting the appropriate Bolshevik authorities, defied its officers. An attempt to raise the Neva River drawbridges connecting the heart of the city with the working class section was also unsuccessful.

At Smolny the Bolshevik Central Committee met during the day to take stock of the situation. The sketchy record of its deliberations does not reveal a decision to seize power, but it does demonstrate that the eleven members present (Lenin, Zinoviev, and Stalin were absent) took determined action to blunt the government's offensive. Trotsky's suggestions as to the disposition of assignments among the committee members and the designation of the Peter and Paul fortress as emergency headquarters should it be necessary to evacuate Smolny were accepted.

Trotsky, whose moments of leisure since his release from prison in September had been few indeed, maintained an even more frantic pace as the decisive confrontation drew near. Seldom leaving Smolny, he slept fully clothed on a leather couch and was frequently interrupted by couriers and telephone calls. On the afternoon of the sixth, after the meeting of the Central Committee, he spoke to the

Bolshevik delegates who were to attend the Second Congress of Soviets the next day. His remarks were basically "defensist" though laced with belligerent phrases. "The arrest of the Provisional Government," he maintained, was "not on the agenda as an independent task. If the congress establishes a government and Kerensky does not submit to it, then it would be a police question rather than a political one."[20]

In the evening, at a meeting of the Petrograd Soviet, Trotsky recounted the morning's events, including the incidents involving the Bolshevik press and the cruiser *Aurora*. He denied that an insurrection had begun: it was simply "revolutionary self-defense." Kerensky's "semi-government," he asserted, was already "inwardly dead," awaiting only "the sweep of history's broom to clear the way for an authentic government." But if it should make a "hazardous attempt to revive its own corpse" and "stab the revolution, then we declare that . . . [we] will answer blow with blow and iron with steel."[21]

Were these ambivalent pronouncements simply "a political screen for the forthcoming night attack," as he later maintained? It seems more likely that in the absence of a clear mandate from the party he assumed that the Soviet congress would peacefully take over the responsibility of governmental authority.

As the two sides continued, in a kind of escalating probing action, to reconnoiter the strength of the other, the Soviet Central Executive Committee met about midnight at Smolny in what was destined to be its last session. The moderate socialists, who had earlier in the day censured Kerensky's government at the Pre-Parliament, sought a compromise. Their spokesman, the Menshevik Fyodor Dan, received an apathetic response except for some sharp heckling as he warned of the counterrevolutionary danger that a Bolshevik rising would set in motion. Trotsky rose to reply, "his thin, pointed face . . . positively Mephistophelian in its expression of malicious irony." "Dan tells you that you have no right to make an insurrection," he declared. "Insurrection is the right of all revolutionists! When the down-trodden masses revolt, it is their right."[22] The Bolsheviks walked out soon afterward, leaving the moderates to a debate that was becoming more irrelevant by the hour.

During the night of November 6–7, as the government failed to locate any large body of troops willing to take up arms on its behalf, the Bolsheviks, peacefully and almost by default, took over the

capital by occupying its strategic buildings and installations. At
dawn only the Winter Palace, the government headquarters, remained as an anti-Bolshevik redoubt. Trotsky had spent a sleepless
night and fainted on one occasion, presumably from exhaustion,
nervous tension, and lack of food, although his propensity toward
fainting spells when under pressure was an established trait. His
combat instructions, repeated many times, were typically melodramatic: "If you fail to stop them with words, use arms. You will
answer for this with your life." Admittedly he lacked confidence in
his own order, for the revolution was "still too trusting, too generous, optimistic and light-hearted." Like everyone else, he overestimated the government's strength, and it was probably Lenin's arrival at Smolny about midnight that converted a timid holding operation into a full-scale offensive. Lenin feared that some kind of compromise solution had been negotiated in his absence, and Trotsky
explained the reports as "only a bit of *ruse de guerre*, military cunning, which we used at the very moment we were opening the
general battle."[23] Perhaps, but there is the suggestion of an unspo-
ken "conspiracy" at Smolny to convince Lenin that his subalterns
had already opened the "general battle" when in fact only preliminary skirmishes had taken place.

The "storming" of the Winter Palace on the evening of the
seventh, a fabled event in the epic of the Bolshevik Revolution, was
in reality an anticlimax in which neither the besiegers nor the besieged showed much inclination to risk their lives. Trotsky had been
among the prominent and slightly premature celebrants at an afternoon session in Smolny of the Petrograd Soviet, together with the
Bolshevik delegates to the Congress of Soviets. As chairman, he led
off the proceedings with a rousing speech: "In the name of the
Military Revolutionary Committee I declare that the Provisional
Government no longer exists. Individual ministers are under arrest. . . . The revolutionary garrison has dispersed the Pre-
Parliament. . . . We don't know of a single casualty. I don't know of
any examples in history of a revolutionary movement in which such
enormous masses participated and which took place so bloodlessly.
The Winter Palace has not yet been taken, but its fate will be
decided in the course of the next few minutes [it was not secured for
another eleven hours or so]. At the present time the Soviet . . .
faces the historically unprecedented experiment of creating a regime which will have no other interests but the needs of the work-

ers, peasants, and soldiers."[24] A Menshevik deputy was over-whelmed: "It was like molten metal, every word burned the soul, it awakened thought and roused adventure, as he spoke of the victory of the proletariat. We listened to him with bated breath, and I saw that many people were clenching their fists as they brought them-selves to the final decision to follow him unwaveringly wherever he might call them."[25]

The Congress of Soviets was postponed until late in the evening to allow more time for the capture of the Winter Palace. The Bol-shevik delegates—to Sukhanov they seemed an "utterly crude and ignorant people whose devotion to the revolution was spite and despair"—formed a sizable majority. And the support of Left Socialist Revolutionaries, who had repudiated the party moderates, clearly placed the anti-Bolshevik socialists in an untenable position. But the Bolsheviks had not yet become a monolithic party, and many greeted Martov's speech on the necessity of creating a broadly based socialist government with warm applause. Other Menshevik speakers were less conciliatory: a "military conspiracy" had been engineered, they charged, and it behooved the conspirators to end the civil strife by opening negotiations with the Provisional Gov-ernment. For the Bolsheviks to repudiate their own revolution would be inconceivable, and some seventy delegates walked out when the rhetorical flourish of the socialist Right had spent itself. Martov renewed his plea for a compromise. Trotsky answered his old comrade with withering scorn: "What has happened is an insur-rection, not a conspiracy. . . . The masses of the people followed our banner, and our insurrection was victorious. And now we are told: renounce your victory, make concessions, reach a com-promise. . . . No, here no compromise is possible. To those who have left and to those who have made these proposals, we must say: you are miserable bankrupts, your role is played out; go where you ought to be: into the garbage can of history."[26] Martov, angry and upset, left the platform, and his faction voted fourteen to twelve to uphold their chief and join the boycotters. It was to be the last confrontation of the two: Trotsky, exulting in the victory of his adopted party and riding the crest of History's immutable wave, and Martov, bitter and stubborn in defeat but ever faithful to his concept of democratic socialism.

CHAPTER 5

Commissar for Foreign Affairs

HAVING seized power with such unexpected ease, the Bolshevik leaders were no more confident of retaining it than they had been of taking it in the first place. Their popular mandate, even among the "toiling masses" for whom they professed to speak, was questionable, but a successful revolution does not seek credentials from the social order it has overthrown. By calling for an immediate general peace and by sanctioning the peasant land seizures, the Bolsheviks gained, if not unanimous approbation, a national consensus more impressive than that of the hapless Provisional Government.

Trotsky's thoughts on the prospects for permanent Bolshevik rule are not on record. But he opposed, as did Lenin, a coalition regime, and the new cabinet, the Council of People's Commissars, consisted entirely of Bolsheviks. Nevertheless, several Left Socialist Revolutionaries were invited to participate but declined, hoping to serve as mediators should a genuine coalition government emerge. Trotsky suggested the revolutionary nomenclature ("commissar" seemed more fitting than the bourgeois "minister"), and Lenin quickly approved: "That's splendid; smells terribly of revolution!"

None of the party leaders had previous government experience. Trotsky, emotionally drained by the nervous tension and exhausting pace of his revolutionary duties ("I felt like a surgeon who has finished a dangerous and difficult operation"), preferred to stay out of the government. He offered to become press director—the non-Bolshevik newspapers, he complained, "kept up a unanimous chorus of wolves, jackals, and rabid dogs." It seemed logical to Lenin that Trotsky, as chairman of the Petrograd Soviet, should also head the cabinet, but when he declined Lenin accepted the post himself. Since the defeat of counterrevolutionary enemies appeared to be the most urgent task, Lenin then insisted that he become commissar for internal affairs. Trotsky again objected and raised, among other arguments, the question of his Jewish origin. Although he believed himself to be a thoroughly emancipated "internationalist"—and as a Marxist he was by definition an atheist—he displayed then and later an abnormal sensitivity to his Jewishness. Lenin, irritated at "such trifles," allowed himself to be overruled, and the Central Committee accepted Jacob Sverdlov's proposal that Trotsky head the Commissariat for Foreign Affairs (Narkomindel).

Lenin's purported remark, "What foreign affairs will we have now?," was well taken, for Russia's allies regarded the new regime with consternation and dismay. From their standpoint Bolshevism was not only a distressing ideology, but its devotees seemed bent on making peace with a more tangible menace—Imperial Germany. To a large extent Trotsky shared Lenin's skepticism about the need for conventional diplomacy, and he almost invariably advised party members who offered their services to look for more gratifying work elsewhere. To one interlocutor, who asked what duties his new office might entail, Trotsky allegedly responded: "I will issue a few revolutionary proclamations to the people of the world, and then shut up shop." He obviously contemplated nothing quite so drastic, but his hyperbole concealed not only disdain for the normal procedures of capitalist government but also the euphoria common to the Bolshevik leadership: the revolution in Russia, they firmly believed, was merely the prelude to a great rising of the European proletariat.

Before Trotsky had an opportunity to serve as foreign minister or properly to organize an office, he was called upon to help repel a Cossack "division" of some seven hundred men marching on Petrograd. Loyal to Kerensky, who had escaped from the Winter Palace to find reinforcements at the front, they met a much larger Bolshevik force at Pulkovo Heights on the outskirts of the city on November 12. The battle itself was inconclusive, but the Cossacks retreated and could not be induced to fight again. Trotsky, who was on the scene, gave much of the credit for the victory to Colonel Valden, a former tsarist officer. "It could hardly have been that he sympathized with us because he understood nothing," Trotsky wrote. "But apparently he hated Kerensky so much that it inspired him with temporary sympathy for us."[2] He and several other professional soldiers at Pulkovo were the first among some fifty thousand who fought for the Reds against the Whites in the long and ferocious civil war that erupted in 1918.

Trotsky and his wife shared a single large room at Smolny Institute. A partition concealed his living quarters from his office, which contained a desk and several wooden chairs. Lenin's office was at the opposite end of the building, and though they could communicate by telephone and messenger service was available, Trotsky "would walk the endless corridor that looked like an ant-hill" several times a day for conferences. He attended the almost daily cabinet meetings where Lenin presided with firm authority over an "immense legislative improvisation." Decrees, many with a large propaganda content to educate the masses, poured forth from Smolny on an amazing variety of subjects. The incipient civil war and problems of food supply and distribution tended to crowd out the "socialist" program of the new regime. Trotsky took on added burdens by presiding over numerous special commissions: transport, food, and publications were among the more important. He also found the time to attend meetings of the party Central Committee and the Central Executive Committee of the Soviet, where he invariably (though not without private doubts) seconded Lenin's demands for an all-Bolshevik government. The "conciliators," led by Kamenev, agitated for a coalition with the other socialist parties. The controversy, which threatened to tear asunder the party in the flood tide of its political success, ended with a Leninist triumph. Three Left Socialist Revolutionaries consented to join the cabinet, but this minor concession to the conciliators did little to conceal the growing party dictatorship. Lenin was always implacable on matters of party discipline, and it was Trotsky's loyalty rather than his other estimable qualities that won from Lenin the ultimate accolade: "There is no better Bolshevik than Trotsky."

At first Trotsky's own commissariat took very little of his time, but as peace negotiations with Germany became a reality his other duties had to be neglected or curtailed. A somewhat disorganized general strike of government employees—anti-Bolshevik almost to a man—piled an added burden on Russia's new rulers, and the Narkomindel was not spared. Several of its high ranking officials were taken into custody until they agreed to cooperate. Trotsky was particularly eager to obtain the secret treaties that the tsarist regime had signed with the Allied governments. When he had an opportunity to examine them, he pronounced them "more cynical in their contents than we had supposed." The documents were published serially in the Bolshevik press, and Trotsky's introduction drove home the lesson that secret diplomacy was "an indispensable tool in the hands of the mighty minority that must blindfold the majority" and that its abolition was the "primary condition for a really honest, popular, democratic foreign policy."[3]

On November 21 Trotsky officially informed the Allied ambassadors of the existence of the new Soviet government and called attention to its peace decree as a "formal offer for an armistice on all fronts and an immediate opening of peace negotiations." The ambassadors agreed to disregard the message, and the Bolsheviks implicitly acknowledged what their own propaganda had previously ignored: peace for Russia could come only through separate negotiations with Germany, not by pretending that all the belligerents would somehow be persuaded to lay down their arms. The chiefs of the Allied military missions attached to Russian army headquarters sent a formal note to the commander-in-chief protesting the proposed armistice and threatening "the gravest consequences" should the 1914 treaty forbidding a separate peace be violated. Interpreted to mean that Japan would be invited to occupy eastern Siberia, the ill-advised protest foreshadowed future Allied intervention in the internal affairs of Russia. Trotsky bitterly denounced this "flagrant interference," asserting that "the soldiers, workers, and peasants of Russia did not overthrow the governments of the Tsar and Kerensky just to become cannon fodder for the Allied imperialists."

A de facto armistice on the eastern front had already existed for several months, and it became official on November 28. In separate notes to the Allied envoys, Trotsky informed them that preliminary peace negotiations were to begin shortly and once more invited their governments' participation. Anticipating refusal—his invitation was again received in silence—he issued an appeal (signed also by Lenin) to the "toiling masses" over the heads of their governments. "Does reactionary diplomacy express their [the people's] thoughts and aspirations?" he asked rhetorically. "We want a general peace, but if the bourgeoisie of the Allied countries force us to conclude a separate peace, the responsibility will be theirs."[4]

A foretaste of Trotsky's tactics against the German negotiators, the manifesto, unfortunately for the Bolsheviks, remained virtually unknown to the "toiling masses" in any of the belligerent countries. But it was a representative sample of his declamatory, pseudo-diplomatic style. When he chose to do so he could be as formal and correct in his official communications as the most conventional of bourgeois diplomats.

On December 2 negotiations for a permanent armistice began at Brest-Litovsk, a town in Russian Poland serving as headquarters for the German army on the eastern front. "History willed it," wrote Trotsky in 1919, "that the delegates of the most revolutionary regime the world has ever known had to sit at the same diplomatic table with the representatives of the most reactionary caste among all the ruling classes." Adolf Yoffe, presumably upon Trotsky's recommendation, led the Russian delegation. It included, aside from the usual complement of diplomats and technical personnel, symbolic representatives from the masses: a soldier, a sailor, a worker, and a peasant. The latter had been fortuitously acquired in Petrograd on the way to the railroad station when Yoffe and his companions suddenly realized that a man of the soil was lacking to round out the party. The talks proceeded with no major complications but were suspended for a week to allow the Russians to consult their superiors in the capital and to give the Allies another opportunity to participate. Trotsky again circulated invitations among the embassies, informing them in some detail of the progress that had been made and requesting a reply. His renewed effort was fruitless, as he must have foreseen, and a formal armistice was signed on December 15.

The party elite did not relish the prospect of a separate peace. The ideal means of avoiding this unpleasant likelihood was a revolution in Germany, but the "science" of Marxism provided no reliable timetable, and as the peace conference drew near Trotsky expressed his grave concern at a mass meeting of Soviet and trade union leaders on December 21. Although his remarks were permeated by the kind of revolutionary eloquence that appeals to the emotions rather than to reason, he faced the issue without flinching: what if the German revolution failed to materialize? "If this dead silence were to continue in Europe much longer, if this silence were to give Wilhelm the chance to attack us and to dictate terms insulting to the revolutionary dignity of our country, then I do not know," he confessed, "whether . . . we could go on fighting." Having so frankly revealed his own inner doubts, he checked himself and reverted to the revolutionary romanticism that in the weeks ahead would come nearer to wrecking the party than the recent controversy over a coalition government. "Yes, we could!" he declared to "stormy applause." "For our life, for our revolutionary honor, we would fight to the last drop of our blood. . . . We have not overthrown the tsar and the bourgeoisie in order to kneel down before the German kaiser." And he used the term "holy war," an expression soon to gain popularity but not, ironically, with Trotsky himself.[5]

The peace conference began the next day. Yoffe, who was still in charge, appeared to believe that Germany would actually restore the Russian territory its army was occupying in Poland and the Baltic littoral. General Max Hoffmann of the German high command corrected his impression: his government did not consider an annexation forceful if portions of the former Russian empire decided "of their own free will" to unite with some other state. Yoffe, "looking as if he had received a blow on the head," eventually threatened to break off the negotiations. But his bargaining position was anemic indeed. The conference recessed on December 28 to allow the Russians to proceed with the futile ritual of urging the Allies to participate. In his proclamation, Trotsky warned that if in the "blind stubbornness which characterizes decadent and perishing classes, [the Allied governments] once more refuse . . . then the working class will be confronted by the iron necessity of taking power out of the hands of those who cannot or will not give the people peace."

The German revolution had not even raised a preliminary tremor, and time, ostensibly a Bolshevik ally, was beginning to run out. "To delay the negotiations," Lenin remarked, "there must be some one to do the delaying." Yoffe's performance had been competent but uninspired, and it seemed to Lenin that Trotsky, unrivaled as a propagandist and rhetorician, should be thrown into the breach at Brest-Litovsk. Trotsky accepted his new assignment with extreme reluctance: "I confess I felt as if I were being led to the torture chamber. Being with strange and alien people always had aroused my fears; it did especially on this occasion."[6] Passing through the Russian lines on his way to the conference, which reconvened on January 9, 1918, he observed with growing despair that the trenches were nearly empty and that a "holy war" was out of the question.

Trotsky was determined to end the air of false camaraderie that the Germans had encouraged: their Russian guests had been treated with hospitable deference, and the two delegations customarily dined together. He regarded the amenities of old-fashioned diplomacy as bourgeois hypocrisy, unsuited to the candor and bluff honesty of a proletarian regime. When Baron Richard von Kühlmann, the polished German foreign minister, remarked pleasantly at their first meeting that it was better to deal directly with the master than with his emissary, Trotsky recoiled involuntarily: "This made me feel exactly as if I had stepped on something unclean." He kept a tight rein on the other members of the delegation, forbidding social intercourse and insisting that they obtain his permission before speaking at the conference table. The four ornaments of proletarian democracy had been unceremoniously dropped, and an impish newcomer, Karl Radek, had signaled his arrival by distributing propaganda leaflets to German troops on the railway platform.

Trotsky spoke for the first time on January 10 and delivered one of many harangues seldom relevant to the business of making peace but well calculated to spin out the negotiations. His remarks, invariably laced with revolutionary propaganda, were designed to seep into the consciousness of the German people. Occasionally he treated his adversaries to beginners' lessons on Marxist principles. A tone of contempt and biting sarcasm pervaded almost every statement, and his malevolent expression indicated to Kühlmann a desire to bring the conference "to a sudden and thorough end by throwing a few hand grenades over the green table."[7] The German foreign minister, the leading spokesman for the Central Powers, possessed more diplomatic finesse and spurned Hoffmann's advice to "give them another touch of the whip." Although a shrewd and experienced debater, he had no conception of the Allied fear of Bolshevism and missed a fine opportunity to parry Trotsky's thrusts by portraying his country as a buffer against the engulfing Red tide.

Hoffmann finally had his chance to interrupt the wordy duel between Trotsky and Kühlmann. "In short, staccato sentences, as if he were snarling at some one or giving orders," he bluntly reminded his opponents that the German army stood victorious on Russian soil and that their demand for the right of self-determination in the occupied area was inconsistent with the Soviet government's practice toward its own people. It was a government "founded purely on power and, indeed, on power which ruthlessly suppresses by force all who think otherwise." Trotsky, anticipating with relish the ways in which the general's mailed-fist approach could be used for propaganda, countered by pointing out that in a class society every government is based on force. Germany used repression to protect big property owners, and the Soviet republic used the same methods to defend the workers. "The thing that surprises and repels the governments of other countries," he declared, "is that we do not arrest strikers but capitalists who subject workers to lock outs, that we do not shoot peasants who demand land but arrest the landowners and officers who try to shoot the peasants." Trotsky was pleased to note that his sally had struck home: "Hoffmann's face," he reported, "grew purple."[8]

After Hoffmann's outburst the negotiations reverted to a more conventional pattern. Trotsky continued to pillory his adversaries as brutal practitioners of power politics, and Kühlmann, with considerable success, sought to embarrass the Russians by inviting representatives of the bourgeois Ukrainian government, which had taken power in Kiev, to address the conference. "I never for a moment doubted," Trotsky reported, "that these over-zealous flunkies would soon be thrown out-of-doors by their triumphant masters." His resourceful brain had already conceived a "pedagogical demonstration" to break out of the straitjacket of a dictated peace. He outlined his scheme in a letter to Lenin: "We declare we end the war but do not sign a peace. They will be unable to make an offensive against us. If they attack us, our position will be no worse than now." Lenin, who spurned the kind of political showmanship that came so naturally to Trotsky, wired that the idea seemed "disputable" to him and suggested that the negotiations be recessed to enable the party leaders to discuss the question in Petrograd.[9] The Russian request for an adjournment was granted, but the terms of what amounted to a German ultimatum were clearly sketched on a map that Trotsky carried back with him on January 18: a blue line stretching from Brest-Litovsk to the Baltic Sea indicated the future boundary of a drastically mutilated Russia.

The top Bolsheviks were in a quandary, and their mood of vacillation between the extremes of signing an annexationist peace and fighting a revolutionary war contributed to the popularity of Trotsky's untested formula. But the rank and file tended to support the so-called Left Communists, led by Nikolai Bukharin, who espoused the "holy war" concept. A party conference on January 21 offered the first full discussion, and the presence of provincial delegates tipped the balance in favor of the Bukharin faction. His policy gained thirty-two votes, Trotsky's "no war, no peace" prescription acquired sixteen, and Lenin's steadfast position in favor of an immediate peace mustered fifteen.

In reconstructing his private conversation with Lenin, Trotsky recorded him as saying:

"All right, let's suppose that we have actually refused to sign a peace, and that the Germans answer it by an advance. What are we going to do then?"

"We will sign the peace at the point of a bayonet," Trotsky replied. "The situation will be clear to all the world."

"But in that case, you won't support the slogans of revolutionary war, will you?"

"Under no circumstances."

"In that case, the experiment will probably not be so dangerous. We will only risk losing Esthonia or Latvia." And Lenin added with a sly chuckle, "For the sake of a good peace with Trotsky, Latvia and Esthonia are worth losing."[10]

On January 22 the Central Committee approved by a vote of nine to seven Trotsky's daring but undeniably risky plan—on the understanding, however, that he would prolong the negotiations as long as possible. He spoke at the Third Congress of Soviets four days later, arousing a spontaneous tribute that reflected his immense popularity, his undiminished powers as an orator, and his audacious policy at Brest-Litovsk. One portion of his speech exposed a curious blind spot in an otherwise informed analysis of the precarious situation in which the Soviet republic found itself. He assumed without a shred of evidence—for there was none—that the Allied governments had come to a secret agreement with Germany. "The peace terms which Germany offers us are also the terms of America, France, and England," he charged; "they are the account which the imperialists of the world are making with the Russian Revolution." His touch of paranoia about a conspiracy among the "imperialists" (a belief that Lenin, among others, apparently shared) stemmed in part from the reluctance of the Allies to make any forthright commitment about military assistance should peace negotiations be broken off. Although the ambassadors remained scrupulously aloof from any direct contact with the Soviet government, unofficial agents maintained a tenuous but serviceable liaison between Smolny and the embassies.

Trotsky resumed his place at the Brest-Litovsk conference table on January 30. He brought with him two Ukrainian Bolsheviks to counteract the German protégés, but the occupation of Kiev by Soviet forces shortly afterward rendered the dispute somewhat academic. To legitimize their expansion, the Germans, nonetheless, found it expedient to sign a treaty with "their" Ukrainians, and Trotsky, "perfectly pale" and with beads of sweat trickling down his forehead, was forced to endure the embarrassment of being "abused by his fellow-citizens in the presence of the enemy."[11] The Bolshevik trump card—a revolution in Germany—had momentarily flashed into view when strikes and demonstations in Berlin, Vienna, Hamburg, and other cities raised hopes that the Central European proletariat was at last heeding its revolutionary duty. By early February, however, these promising developments had collapsed, and Trotsky faced the grim reality of the Russian position. Kühlmann and Hoffmann had grown tired of fencing with their agile opponent. The time had come for Trotsky's bombshell. On February 10 the delegates of the Central Powers listened with something like complacency as he launched into a passionate denunciation of the "imperialist war," a seemingly final gesture of defiance before bowing to the inevitable. But he went on to announce that his government refused "to sanction those conditions which the sword of German and Austro-Hungarian imperialism is ready to inscribe on the living bodies of the people involved" and that it could not "enter the signature of the Russian Revolution under conditions which carry oppression, sorrow, and suffering to millions of human beings." He concluded by reading a signed declaration that unilaterally proclaimed the war at an end. Kühlmann and his colleagues sat in stunned amazement. Hoffmann finally broke the silence: "Unheard of!" he exclaimed.

The Russians departed for Petrograd in a state of euphoria, convinced that they had scored a diplomatic triumph. Kühlmann, loath to "run after the Bolsheviks with pen in hand," was content with a de facto peace. But Hoffmann and the general staff were not squeamish about using force as an answer to unconventional diplomacy. Trotsky, though reasonably confident that he had gambled and won, admitted that the issue had yet to be settled: "I do not want to say that a further advance of the Germans against us is out of the question. Such a statement would be too risky, considering the

power of the German Imperialist Party. But I think that by the
position we have taken . . . we have made any advance a very
embarrassing affair for the German militarists."[12]

Embarrassing or not, the Germans denounced the armistice and
notified the Russians that hostilities would be renewed on February
18. Lenin was attending a meeting when the fateful news arrived by
telegram. Without a word he handed it to Trotsky. "They have
deceived us, after all," he allegedly stated. "There is nothing left,
then, but to sign the old terms, provided that the Germans will
agree to leave them exactly as they are." Trotsky insisted that the
offensive be allowed to get under way as a lesson to the German
workers, but Lenin was adamant: "No, we can't afford to lose a
single hour now. The test has been made. Hoffmann wants to and
can fight. Delay is impossible. This beast jumps fast."

The party's Central Committee met almost continuously for the
next several days. Opinion was so fragmented that a consensus
seemed impossible. The notion of a revolutionary war had lost its
appeal, but Lenin's proposal to sign the peace was defeated by a
single vote. Trotsky sided with the majority, interpreting his
agreement with Lenin to mean that he would support an immediate
peace if an actual offensive as opposed to a mere paper ultimatum
materialized. The reality of the German threat was soon
confirmed—the advance began on schedule—and Trotsky reversed
his position, giving Lenin the necessary authorization to sue for
peace. But the German high command saw no need for haste, and
the mood in Petrograd grew panicky as enemy troops approached
and Berlin remained silent.

The question of Allied assistance suddenly assumed a higher
priority in Bolshevik calculations. The Central Committee voted
narrowly to accept (as Lenin put it) "potatoes and arms from the
bandits of Anglo-French imperialism." After the meeting, the emotional Bukharin flung his arms around Trotsky, who had sponsored
the resolution, and sobbed, "We are turning the party into a dung-
heap." The Allied ambassadors, despite silence in their respective
capitals and a lingering suspicion that Lenin and Trotsky were German agents, gave assurances that support would be forthcoming.
Bruce Lockhart, Britain's unofficial envoy, had previously called on
Trotsky and judged him to be "perfectly honest and sincere in his
bitterness against the Germans" and a man "who would willingly die
fighting for Russia provided there was a big enough audience to see

him do it." To Raymond Robins, who fulfilled a somewhat similar role for the United States, Trotsky was "a four kind son of a bitch, but the greatest Jew since Christ. If the German General Staff bought Trotsky, they bought a lemon."[13]

Now that the strategy of "neither war nor peace" had proved bankrupt, Trotsky raised the question of resigning as commissar for foreign affairs. Lenin, who scorned "bourgeois democracy" and its "parliamentary procedures," wondered why. Because, Trotsky explained, his resignation would imply to the Germans "a radical change in our policy" and would "strengthen their confidence in our willingness actually to sign the peace treaty this time." Lenin agreed that the proposal made good political sense, but the Central Committee urged Trotsky to remain at his post until peace had been formally concluded. He compromised by keeping his resignation a secret for the time being. His successor, Georgi Chicherin, had already taken charge of routine Narkomindel business during his superior's absence at Brest-Litovsk.

The new German terms, when finally submitted on February 23, were harsher than the old ones. Again the party leaders became embroiled in a furious debate. Trotsky's views were ambivalent: emotionally drawn to Bukharin's arguments, he recognized the intellectual force of Lenin's stand. In the end he sought the neutrality of abstention. "There is much subjectivism in Lenin's position," he told his colleagues. "I am not sure that he is right, but I do not want to do anything to disturb the party's unity."[14] Three others followed Trotsky's lead in refusing to vote, giving Lenin a seven to four majority.

This was Trotsky's last "official" act prior to the signing of the peace treaty. His prestige suffered a sharp drop; his conduct at Brest-Litovsk, once seeming so daring and courageous, now appeared vainglorious and foolhardy. He went into seclusion for several days, apparently indisposed because of nervous tension. Reappearing at a meeting of the Soviet Central Executive Committee on February 27, he excoriated the "imperialists" with his old vigor and scornful eloquence. The rumor flourished that "he was so overcome with mortification that he broke down and wept."[15]

On March 3 a Russian delegation, refusing to discuss the terms as a demonstration of its submission to brute force, signed the treaty at Brest-Litovsk. Russia's wealthiest provinces were torn away, an area containing a third of its population, a third of its cultivated land, and half of its industry. With Petrograd in danger—the offensive had been virtually unopposed—the government was in the process of moving the capital to Moscow. Before the leaders departed a special party congress convened on March 6–8 to review the peace terms and to make a formal recommendation to the Congress of Soviets about ratification. The two major antagonists, Lenin and Bukharin, restated their positions. Lenin called attention to Trotsky's "profound mistake," his "bitter overestimation of events," but Radek came to his defense: Trotsky's strategy had "not been an illusion but a policy of revolutionary realism." Radek nevertheless reproached him for not joining the Left Communists. Outwardly unrepentant and quite able to assume his own defense, Trotsky again used the danger of a party split to justify his vacillation: "We who abstained performed an act of great self-restraint, for we sacrificed our 'Ego' in the name of saving the unity of the party."[16] His supporters proposed a resolution commending his conduct of the negotiations. It presented an awkward dilemma, for most of the delegates were convinced of the necessity of ratification and hesitated to go on record in praise of one whose handiwork was now being repudiated. Its defeat, though not intended as a vote of censure, hurt Trotsky's pride, and in his resentment he tendered a resolution that offered a blanket indictment of his own record at Brest-Litovsk. It too was defeated. That he had not lost the party's confidence was amply demonstrated when he and Lenin received the largest number of votes in the election of a new Central Committee.

With Lenin now securely in command of the party, ratification by the forthcoming Congress of Soviets was, if not certain, reasonably assured. But preferring to keep his options open, he encouraged Allied hopes that a separate peace might be thwarted at the eleventh hour. The ambassadors, anticipating a German takeover, had already left Petrograd. The unofficial agents remained and, though Trotsky was technically no longer in charge of foreign affairs, they kept in close touch with him. Robins and Lockhart conveyed to their governments his strong intimation, endorsed by Lenin, that a firm promise of Allied help and the discouragement of Japanese intervention in Siberia would lead to non-ratification of the treaty. That a favorable response—and none came—would have accomplished the desired result seems unlikely. Trotsky took no part in the debates at the Congress of Soviets (according to Robins he remained "sulking" in Petrograd), and Lenin gave no indication that he had wavered in his determination to take the final step.

On March 13 it was announced that Trotsky had resigned as commissar for foreign affairs and had been appointed commissar of war and chairman of the Supreme War Council. He left for Moscow to undertake his new assignment on the sixteenth. At a stopover on the way he was playing the genial host to Lockhart and the members of the British mission at the station restaurant when a telegram informed him that the peace treaty had been ratified by an overwhelming majority. The prolonged melodrama of Brest-Litovsk had tarnished his reputation, but it was to be newly enhanced when the foreign war gave way to a civil war.

CHAPTER 6

Commissar of War

TROTSKY'S new position seemed less than demanding at the time the appointment was made. Although there were ominous rumblings in South Russia, where a number of former tsarist generals had congregated after the Bolshevik Revolution, peace with Germany offered the Soviet regime a chance to set its own house in order. The ailing economy claimed first priority, and Trotsky (unlike the Left Communists) supported Lenin's policy of moderation, loyally calling for "labor, discipline, and order" and the full use of *spetsy*—bourgeois specialists with the necessary technical and managerial experience.

Trotsky's principal duties, however, lay in a field in which he admittedly lacked training and expertise. He had grave reservations about accepting the post, but Lenin, with an assist from Jacob Sverdlov (the Soviet republic's titular president), persuaded him "because there was no one else to do it." Only marginally interested in military organization and tactics, he was fascinated by the psychology of an army—"its barracks, trenches, battles, hospitals, and the like." To compensate for his ignorance of technical matters, he delegated authority by "putting the right man in the right place." As his chief deputy he chose Efraim Sklansky, a young army doctor, whom he described as "always exact, indefatigable, alert, and well-informed." Unlike his quarters in Petrograd, where his residence and office were combined, his Moscow accommodations were separate. He obtained a modest apartment within the massive walls of the historic Kremlin, the seat of Russia's government before the era of Peter the Great. The War Commissariat was situated in a requisitioned building in the square behind the Cathedral of the Savior. None of the Bolshevik leaders had much time for domestic tranquility. Nor did their wives, since most of them worked in government offices. Sedova found employment in the Commissariat of Education, where she supervised museums and ancient monuments. Military necessity often clashed with the sanctity of institutional culture, and at times it looked as if Trotsky and his wife were engaged in an endless jurisdictional quarrel. "Many jokes were made about us on this score," he reported.

In anticipation of future German aggression against Russia, the Allied military missions moved to Moscow. Trotsky shared this concern, and in the interest of harmony and future cooperation he formally received some twenty officers in the latter part of March. Usually at a loss for small talk, he soon exhausted his meager store and was uncertain how to bring the ceremonial visit to a close. The officers were equally inexperienced about the protocol of leave taking, and finally a French general found an appropriate formula by asking whether Trotsky would object if the military representatives were to take no more of his valuable time. Trotsky took his cue and the officers departed, but he recalled the episode with an acute sense of embarrassment. A vibrant personality in the dramatic tableau of History's inexorable march, he was uncommonly maladroit in managing the social amenities of daily life, especially when confronted with strangers of a different class and nationality.

The expected collaboration between the Soviet republic and the Allies never materialized, although an Anglo-French landing in March at the port of Murmansk in North Russia to forestall alleged German designs in that area was accepted with an equanimity that amounted to tacit consent. That the Allies would prove to be a greater menace than Germany to the vulnerable Communist state neither Trotsky nor the other Soviet leaders could possibly foresee.

It was therefore with no sense of emergency that Trotsky set about the task of molding the infant Red Army into a professional fighting force. The early recruits were volunteers, and he soon recognized that improvisation and the mystique of a victorious revolution were not substitutes for the conventional attributes of a regular army: proper training, adequate equipment, strict discipline, and a corps of experienced officers. Since the latter could only be found among the unemployed professionals who had fought for the old regime, he reached the logical conclusion that they might, with appropriate safeguards, serve Russia's new masters as "military specialists." Although the scheme remained morally and politically repugnant to many Bolsheviks—Lenin had been rather dubious at first—Trotsky had his way. By midsummer, as civil war threatened to engulf the fledgling Soviet republic, these veteran officers were eagerly recruited and ultimately made a vital contribution to the Red Army's military success.

The smoldering embers of what was to become a savage and exhausting conflict were ignited on May 14, 1918, with a chance altercation at Chelyabinsk, a city just beyond the Ural mountains on the main line of the Trans-Siberian Railroad. The combatants were Czech troops eastward bound for Vladivostok and Hungarian war prisoners returning to their homeland. The Soviet government, considering the impotence of its armed forces, reacted with undue severity. The Czechoslovak Legion, numbering perhaps thirty-five thousand and strung along the rail line for some five thousand miles, was to be disarmed and detained. Trotsky himself sent a peremptory telegram on May 25 instructing local Soviets as to their responsibility. "Every armed Czechoslovak found on the railway is to be shot on the spot," he ordered.[1] This empty bellicosity merely spurred the Czechs to take over the Trans-Siberian and the major cities from the Volga to the Pacific, an act that Trotsky (and Soviet historians generally) maintained was a conspiracy hatched by Britain and France. But the Allied powers, no less than the Soviet republic, had been caught by surprise. They soon perceived, however, that "rescuing" the Czechs furnished an excellent pretext for intervening in Russian affairs, and in early August the first installment of a sizable number of foreign troops landed at Vladivostok.

During the summer months Trotsky retreated from the notion of a volunteer army but insisted that mobilization be confined to workers and poor peasants. The "bourgeoisie" (the term was loosely applied), not to be trusted with arms, were to be drafted for labor service. "Our grandfathers and fathers served your grandfathers and fathers, cleaning up dirt and manure," Trotsky announced in his best demagogic style, "and we will force you to clean up filth."[2] However dubious as an efficient method of utilizing manpower skills, the scheme offered the masses certain psychological satisfactions by humbling the former "exploiters."

By early August, Czech legionnaires and White detachments had seized control of the upper Volga. The Soviet regime was suddenly in grave peril, and Trotsky was dispatched to the scene in an attempt to rally the disorganized and dispirited Red troops. On August 7 he left Moscow with fifty zealous party workers on a special armored train, never suspecting that it was to become a kind of roving command post for the next two years. He established his headquarters at Sviyazhsk, a small town across the Volga from Kazan, recently captured by the enemy. Still without practical military experience, he sought by fierce eloquence and stern discipline to check the infectious mood of panic and to build up a reliable combat force. For a month "the fate of the revolution was trembling in the balance." Fresh units arrived but were often "ingulfed by the inertia of retreat." "The sort of Communists that need to be sent here," Trotsky telegraphed Lenin, "are those who know how to obey orders and are prepared to undergo deprivations and ready to lay down their lives. Lightweight agitators are not needed here."[3]

Trotsky believed in applying a "red-hot iron" to a "gangrenous wound" and warned his troops "that if any unit retreats without orders, the first to be shot down will be the [political] commissar of the unit, second the commander. Brave and gallant soldiers will be appointed in their places. Cowards, scoundrels, and traitors will not escape the bullet. This I solemnly promise before the whole Red Army."[4] This was no idle threat. In one mutinous regiment he ordered the commissar, the commander, and every tenth man shot as an example to others whose loyalty and courage might falter under the stress of battle.

Slowly, as reinforcements arrived (the initial Red detachment of three or four thousand expanded to perhaps twenty-five thousand), "a vacillating, unreliable and crumbling mass was transformed into a real army." Trotsky modestly ascribed the improvement to "propaganda, organization, revolutionary example and repression," but it was his fiery leadership that supplied the vital ingredient. Somewhat cavalier abut his personal safety, he was eventually persuaded to transfer his quarters to a river steamboat—not, however, the comfortable passenger vessel that had been assigned but the more spartan accommodations provided by a torpedo boat.

As plans were readied for an attack on Kazan, word came that Lenin had been wounded by an assassin. Trotsky left hastily for Moscow. He found the mood of the party leaders "sullen and dismal" but resolute, and he gave an encouraging report about the military situation on the eastern front. Since Lenin was recovering with no complications, Trotsky returned to his post and launched an assault that took Kazan on September 10. Two days later Red troops seized Simbirsk to the south; within another month the Volga waterway had been secured and the Whites were in full retreat.

Back in Moscow in late September, Trotsky presided over the Revolutionary War Council of the Republic, a reorganized version of the Supreme War Council. Yoakim Vatsetis, a colonel in the tsarist army, was named commander-in-chief, while Sklyansky assumed the post of de facto chairman of the Council during Trotsky's frequent and prolonged absences from the capital.

For military reasons and because his authority continued to be flouted by the so-called Tsaritsyn group, Trotsky soon found pressing business on the southern front. The city of Tsaritsyn (later Stalingrad, now Volgograd) commanded the lower Volga and had successfully withstood repeated attacks by White forces during the summer months. It was defended by the Tenth Red Army under Klementi Voroshilov who had acquired a powerful patron in Joseph Stalin. They represented a strong current in the party that never became reconciled to the use of former tsarist officers. As Lenin's troubleshooter in the south, Stalin acted with ruthless efficiency but resented his inability to dismiss "army commanders and commissars who are ruining the work." "Not having a paper from Trotsky" would not deter him, he protested to Lenin. Recognizing the temperamental differences as well as the indispensability of both men, Lenin mediated the dispute with tactful diplomacy. Stalin gained the special powers that he sought, while Voroshilov and his associates tacitly accepted the normal chain of command. But in October Trotsky charged that new acts of insubordination had violated the previous agreement. In a telegram to Lenin, he insisted that Stalin be recalled and threatened to court-martial Voroshilov.

In the end Trotsky's will prevailed. Sverdlov was dispatched to escort Stalin back to Moscow on a special train, thereby concealing the reprimand with ceremonial honors befitting a hero of Tsaritsyn, the "Red Verdun." Sverdlov arranged a meeting between the two antagonists, and Trotsky's account depicts Stalin inquiring in a tone of exaggerated humility: "Do you really want to dismiss them all? They're fine boys." Trotsky's reply was typically brusque: "Those fine boys will ruin the revolution, which can't wait for them to grow out of their adolescence. All I want is to draw Tsaritsyn back into Soviet Russia."[5]

Trotsky spent most of the autumn and part of the winter on the southern front. But the "Tsaritsyn tendency" persisted. In December the refractory Voroshilov was transferred to the Ukraine with no better results, and Trotsky complained to Lenin, who again sought a compromise. Trotsky replied testily: "A compromise is of course necessary, but not a rotten one . . . . I consider Stalin's patronage of the Tsaritsyn trend a most dangerous ulcer, worse than any treason or betrayal by military specialists."[6]

Lacking finesse in human relations and insight into the aspirations of what came to be called the "military opposition," Trotsky dismissed his adversaries as fools and troublemakers. But they had legitimate grievances. Lenin, fully acquainted with Trotsky's extraordinary talents as well as his arrogant personality, was reluctant to take a definite stand in the recurrent controversy. Trotsky's critics not only condemned his use of "military specialists" but his "system of organized panic," as one disgruntled observer put it. "Frequent changes of political workers and commanders, crowding the . . . southern front with a great number of party members, and Trotsky's princely journeys along the front" were, he charged, symptomatic of poor overall leadership.[7] Moreover, aside from coddling former tsarist officers, Trotsky was reproached for his draconic punishment of loyal Bolsheviks. The executions at Sviyazhsk, in addition to his propensity for violent threats against those derelict in their duty (though excusable in a time of military crisis), inevitably typed him as excessively bloodthirsty and autocratic in his methods. Having already acquired, at least in the upper echelons of the party, an unenviable reputation as a prima donna, he now aroused fresh doubts, if not hostility, just as his public reputation reached new heights.

Trotsky achieved a measure of vindication at the Eighth Party Congress in March, 1919. Unfortunately, he was unable to argue his case in person because the Whites were again advancing on the eastern front, and the situation required his immediate attention. Lenin spoke out in his defense, thus virtually assuring a favorable verdict from the congress as a whole. Yet the opposition had become a strong minority, and in the separate debates of the military delegates Trotsky's policies were sharply attacked, though these deliberations remained confidential.

Trotsky's "princely journeys along the front" were made in his special train. It was continually augmented with extra equipment and services, including a printing press, a library, an electric generator, a radio receiver, telegraphic apparatus, and a "garage" for automobiles. The train also carried a reserve complement of picked troops, a few dedicated party members for special assignments, and supplies of guns, ammunition, clothing, medicine, field glasses, watches, and a variety of other items useful to an army in the field. It was pulled by two engines, and eventually two trains were organized. Trotsky estimated that he traveled at least sixty-five thousand miles by train, excluding trips by automobile from the railroad to various fighting fronts. The train grew to almost legendary stature, "as good as a division in reserve" according to some commanders, and to the enemy it sometimes had the opposite effect of a devastating blow to morale.

The threat to the Muscovite heartland, barely averted in 1918, was renewed in the spring of 1919 when a White army led by Admiral Alexander Kolchak advanced upon the upper Volga from its Siberian base. Although the southern front was active, depriving the defenders of their strongest units, Trotsky had far more men and matériel available than he had had at Sviyazhsk. After two months of preparation, troops under the command of Sergei Kamenev, a former colonel in the tsarist army, mounted a counterattack in late April that sent the White forces reeling back toward the Urals. Lenin favored a "hot pursuit," as did Kamenev, but the conventional military wisdom maintained that Kolchak had strong manpower reserves in Siberia. Trotsky argued that it would be too dangerous, considering the buildup of General Anton Denikin's White army in South Russia, to commit any large force to the Kolchak operation. Vatsetis agreed, but both were overruled by the Central Committee.

Trotsky meanwhile had departed for the Ukraine, where he found conditions chaotic. He reported to Lenin on June 1 that the steppes had turned into "a sea of mud in which I have been floundering for four days." The impatient and occasionally querulous tone of Lenin's messages to Trotsky suggest that he had become temporarily disenchanted with his war commissar. At any rate, the Central Committee decided on July 3 to replace Vatsetis with Kamenev as commander-in-chief, and the Revolutionary War Council, heretofore dominated by Trotsky's appointees, was reorganized with new personnel. Trotsky, who attended the meeting, remained chairman, but he took both decisions as a personal affront and is said to have slammed the door upon leaving and to have become ill for several days.

Trotsky later ascribed his setback to Stalin's "intrigue," a simplistic assessment that cannot be taken seriously, for the other members of the Central Committee—certainly not Lenin—were in no sense manipulated by Stalin. Trotsky soon found himself in disagreement with the new commander-in-chief on the proper strategy to check Denikin. Again outvoted, he submitted his resignation as commissar for war and as chairman of the Council. A typically melodramatic gesture—one that could not have endeared him to his less temperamental colleagues—it was unanimously rejected by the Politburo (Political Bureau), which was soon to supplant the Central Committee as the supreme party organ. An openly acknowledged disruption in the party's high command at such a time was politically impermissible. The members delicately rebuked him by requesting that he refrain from raising the question again and that he carry on his duties, curtailing them if they were too onerous, and concentrating his attention on the southern front.

Well aware that Trotsky's vanity had been severely wounded, Lenin made a mollifying gesture by signing a "blank check" offering to endorse any order that the offended war commissar might care to give. Nevertheless, the relationship between the two men—never really close despite Trotsky's protestations to the contrary—continued to deteriorate. Trotsky returned to his post in the south, apparently in a petulant mood, though his ceaseless energy was wholly committed to victory over Denikin.

Still convinced that Kamenev's plans were in error, Trotsky refrained from criticizing him further. However, he did suggest that the commander of the southern front, Vladimir Yegoryev, be replaced because he had no confidence in the proposed campaign: "I consider . . . wholly inadmissible a situation in which the plan is being put into effect by someone who does not believe in its success."[8] His recommendation was eventually acted upon, but the irritable tone of the Trotsky-Lenin correspondence (usually conducted through intermediaries) during the summer and fall, as Denikin pushed onward, indicated exasperation and anxiety on both sides. Trotsky complained about a lack of supplies, especially ammunition, and commented rhetorically that "neither agitation nor repression can make an unshod, unclothed, hungry, lice-ridden army combat ready." Nine days later, on August 9, he protested that he had not received "a single sensible answer to [his] direct and practical demands." Lenin was equally querulous. While deploring the cowardice displayed by some Red Army troops, for example, he censured Trotsky in all but name: "In dispatching such units, the Revolutionary War Council of the Republic *covers itself with shame.*"[9]

In September, as Denikin's forces threatened Moscow from the south, Trotsky renewed his strictures on Kamenev's operational plans. The substance of his argument, that the Ukraine had been denuded of troops to reinforce the eastern sector, was stubbornly disregarded. Lenin and his Politburo colleagues, for understandable reasons, were inclined to write off Trotsky's objections as self-serving. But by mid-October, when it seemed that Moscow might fall (and when a White army under Nikolai Yudenich simultaneously advanced on Petrograd), they were prepared to admit that his analysis had been basically correct.

Back in Moscow, Trotsky attended a special session of the Politburo on October 15 which took emergency measures to save the two capitals. Lenin proposed to abandon Petrograd because of its limited strategic value, but Trotsky stressed its symbolic importance as the cradle of the revolution and pointed out the danger of a link between Yudenich and Denikin. He finally received permission for a twenty-four hour visit to "Red Peter" to see what could be done. Already he had conceived of a formula for victory through urban guerrilla warfare. Even if Yudenich's army of some twenty-five thousand stormed its way into the city, he reasoned, its fate would be sealed if the million or more inhabitants organized serious resistance.

Trotsky arrived in the stricken city on October 16 and immediately took charge of its defense with that impetuous élan and passionate conviction so characteristic of his working style when confronted with a crisis en masse. Zinoviev, the local party boss, had become panicky, infecting his aides with the apparent hopelessness of the cause. There were courageous men in his entourage, "but even their hands hung limp." Trotsky's confidence not only bolstered the morale of the besieged but won from Lenin a full measure of what had been rather tentative support. "Petrograd is to be defended to the very last drop of blood," he wired Trotsky on the seventeenth.

On October 18 Yudenich neared the outskirts of the city. Petrograd had been converted into an armed camp, with trenches in the suburbs, artillery at strategic points, and barricades in the streets. For the first and only time during the civil war Trotsky assumed the role of a regimental commander, though his tour of duty was brief and impromptu. Observing a retreating unit near the front, he mounted the first horse he could find and eventually rallied the men by a combination of intimidation and personal example. He was exposed to enemy fire for a time and returned to staff headquarters in a truck that stopped intermittently to pick up the wounded. But the White advance continued, and he admitted in a message to Lenin on the twentieth that the Red position was faltering.

October 21 was the critical day. The defenders retreated to the Pulkovo Heights, where Kerensky had been repulsed nearly two years before. Reinforced with factory workers and military students, the Seventh Red Army fought with "heroic frenzy" (according to the White commanders) and passed over to the offensive the next day. His momentum checked, Yudenich lacked reserves in men and matériel to sustain a siege and never regained the initiative. Trotsky left for Moscow during the second week of November when the issue was no longer in doubt.

Denikin's troops had also been put to flight, and Kolchak's army was at the point of total disintegration. Although Allied soldiers remained on the Russian periphery, the civil war seemed all but over. Trotsky's dramatic role in saving Petrograd furnished a fitting climax to his military career which had become somewhat tarnished through no fault of his own during the campaign against Denikin. He was presented with the Order of the Red Banner at an elaborate ceremony in Moscow and gave a report on the military situation. Stalin also received the award but was absent from the meeting, "wisely," Trotsky later commented with ill-concealed satisfaction, for "a sort of cold bewilderment crept through the hall" at the announcement.

The ravages of domestic conflict left the nation hungry, exhausted, and demoralized. The policy of "War Communism," a mélange of economic regimentation, Marxist dogma, and military exigency, had led only to a crisis of production that threatened the very fabric of organized society. The industrial proletariat, in whose name the Bolsheviks had taken power, was depleted by a mass exodus to the countryside, where the peasants, though subjected to grain expropriations, were better fed than urban dwellers.

Lenin was eventually able to provide a partial solution to Russia's economic woes through the New Economic Policy. But in the interim he supported Trotsky's view that the draconic methods that had helped to win the civil war might work equally well with civilian labor. From the beginning, there were skeptics who anticipated that the "militarization of labor" was impractical. Yet the party leaders were desperate and unwilling to abandon their Marxist premises, even temporarily, for a return to capitalist norms. The initial experiments, however, were confined to idle units of the Red Army. During the early months of 1920 several "labor armies" undertook such tasks as peat mining, timber cutting, and railroad repair. Despite incessant propaganda and other morale building schemes, the soldiers who had fought the Whites with dogged endurance if not always with enthusiasm resented their status as "serfs." Low productivity, disciplinary problems, and large-scale desertion, coupled with the prohibitive expense of maintaining a sullen work force of such magnitude, inevitably led to an abandonment of the project. In the caustic verdict of one observer, the experiment proved "an empty bureaucratic fantasy."[10]

In the end, Trotsky, too, became disillusioned, though he never admitted that his (and the party's) policy had been mistaken. Meanwhile he sought to convince the hapless conscripts that they were not performing "slave labor but supreme service to the socialist fatherland." During the course of his inspection of the labor battalions in the Urals in February, 1920, Trotsky realized that the peasants needed incentives to produce and that the state's requisition squads did not offer a long-term answer to the country's chronic food shortage. But his remedy, essentially a return to the free market and an anticipation of the reforms of the next year, was premature. He did not persevere once the Central Committee dismissed his suggestion. At the Ninth Party Congress in late March he declined to draw the obvious analogy between the industrial and agrarian sectors of the economy and reverted instead to the notion of strict military discipline for civilian workers. Deserters, he declared, should be punished by forced labor or sent to concentration camps. Once Russia's "miserable poverty" could be overcome, a rapid advance would occur on the economic front: "We will be able to leap over a whole series of intermediate stages."[11] Always intrigued with the idea of History as paradox, Trotsky considered Russia a prime candidate for this "leapfrogging effect, phenomena that he would elevate to the status of historical "laws" in later years.[12] His "universal law of unevenness," leading to the "law of combined development," was essentially a pretentious way of saying that material and cultural "progress," especially in backward countries such as Russia, was erratic and unpredictable but could be telescoped and surpass that of the industrial West.

In March, 1920, in response to Lenin's request, Trotsky reluctantly assumed the post of commissar for transport while retaining his position as war minister. It was a forbidding task, for rail service was "quite catastrophic" (Lenin's phrase), and the workers were traditionally an independent lot, seldom amenable to the kind of party discipline that had proved more successful in other sectors of the economy. Trotsky approached his job with the kind of ferocious energy and relentless determination that had galvanized the defenders of Sviyazhsk and Petrograd. He obtained reasonably impressive results, but his tactlessness and inflexibility, as in the case of the military opposition during the civil war, aroused needless antagonism. Furthermore, his willingness, indeed eagerness, to suppress free union activity among the transport workers, though in accord with a party decision to subordinate the trade unions to the state apparatus, placed him in a politically awkward position.

Trotsky's zeal helped prevent the complete disruption of rail transport during the war with Poland which erupted in the spring of 1920. The Polish invasion of the Ukraine was not only rebuffed but provided a tempting opportunity for Soviet counter-aggression—not, however, for territorial aggrandizement, the customary reward of the conqueror, but for essentially ideological reasons. Poland was the gateway to Germany, and Germany, as the Bolshevik leaders fervidly believed, was a nation ripe for Communist revolution. The delegates to the second congress of the Communist International, which was meeting in Moscow as the Red Army launched a drive on Warsaw, waited with "breathless interest, with palpitating heart" (in Zinoviev's words) to see if military success "would mean an immense acceleration of the international proletarian revolution."

Despite Zinoviev's hyperbole, there is evidence that the party leaders, including Lenin, were not so enamored by the Red Army's Polish venture that they overlooked the risks involved. Trotsky, if we accept his own testimony, was the only one of prominence who consistently opposed the enterprise from beginning to end. Perhaps for this reason—or more likely because of the independent policy of the commander, Mikhail Tukhachevsky—his part in the military campaign seems to have been nominal, and on August 17, while the battle of Warsaw was still in doubt, he even declined Lenin's appeal to make a "lightning" journey to the front. But on the twentieth, presumably in response to a Politburo decision, he left Moscow for Minsk. By this time the Poles had thrown back the Soviet onslaught, and he turned his attention to the threat posed by Baron Peter Wrangel, the "German hireling of the French loan-sharks" (to use Trotsky's biting phrase).

The ablest of the White commanders, Wrangel, had taken over the remnants of Denikin's vanquished army, but his prospects for more than local success were minimal until the war with Poland offered fresh possibilities. Moscow's armistice with the Poles in October, however, allowed the Red Army to bear on Wrangel, and after his troops retreated into the Crimean Peninsula they were crushed in the final campaign of the civil war. Trotsky regarded Wrangel's defeat as a foregone conclusion but did supervise the preliminary operations before going on to the Ukraine for a tour of inspection. From an economic standpoint, he commented in a report to the Politburo sent from Kursk on November 2, "the Ukraine is still the embodiment of anarchy sheltering under the bureaucratic centralism of Moscow."[13]

The party had not yet decided on peace with Poland. Trotsky returned to the capital to find that a majority of his colleagues favored a resumption of the war. He argued that the units available on the western front were "morally defeated" and that it would be "senseless" to think that such an army would be capable of "raising itself to a victorious advance along a road strewn with its own fragments." He put his case too exclusively in military terms when he might have contended (as he did later) that the exportation of Communism by military force was a dangerous precedent, especially unbecoming for a Marxist state whose leaders had once espoused the idea of an independent Poland. Lenin no doubt recognized the incongruity of his position and began to waver. He proposed that the decision be postponed until Trotsky could make a first-hand report on the state of the army. Trotsky found that the commanders at the front favored another war, but digging more deeply, he concluded that their apparent bellicosity reflected the prevailing winds from Moscow, not their true conviction. Although his opinion is open to question, he was nevertheless correct in asserting that the army was in no condition to undertake an offensive against Poland. Most of his Politburo associates concurred with this judgment upon his return to Moscow, and a formal peace, the Treaty of Riga, was signed on March 18, 1921.

In assessing blame for the Red Army's failure to take Warsaw, Trotsky's verdict has been accepted rather uncritically in the West. He charged Stalin, the political commissar of the southwestern front, with vainglorious conduct in seizing the Polish city of Lvov rather than supporting the main drive on Warsaw.[14] But the evidence is far from conclusive, and in any case it does not support the notion that Stalin's actions, however irresponsible, had much bearing on the Warsaw campaign.[15]

When the war emergency had passed, Trotsky once more found himself embroiled in the trade union dispute. Failing to perceive or perhaps simply ignoring the psychological mood of the population, including the working class, which had grown sullen, even rebellious, after years of grinding toil and unremitting sacrifice, he renewed his strictures on the trade unions. Trotsky demanded a "shake-up" of the labor leaders and decided that their proper function should be to increase production, not to represent the workers. Although no apostle of trade union democracy, Lenin recognized that in a time of economic crisis, conciliation and diplomacy were better weapons than threats and compulsion. He parted company with Trotsky on the issue, and his proposals won a narrow majority at a Central Committee meeting on November 9. But there were so many abstentions that the uncommitted sought a compromise, hoping to avert a party split and to avoid a public controversy. Zinoviev, as chairman of a special mediation committee, was authorized to speak in the party's name on the trade union question, while alternate views were temporarily denied expression. Trotsky, who was among those appointed to the committee, refused to serve. Zinoviev had already emerged as a champion of party democracy, a self-appointed and unaccustomed role that sought by indirection to expose Trotsky's dictatorial propensities. Although Trotsky's disdain of a "loaded" committee is understandable, his stance was probably a political mistake: it sharpened personal rivalries in a factional struggle that many hoped could be decided on the merits of the case.

The dispute remained in abeyance while Trotsky investigated labor unrest in the Donbas region of the eastern Ukraine (the workers, he reported, were "starving," and it was a surprise to him that they were working at all). The debate was renewed in December when Zinoviev's committee recommended the dissolution of Tsek-

tran, an acronym for Trotsky's bureaucratic creation that controlled
the transportation system (and its workers) with a heavy hand.
Trotsky refused to budge, and despite the "bloc" arrayed against
him, including Lenin, Stalin, and Zinoviev, the Central Committee
declined by a single vote to abolish Tsektran. Bukharin succeeded
Zinoviev as a spokesman for compromise, but the ban on open
discussion was lifted soon afterward, and the party launched upon
the bitterest public quarrel since the Brest-Litovsk negotiations.

Trotsky published a pamphlet, *The Role and Tasks of the Trade
Unions,* and supplemented his trenchant views with speeches and
statements in the press. Lenin professed to be "amazed" that the
pamphlet contained so many "theoretical mistakes and glaring
blunders." "The sum and substance" of Trotsky's policy, he
complained, "was the bureaucratic harassment of the trade
unions."[16] Trotsky did not offer a response in kind: such an act
would have been politically unrewarding in the light of Lenin's
immense prestige. Nor did his personal regard for Lenin permit the
astringent tone that had been almost routine before 1914. But there
was no such compunction in the case of Zinoviev, who continually
sniped at Tsektran. Always something of a charlatan, he was an easy
target for Trotsky's barbed wit: "Every village now knows what
Tsektran is: it's a sort of animal that takes away the grain; it has a
stick in its hand and doesn't allow the workers to breathe freely; and
then, when the worker is tired, it offers him vinegar instead of the
milk which Comrade Zinoviev has at his disposal."[17]

By the time the Tenth Party Congress met on March 8, 1921, the
numerous "platforms" had shrunk to three. Bukharin's "buffer
group," unable to provide effective mediation, joined Trotsky's faction. Trade union democracy was espoused by the so-called Workers' Opposition, allowing Lenin and his supporters to pose as
moderates between the two "extremist" blocs. Since the Leninist
delegates constituted a huge majority, the debates at the congress
were almost perfunctory compared to the acrimonious give and take
of the preceding months. The Trotsky-Bukharin resolution received
only fifty votes, the Workers' Opposition a mere eighteen, while the
Leninist "machine" recorded three hundred twenty-six. The results, however one-sided, remained ambiguous, for the status quo
tended to prevail, and the Soviet regime never did solve the problem of how the trade unions could function independently of the
state bureaucracy. In the long run, judging from the experience of

the Five Year Plans in the Stalin era, Trotsky's draconian labor policy had greater relevance to the Soviet economy than the "moderate" but distressingly vague formulation propounded by Lenin.

The formal deliberations of the party were overshadowed by a political trauma that in retrospect made the trade union controversy seem innocuous indeed. The sailors of the Kronstadt naval base, whom Trotsky had once saluted as the "pride and glory" of the revolution, came out in open rebellion. Symbolic of mass discontent with War Communism (and the attendant political and economic straitjacket), the revolt was touched off by strikes in Petrograd and threatened to spread beyond the island redoubt of the mutineers. Official propaganda denounced it as a counterrevolutionary uprising—a veritable White Guard conspiracy—for it was imperative that the Kronstadters be discredited. No one proved more adept than Trotsky in embellishing the party line. Not only was the insurrection hatched in émigré circles with Western support, he declared, but the redoubtable sailors of 1917 had for the most part perished in the civil war or had in any case been replaced by raw recruits from the countryside. Obviously there had been a considerable turnover at Kronstadt and in the Baltic fleet. But that class origin and diluted revolutionary consciousness had anything to do with the revolt is highly unlikely. In later years Trotsky dropped his conspiracy thesis while stoutly maintaining the "petty bourgeois" character of the rising and the "tragic necessity" of suppressing it.

Trotsky had been investigating peasant disturbances in western Siberia when the uprising occurred on March 2. He rushed back to Moscow to consult his colleagues, reaching Petrograd on the fifth. Making no attempt to negotiate, he issued an ultimatum demanding unconditional surrender of "all who have raised their hands against the socialist fatherland." Only those who complied could "count on the mercy of the Soviet republic . . . . This is a final warning."[18] His blunt tone could only have stiffened the sailors' defiant mood. Two days later military operations began. Trotsky interrupted his duties to report the situation to the party congress, and many of the delegates departed for Petrograd to take part in the final assault. Not until March 17, after a bloody advance across the frozen Gulf of Finland, did the fortress capitulate.

Trotsky appears to have played a secondary role in the military campaign, but it was not as negligible as he afterward pretended. "I personally did not participate in the least in the suppression of the

Kronstadt rebellion, nor in the repressions following the suppression," he wrote, adding that he had remained in Moscow during the whole affair while Zinoviev took charge in Petrograd.[19] This version of his conduct, while an understandable exercise in apologetics, cannot be recommended as either reliable or convincing. He also did not attempt to explain the brutal reprisals that disfigured the Soviet victory. As for his justification of the government's policy on Kronstadt, opinions may legitimately differ. Internal disorder, even in countries with a democratic tradition, is impermissible beyond the limits of peaceful protest, and the Communist leaders were faced with a military insurrection that could prove fatal to their rule. The sailors had a good case, morally speaking, but politically it was exceedingly naive. Without outside intervention or a groundswell of popular support their cause was doomed.

CHAPTER 7

NEP and the Close of the Lenin Era

HAD Lenin introduced his New Economic Policy (NEP) at the beginning of 1921 the Kronstadt tragedy might well have been averted. A strategic retreat from premature socialism to small-scale capitalism and a free market for agricultural produce, the NEP pumped adrenalin into the prostrate economy and restored a measure of popular confidence in the party's ability to rule. Young Communist idealists considered it an unpardonable offense to the integrity of the Bolshevik Revolution. Yet even its staunchest advocates (Trotsky was not among them, though he gave it his support) never pretended that it was more than an evil necessity to be endured until the march toward socialism could once again resume.

One of the paradoxes associated with launching NEP was that economic freedom, now permissible even though the state held the "commanding heights" of heavy industry, had no equivalent in the political sector. Apparently Lenin felt that the revival of "petty bourgeois" economic ideas might be politically contagious, and he resolved to close ranks and eliminate potential outlets for dissenting views. The Mensheviks and Socialist Revolutionaries, who had retained some cohesion despite the tribulations of the civil war, were now virtually outlawed. The intra-party factions, notably the Workers' Opposition, were also proscribed, though it was well into 1922 before Leninist orthodoxy could prevail. Trotsky loyally dissolved his own "faction" on the trade union question and supported Lenin's proposals for a more monolithic party, never suspecting that he too would become a dissenter and thus a victim of his own logic.

If not precisely oblivious to the infighting among his colleagues (Lenin was naturally above the battle), Trotsky was singularly inept as a practicing politician. He considered it unseemly to engage in a sordid struggle for personal power—not that he spurned it. Quite the contrary. But he tended to equate fame and glory with the

113

exercise of power and disdained the notion that they should come to him by other means than the rightful reward of a grateful nation. His talent, so useful—indeed indispensable—during the heroic period of revolution and civil war, was ill-suited to the bureaucratic routine and organization politics that began to shape the party in Lenin's last years. Overly enamored with his extraordinary intellectual gifts, he had limited insight into the aspirations of his nascent rivals. His aversion to Zinoviev, whom he could at least respect as an "intellectual" of sorts, was of a different order from his dislike of Stalin, a man of remarkable ability who at the same time lacked sophistication in the world of ideas. Trotsky, content to dismiss him as a boorish mediocrity, never shared (or even understood) Lenin's high regard for the "wonderful Georgian," as the party chief had put it in 1913. Nor did Trotsky consider him a serious contender for power until well after Lenin's death.

Stalin's credentials as an Old Bolshevik were far superior to Trotsky's, and if the evidence is tenuous, it seems apparent that he resented (to use no stronger a term) Trotsky's status as an international celebrity while he remained in relative obscurity. The Tenth Party Congress, at least in retrospect, was something of a watershed in the waxing fortunes of Stalin and the waning of Trotsky's. A number of Stalin's associates were elevated to the Central Committee, while several of Trotsky's supporters on the trade union question lost key positions. Increasingly involved in the administrative routine of party affairs, Stalin was the logical candidate to head the Secretariat, a body charged with maintaining the party's personnel records and other organizational tasks that held little appeal to such charismatic figures as Trotsky and Zinoviev. In April, 1922, the appointment became official—Stalin's title was that of general secretary—and two of his disciples, Vyacheslav Molotov and Valerian Kuibyshev, joined him as junior associates. Trotsky recalled that Zinoviev proposed Stalin for the post "quite against Lenin's will" and that Lenin would say of the general secretary, "This cook will make only peppery dishes."[1] But the clarity of his recollection is suspect because he places the appointment in 1921, and in any case there is no indication that either Lenin or Trotsky opposed it in the Central Committee. No one (and this may well have included Stalin) anticipated that the office would be politically rewarding, for it was then regarded as one of paper shuffling drudgery.

Shortly after Stalin became general secretary Lenin proposed that

Trotsky be named a deputy chairman of the Council of People's Commissars—that is, a vice premier. The position was more than ceremonial. Lenin obviously saw it as a promotion, perhaps as the governmental equivalent of Stalin's in the party apparatus. But Trotsky declined it so abruptly and tactlessly that Lenin was offended, though he renewed the offer on subsequent occasions. Trotsky regarded it as a demotion since there were already three deputies ("practical, obedient assistants") whom he considered his inferiors. Later realizing his mistake, he distorted the incident in his autobiography by claiming that he was "unsuited to the role" and that he was "grateful to Lenin for not offering" the deputyship.

At the time of his overture to Trotsky, Lenin had been in poor health for over six months, and on May 26 he suffered the first of a series of cerebral strokes. Trotsky was bedridden himself when Bukharin brought him the news. He had fallen accidentally while fishing and injured the ligaments in his foot. Lenin never fully recovered but did return to work briefly in October. For all practical purposes his political career was finished, yet his colleagues could not openly scramble for positions of power. They continued to regard their leader with respect and even affection, maintaining a public stance that he would soon resume his duties, and it may be that this was also their private view. Trotsky's admiration for Lenin from 1917 onward was unquestionably sincere: whatever his defects of personality and character, Trotsky was never hypocritical. Lenin's illness was, he reports, an "overwhelming" blow, and since Bukharin had been two days late in informing him, he later concluded that the delay had been "no accident" and that Zinoviev, Kamenev, and Stalin were already conspiring against him. That the "troika" acted this swiftly is doubtful. But his air of aloof superiority won him no friends or admirers, his belated conversion to Bolshevism made him inevitably an outsider, and his fame aroused only ill-concealed envy. The only possible exception among the senior Bolsheviks was Bukharin, who held Trotsky in high personal esteem. ("Bukharin," says Trotsky patronizingly, "was attached to me in his characteristic 'Bukharin' way, half hysterically, half childishly.") But this "flirtation" did not carry over to the political struggle that lay ahead.

Trotsky's "power base" outside the party structure remained the Red Army. As commissar of war he supposedly elicited the loyalty and talent of an imposing array of battle tested officers. But such was hardly the case, for he had never attempted to create a personal military "machine" analagous to that which Stalin was building in the party, and the end of the civil war emergency had inevitably lowered his prestige and reduced his public profile. Nor had his brusque manner and autocratic personality attracted any discernible group of "Trotskyists." He was temperamentally incapable of organizing a military coup despite his alleged propensities toward "Bonapartism," a charge that was to gain currency through rumors traceable to his political enemies. Even had he been inclined toward military adventurism, the prospects for success would have been poor. The Red Army never emerged from strict party control to become an independent political force.

Trotsky's other interests and responsibilities constituted an impressive list and would seem adequate to keep half a dozen lesser mortals well occupied. Few of them were publicized and none carried any tangible political benefits. Perhaps his most unique assignment involved anti-religious propaganda, one of Lenin's special concerns. Trotsky headed the League of the Militant Godless, and though the nature of his task demanded a dogmatic attitude, he nevertheless sought to avoid the more outrageous insults to organized religion that could only confirm the pious in the certitude of their faith. His successor, Emelian Yaroslavsky, chose to ignore his example of moderation.

In the broader sphere of the country's intellectual and cultural life, Trotsky was more disposed toward tolerance and the free marketplace of ideas than most party members. He criticized those who, in the name of Marxism, condemned "bourgeois" culture and espoused a specifically "proletarian" culture, and he implicitly recognized that party dictation on matters of art, literature, and scholarship would lead only to stultifying mediocrity. "It is childish to think that bourgeois *belles lettres* can make a breach in class solidarity," he argued. "What the worker will take from Shakespeare, Goethe, Pushkin, or Dostoyevsky will be a more complex idea of human personality, of its passions and feelings, a deeper and more profound understanding of its psychic forces and of the role of the subconscious, etc. In the final analysis, the worker will be the richer."[2]

For all his indulgence in matters of the intellect, Trotsky was hardly the classical liberal championing the right to free speech and a free press as a matter of principle. He contended that counter-revolutionary ideas, even when expressed in such relatively harmless forms as art and literature, might be suppressed to protect the safety of the socialist state. Until the early thirties, when Stalin solved to his own satisfaction the problem of how much political and ideological freedom was permissible, Soviet Russia contrived an uneasy compromise between two extremes: that of Western democracy and its traditional civil liberties and that of doctrinaire Communism, which maintained that since the party held a monopoly on truth and wisdom it was morally obliged to repress falsehood and to provide society at large with cultural as well as political guidelines. Trotsky himself was rather equivocal about the role of the party and never properly examined the contradictions of his own position, but it is to his credit that he opposed the kind of intellectual vigilantism that was never far below the surface even in the pre-Stalinist era.

Literary criticism was Trotsky's nonpolitical specialty, but the range and variety of his knowledge in other fields commands respect and admiration. Most of his articles and speeches were those of a well-informed publicist, and he made no claim to originality or special competence, though he was characteristically opinionated and inclined to render judgments with an air of infallibility. Yet he never patronized his audience, either by the written or the spoken word. Whether his subject was Freudian psychoanalysis, atomic physics, or the role of women in society, he maintained the highest standards of intellectual integrity, and his exposition was always lively, if sometimes overly rhetorical. In his self-appointed capacity as propagandist and educator, he was only too familiar with Russia's historic backwardness, especially its legacy of poverty and illiteracy. While not ignoring these larger questions, which he confidently expected would be solved in time, he conducted something of a one-man crusade against the incivilities and degraded values of his countrymen. He deplored the decay of both literary and oral Russian, reserving special indignation for the routine use of profanity as spiritually debilitating. Drunkenness, lack of personal hygiene, uncouth manners—these were manifestations of an uncivilized past which the "new Soviet man" (to borrow a phrase from Stalin's Russia) would do well to avoid. But the quality of life could not be improved very rapidly by moral exhortation. However desirable, "primitive cultural accumulation," as Trotsky put it, remained slow paced, if not stagnant. And the vanguard of Soviet society, the Communist party membership, not only failed to provide moral tone and leadership but by the mid-twenties became in some ways a deterrent to upgrading the social amenities. The "organization men" favored by the Stalinist apparatus possessed neither the intellectual equipment nor the social sophistication of the first generation Bolsheviks, few of whom survived to enjoy a ripe old age.

In Trotsky's concern about moral uplift there is an element of prissiness—or what some might prefer to call Bolshevik sanctimoniousness. Like Lenin, he was ascetic in his personal habits and prudish about the subject of sex. His set of values and his life style may properly be identified with a strain of Bolshevik puritanism that in some respects carried over to the Stalin era. But that he spent so much time and energy on "good works" while his career hung in the balance reveals not only a self-imposed handicap but, more importantly, a curious block in his understanding of the political process. His subconscious seemed to rebel at the sordid reality of human nature and its grubby offspring—power and the means of obtaining it.

A more significant but little known aspect of Trotsky's career in the early twenties was his involvement with foreign affairs. Ostensibly he had abandoned or at least had become less concerned with conventional diplomacy when he took over the Commissariat of War. But even during the civil war he had been consulted on important decisions, and later he became a regular member of a small group of "experts" headed by Lenin (Kamenev, Chicherin, and occasionally Karl Radek participated) who discussed specific issues and to a considerable extent determined foreign policy. Trotsky had long since jettisoned his cavalier attitude toward traditional diplomacy as somehow a "bourgeois" enterprise and therefore rather disreputable when pursued by a "proletarian" state. The Bolsheviks, still hopeful that their revolution would spread to industrial Europe, were anxious to forestall any anti-Soviet moves by the capitalist enemy. None of the powers had formally recognized Soviet Russia, although Great Britain signed a commercial treaty in 1921.

This diplomatic boycott was broken in April, 1922, when the Treaty of Rapallo was signed with Germany. The occasion marked the beginning of a historic friendship based on political expediency and was to be severed only when Adolf Hitler destroyed the Weimar Republic in 1933. Trotsky's part in the long and tangled negotiations leading to Rapallo was rooted in his desire, as commissar of war, to obtain munitions and equipment for the Red Army. Germany, chafing under the armament restrictions of the Versailles

Treaty, possessed the needed technical skills and industrial capacity. Early in 1921 Victor Kopp, a former Menshevik and associate of Trotsky's in Vienna, returned from a diplomatic assignment in Berlin and informed the war commissar of his contacts with highly placed Germans, presumably in government and industrial circles. Trotsky encouraged him to pursue the subject of collaboration, and in April, Kopp reported that several German firms had agreed to manufacture airplanes, submarines, and artillery on Russian soil.[3] Later on the groundwork was laid for cooperation between the Red Army and the Reichswehr: German officers trained their Russian counterparts and secretly developed a military cadre for their own armed forces. Trotsky did not participate in the diplomatic preliminaries of the treaty which was signed by Chicherin in Rapallo, Italy, in conjunction with his leadership of the Soviet delegation to the European economic conference in Genoa.

Trotsky's forays into personal diplomacy rather than policymaking were infrequent. But he did receive several Western politicians, including Edouard Herriot, shortly to become the French premier, and Senator William H. King of Utah, one of America's most vociferous anti-Communists. On such occasions Trotsky was tactful and conciliatory and proved to be a convincing spokesman for peace and normal trade relations with the West. These sentiments, while they clashed to some extent with his militant image as a leader of world Communism, were sincerely held. His moderation and his mastery of the written word were perhaps instrumental in the decision to draft him as a ghostwriter in May, 1923, when a minor war scare erupted in Soviet Russia because of a peremptory diplomatic note from England. Popularly known as the "Curzon ultimatum" (Lord Curzon was the foreign secretary), it demanded satisfaction on a number of secondary issues involving British subjects and complained of Communist propaganda and activities in India and the Middle East. Alarmed by the strident tone of the protest, the Soviet leaders were prepared to return a soft answer. "Cursed be any one in this country who favors hostilities or a future war," Trotsky declared. "We will not take a single step or say a single word that could make the situation more acute." He later referred to the Curzon note as a "clumsy trap" which had deliberately sought to provoke a sharp retort "that would insult the English Philistines and thus arouse public opinion against us."[4] The formal Soviet reply, drafted by Trotsky, amended by his colleagues, and signed by Maxim Litvinov, one of Chicherin's assistants, skillfully blunted the charges and promised, if not complete satisfaction, a redress of grievances that eventually proved acceptable to the British government.

There was one point that Trotsky refused to concede—Soviet responsibility for the activities of the Communist International. Founded in Moscow in 1919 during the darkest days of the civil war, the Comintern not only began as a Russian-dominated venture but spoke in the name of a world Communist movement that had not yet materialized. Trotsky drafted both the initial invitation to the congress and a rousing manifesto to the "workers of the world" summoning them to a "struggle against imperialist barbarism, against monarchy, against the privileged estates, against the bourgeois state and bourgeois property, against all kinds and forms of class or national oppression." Busy at the front, he attended only one session of the founding congress in order to sum up the military situation and to present his manifesto. Zinoviev, presumably Lenin's choice behind the scenes, became president of the new organization. Trotsky was later appointed a member of the Russian Bureau of the Comintern's Executive Committee.

The second Comintern congress in the summer of 1920 was less conspicuously a Russian affair, although Bolshevik control, if not intended, was inevitable without a successful revolution outside the Soviet republic. The delegates represented a broad spectrum of radical socialism, including a few from Asian countries, whereas the credentials of many who had served in 1919 were questionable. Trotsky, preoccupied with the war with Poland, made only brief appearances. But he did address the closing session on August 7, presenting another manifesto which assessed the prospects of international Communism in typically optimistic terms. The dedicated Communist, he proclaimed, was a "zealous fighter, a mortal enemy of capitalist society, its economic foundations, its state forms, its democratic lies, its religion and its morality. . . . a self-sacrificing soldier of the proletarian revolution and an indefatigable herald of the new society."[5]

None of the Soviet leaders, Trotsky least of all, were capable of a sober appraisal of the Comintern's immediate future. Their messianic faith in the imminence of European revolution had not dimmed in spite of repeated disappointments. The "twenty-one conditions," established at the second congress to test the political reliability of organizations seeking admittance to the Comintern, split the European socialist movement asunder. Until 1921 the latent contradiction in Soviet policy between the aim of world revolution and the national interest of the Russian state had been concealed by mutual hostility with the capitalist West. But lessening antagonism and another discouraging failure of the German Communists to seize power—this time the so-called March Action centering in Mansfeld—prompted what Trotsky later called the "strategy of temporary retreat" in Comintern affairs. Lenin himself initiated the change and received the support of Trotsky and Kamenev, while Zinoviev, Bukharin, and others upheld the minority view that a frontal assault on the bourgeois redoubt remained the proper revolutionary path.

The Comintern's third congress in the early summer of 1921, a far more resplendent affair than the first two, was essentially devoted to shifting the emphasis from the tactics of *Putschism* and "splitting" to those of building mass parties. Trotsky, no longer harassed by military duties, attended many of the sessions and spoke frequently. He even found time for housekeeping details and complained indignantly to Lenin about the "rude disregard of visiting comrades" forced to do without mattresses, pillows, and washbasins. They "get a horrifying impression of the way we do things."[6] He was still at the height of his reputation as far as the delegates were concerned, and there was talk among them that he might replace Zinoviev, but nothing came of it. A Communist observer, Victor Serge, has described Trotsky's appearances: he was "dressed in some kind of white uniform. . . . his bearing [was] superbly martial, with his powerful chest, jet-black beard and hair, and flashing eyeglasses." Serge thought there was "something authoritarian" and "basically dictatorial" about him: "We had much admiration for him, but no real love. His sternness, his insistence on punctuality in work and battle, the inflexible correctness of his demeanour in a period of general slackness, all imparted a certain demagogic malice to the insidious attacks that were made against him."[7] If there was indeed a dictator waiting in the wings as early as 1921, it is entirely understandable that an obscure party functionary—Stalin—would be ignored and that a self-consciously "historic" figure—Trotsky—would be cast in the role.

Trotsky delivered a lengthy "Report on the World Economic Crisis and the New Tasks of the Communist International" at the second session. No less convinced that the "contradictions" of capitalism would lead to its inevitable demise, he conceded that the timetable had been altered and that if in 1919 the world revolution seemed only a "question of months," now it had become "perhaps a question of years." The Leninist premise of imperialist rivalry led him to forecast war between Britain and the United States in 1924, a rash prediction that he obliquely retracted (as far as the "accursed date") the next day.[8]

A ground swell of opposition arose to challenge the timidity of the Soviet leadership. A German delegate accused Trotsky of "putting the revolutionary energy of the proletariat in cold storage," and a Polish delegate proposed to conquer the bourgeoisie "with sword in hand and not with statistics." No amateur in the art of debate, Trotsky responded with some sharp but humorous thrusts that aroused appreciative laughter. While condemning "revolutionary adventurism," he contrived to appear as eager as his critics for the annihilation of capitalism: "We must pin both shoulders of the bourgeoisie to the ground and strangle it to death. That is the task. And to solve this task . . . one must combine the icy language of statistics with the passionate will of revolutionary violence."[9]

Soviet orthodoxy prevailed, but it was less a clear-cut victory for the "correct" ideology and strategy than a personal triumph for Lenin and Trotsky as the incarnation of the Bolshevik mystique. Passive resistance to the Comintern "retreat," especially among French and Italian Communists, continued to threaten the surface unity achieved at the third congress, but the larger and more prestigious German party went a step further and subscribed to a "united workers' front" the following August. The new formula was certified by the Comintern Executive Committee in December as applicable to the international movement. The aftermath was discouraging. The working masses to be lured into the Communist fold were either unresponsive or, if politically committed, loyal to the "trade union" socialism that Lenin and Trotsky had once found so reprehensible.

When the fourth congress of the Comintern met in November, 1922, the mood of militant expectancy, already diminished in 1921, had at best become one of contrived optimism. No one was brash enough to complain that the Soviet national interest was beginning to transcend the goal of world revolution, but there was now a frank recognition that the preservation and strengthening of the Marxist "fatherland" was the prime duty of all Communists. "The Soviet frontier," Trotsky wrote, "is the trench line beyond which counter-revolution shall not pass and where we will stay at our posts until the reserves arrive."[10]

The congress was the last in Lenin's lifetime, and the ailing leader made only one short speech. Trotsky, who received a standing ovation, devoted his major address to the NEP and the world revolutionary situation. Trotsky's performance was eclectic: he touched on many facets of Soviet history and policy and digressed occasionally into the tsarist past. Russia, said Trotsky, was passing through a stage of "primitive socialist accumulation," and he took pains to deny Social Democratic charges that the NEP signified a capitulation to capitalism. He admitted that capitalism in the West was again flourishing after a postwar depression and that an "epoch of European Kerenskyism" was entirely possible. Yet his prescription for the future revolution had not changed: "under the general slogan of the proletarian united front" Communism must teach the working class to "shake off disillusionment, passivity, and dilatoriness." Hardly an inspirational message, it was an implicit admission that the Comintern retreat would have to continue.

Trotsky apparently made no attempt to visit Lenin during the latter's convalescence in the summer of 1922. Their only contact was a routine exchange of letters on August 1. But his appointment as deputy premier was broached once more in September when Lenin delegated Stalin to place the matter on the Politburo's agenda. There was no opposition, though two abstentions, and again Trotsky declined to serve on the grounds that other duties were pressing upon him. He abruptly left Moscow for a vacation, but the timing suggests that he sought to avoid further controversy. The Politburo, presumably at Lenin's behest, formally censured him for what amounted to a breach of party discipline.

Another period of strained relations between Lenin and Trotsky followed, although there is no indication that the two became formally estranged. Lenin eventually proved the more conciliatory. He had not warmed toward Trotsky in any personal way, but his close working relationship with Stalin had broken down, and he needed a political ally. Stalin, as the chairman of a drafting commission for a new constitution, had gone further in the direction of government centralization than Lenin thought appropriate. It is ironic that Stalin, a Georgian nationalist in his youth, now came under Lenin's definition of a "Great Russian chauvinist" for his treatment of his homeland, which had been forcibly annexed in 1921. The relatively minor but vexed question of foreign trade led to a fuller reconciliation between Lenin and Trotsky and prepared the way for political cooperation on other matters. The Central Committee, in Lenin's absence, had approved a weakening of the government's monopoly on foreign trade, a policy of "socialist protectionism" (as Trotsky called it) that had not previously been violated despite the partial return to capitalism under the NEP. Convinced that a serious error had been made, Lenin busied himself with overturning the decision. He wrote to Trotsky (among others) to enlist his support and received a favorable response the same day (December 12, 1922). Trotsky used this opportunity to raise the subject of Gosplan (the State Planning Commission), for he had insistently urged that it be given more authority over the economy. Lenin was noncommittal about Gosplan but expressed satisfaction that they were in "maximum agreement." His health had again become precarious, and he asked Trotsky to assume the defense of "our common point of view" at the forthcoming session of the Central Committee.

Undoubtedly surprised that Lenin was making such an issue of the foreign trade monopoly, Stalin and his associates declined to press the argument, and on December 18 they rescinded the original decision. Lenin, now bedridden after a second stroke but able to communicate by dictation, sent a congratulatory message to Trotsky: "It seems that we have captured the position without firing a shot, simply by a tactical maneuver. I propose that we do not stop but continue the attack."[11]

Lenin had again tried to persuade Trotsky to accept the deputy premiership in a private meeting—it was to be their last—that took place in the Kremlin early in December, 1922. Lenin had become greatly exercised about the growth of bureaucracy ("something monstrous"), and in his search for solutions to the problem he proposed a "radical realignment of personnel." Trotsky balked once more, but this time he took a different tack, complaining about the "apparatus"—that is, the Stalinist party organization. "Well, that will be your chance to shake up the apparatus," Lenin pointed out, and he proposed a "bloc against bureaucracy." Trotsky's rejoinder, "It is a pleasure to form a bloc with a good man," sealed a tentative political partnership that was cut short by Lenin's illness.[12]

Isolated from direct participation in political activity during the winter of 1922–23, Lenin struggled to keep abreast of current affairs. Resigning himself to neither political nor physical disability, he managed to dictate a "journal" that dealt with a variety of internal problems. The best known of these memoranda, a document dated December 25 that came to be known as his "Testament," discusses the future of the party and appraises his colleagues. He reveals concern about a party split between Trotsky and Stalin, "the two outstanding leaders of the present Central Committee." Belatedly recognizing Stalin's hold on the party machinery, he expresses doubt that the general secretary knows how to use the "enormous power" that he holds with "sufficient caution." Lenin also remarks that Trotsky, although distinguished by his "exceptional abilities" and "perhaps the most capable man" in the Central Committee, is inclined to excessive self-confidence and to excessive involvement with the purely administrative side of affairs" (apparently an oblique reference to his vanity and arrogance). Invoking Trotsky's "non-Bolshevism," he states that it can no more be held against him than the "October episode" of 1917 when Zinoviev and Kamenev had opposed the seizure of power. If this was truly the case, then why did he bring up the past at all? On balance, Stalin emerges from Lenin's scrutiny with a more positive image than his rivals. It must have been something of a shock to Trotsky that he was not designated as Lenin's favorite, and one may suppose that Zinoviev and Kamenev were equally disconcerted that they were ranked below Stalin.

Lenin soon revised his original verdict. On January 4, 1923, he added a devastating postscript recommending Stalin's removal as general secretary because of his rudeness and other personal defects. Presumably, new and derogatory information about Stalin—most likely relating to the Georgian question, although there are other possibilities—had reached him in the interval. Stalin and his aides had purged the Georgian Communist party of dissenters, and Lenin was determined to assist these "nationalists" even though his own investigation remained incomplete. Trotsky was not particularly knowledgeable about Georgian affairs, nor was he aware of Lenin's anxiety about the problem, especially as it related to Stalin's conduct. But he had spoken at a Central Committee meeting in a vein that reassured Lenin when he asked his secretaries about

Trotsky's views. On March 5 he dictated a letter to Trotsky seeking his help in the "Georgian case." "The matter is now being 'prosecuted' by Stalin and Dzerzhinsky [the secret police chief], and I cannot rely on their impartiality," he stated. "Indeed, quite the contrary. If you would agree to undertake its defense, I could be at ease. If for some reason you do not agree, please return the dossier to me. I will consider that a sign of your disagreement."[13]

Trotsky was also in poor health, suffering from a prolonged siege of lumbago, and received the message by telephone. His response seems to have been vaguely affirmative, though his later comment on the incident fails to make his attitude clear. At any rate, Lenin sent him the Georgian material, including the so-called "Letter on the National Question" that Lenin had dictated on December 30–31. Lydia Fotieva, one of Lenin's secretaries, informed Trotsky that Lenin did not trust Stalin and that he was "preparing a bombshell" for the forthcoming party congress. Still unable to comprehend that the uncouth Stalin was a serious political rival, Trotsky backed away from the impending struggle, and with a foolhardiness that in retrospect borders on the unbelievable he chose to abandon his Leninist mandate. Through Kamenev he arranged a "rotten compromise" with Stalin—an outcome that Lenin had warned would be the result of any bargain with the general secretary. Opposed to punishment for Stalin and his assistants, Trotsky did demand a "radical change in the policy on the national question, a discontinuance of persecutions of the Georgian opponents of Stalin, a discontinuance of the administrative oppression of the party, a firmer policy in matters of industrialization, and an honest cooperation in the higher centres."[14] Stalin accepted the terms with alacrity, relieved—and probably mystified—that Trotsky had shown such forbearance. But he still had Lenin to contend with, a problem that was substantially reduced when the invalid leader suffered another cerebral stroke on March 10. The stroke put an end to Lenin's political influence, though there was always the possibility that he might rally again. While he lived, Stalin observed the amenities within the Politburo and at times displayed a hypocritical deference to Trotsky.

For his part, Trotsky showed little disposition to upset the status quo. On March 20 he offered some criticism of the "official" Georgian policy in an article in *Pravda*—without naming Stalin—and followed this statement with a more vigorous speech before the

Central Committee that failed to mention Lenin's views. But Stalin contrived to "doctor" the verbatim record by omitting several key statements, much to Trotsky's indignation.[15] Lenin's "Letter on the National Question" remained in Trotsky's custody for some time, and at the request of one of Lenin's secretaries he returned it after making a copy for possible future use. Fotieva took it upon herself to reveal its existence to Kamenev, who promptly informed the Central Committee. Stalin, assuming a pose of moral rectitude, circulated a memorandum on April 16 scolding "Comrade Trotsky" for withholding vital information from his own colleagues for over a month. Trotsky had indeed been placed in an unflattering light, but instead of counterattacking—the appropriate response of an astute politician—he sought to justify his conduct with a lame explanation that he had abided by Lenin's wishes as far as he understood them. He offered to submit the matter to a party investigation and obtained Stalin's personal assurance that he had not acted improperly. However, the general secretary's promise of a written declaration to that effect was not immediately forthcoming, and Trotsky sent him a letter with a veiled threat: "You can understand and appreciate better than anyone else that if I have not done so until now"—that is, request a full investigation—"it was not because of fear that my interests would suffer."[16]

Whether Stalin complied is unknown. Presumably he did, for Trotsky scrupulously refrained from any kind of provocation at the Twelfth Party Congress, which had already begun its deliberations. Zinoviev gave the keynote address in Lenin's absence. Seeking to avoid the appearance of being eager to assume Lenin's mantle, Trotsky had proposed Stalin for the honor, and he in turn had suggested Trotsky as the "most popular member of the Central Committee." Zinoviev thus became by default the party's titular leader, and it was he, along with Kamenev, who founded the cult of Lenin while the party chief was still alive. Stalin, less florid in his tributes, made a more dignified impression as simply a humble disciple of the great man. He was content to appear as an apostle of moderation and party unity, and few of the delegates were aware that the congress, though not "packed" in any conspiratorial sense, was essentially a product of the party Secretariat. Stalin delivered the principal report on the nationalities question and handled himself with aplomb. He referred only by indirection to Lenin's "letter" on the subject. The Politburo had decided against publication, but

the delegates were briefed on its contents. The Georgian opposition, defeated at a party conference in March, was poorly represented at the congress. Trotsky maintained a discreet silence,
avoiding the debates—they were occasionally somewhat acrimonious—on Georgia and the whole problem of nationalities. Bukharin
was the only prestigious figure to take up the Georgian case, while
Rakovsky, Trotsky's old associate, made some tart comments on
Stalin's policy that invited retaliation: he was honorably "exiled" the
following summer as the Soviet representative in London.

Trotsky deliberately avoided controversy by confining his major
address to the relatively safe area of economic theory and practice.
Long an advocate of industrial planning, he stressed the desirability
of gradually eliminating the NEP as the state enlarged the public
sector at the expense of the private. But where would the state
acquire its investment capital? He frankly declared that it would
have to come from the workers: the state, not the capitalist entrep-
reneur, would acquire the Marxian "surplus value" to push onward
toward socialism. It was not a prescription with mass political appeal, though Stalin eventually proceeded with a grandiose industrial
plan that dwarfed Trotsky's modest and tentative proposals. For the
sake of the political armistice, it had been agreed beforehand that
Trotsky would be allowed to convey the "official" line on the
economy. Criticism was therefore more perfunctory than it would
otherwise have been, and his recommendation for a "more harmonious, more concentrated economic offensive," rephrased as a
resolution on industrial development, was approved without opposition. Yet his "victory" was a hollow one, for the idea of planning
came to be associated with Trotskyism, and Leninist orthodoxy as
determined by Stalin required an indefinite perpetuation of the
NEP.

The Twelfth Congress represented Trotsky's supreme opportunity to rally his supporters and to take over the party leadership. It
was never to recur again, and in later years he confessed his mistake:
"I have no doubt that if I had come forward on the eve of the twelfth
congress in the spirit of a 'bloc of Lenin and Trotsky' against the
Stalin bureaucracy, I should have been victorious. . . . [for] it was
still possible to capture the commanding position by an open attack
on the . . . usurpers of the apparatus, of the unlawful heirs of October, of the epigones of Bolshevism." Then why did he not do so?
He not only declined to attack, but in rebuking a delegate who

complained that Trotsky's services were not being fully utilized he all but announced his unwillingness to engage in political combat. His own explanation is less than adequate but psychologically revealing: "Independent action on my part would have been interpreted, or, to be more exact, represented as my personal fight for Lenin's place in the party and the state. The very thought of this made me shudder. I considered that it would have brought such a demoralization in our ranks that we would have had to pay too painful a price for it even in case of victory."[17]

It is a rare and fortunate politician who has power thrust upon him. Trotsky obviously expected that he was to be among the elect whom History had chosen. He had only to bide his time. Subconsciously he shrank from a test of strength and rationalized his lack of moral courage—of physical courage he was seemingly well supplied—with a variety of excuses: Lenin's illness and possible recovery, the mediocrity and philistinism of the opposition, the danger of demoralizing the party rank and file. But in all fairness, it should be acknowledged that in 1923 he lacked the knowledge and wisdom that hindsight confers so readily upon those who can examine the past at their leisure. He was not alone in his underestimation of Stalin. The other triumvirs, Zinoviev and Kamenev, had joined Stalin in a temporary alliance because of Trotsky, assuming that they could discard him at their convenience. Despite his political shrewdness, Lenin too had not properly assessed the true character of the man until illness allowed him time for reflection.

The political moratorium achieved at the Twelfth Congress lasted until the fall. Isolated in the Politburo and the Central Committee, Trotsky remained politically lethargic and reputedly showed his contempt for his associates by reading novels at some of the sessions. Stalin, with quiet efficiency, proceeded to consolidate his hold on the party apparatus. Neither he nor his partners ventured the slightest public criticism of Trotsky, but the circulation of underground leaflets directly attacking him could hardly have been accomplished without the connivance, if not the instigation, of one of the party leaders, probably the general secretary himself.

The outward serenity among the oligarchs was shattered on October 8 when Trotsky, provoked by an accumulation of grievances, sent a scorching letter to the Central Committee citing the "radically incorrect and unhealthy regime within the party" and "flagrant" errors which had brought on a "grievous economic situation" during the summer.[18] Discontent among the workers had led to wildcat strikes and political agitation. The "scissors crisis" (high industrial prices and low agricultural prices), which Trotsky had analyzed so convincingly at the Twelfth Congress, continued to squeeze the economy, and he complained that the basic remedy—industrial planning—was being virtually ignored. Sympathetic to the workers' demands, he nevertheless refrained from protesting the arrest of numerous dissenters who might spark another Kronstadt in the factories. But he was repelled by Dzerzhinsky's insistence that party members should act as informers for the secret police, though he avoided repudiating the idea in his letter. The whole problem of dissent and opposition within a one party state was becoming less abstract: he openly scorned bourgeois democracy, yet protested the "unheard of bureaucratization of the party apparatus" and the suppression of free intraparty discussion.

Another sore point to Trotsky—and this may have festered more than the "incorrect" economic policy and the "bureaucratization" of the party—was the troika's attempt to weaken his hold over the War Commissariat. A year before he had been able to oust one of his old civil war adversaries, Sergei Gusev, as head of the army's political administration and to replace him with a trusted aide, Antonov-Ovseyenko, who had gained a measure of fame during the Bolshevik insurrection. In September, 1923, the troika sought to weaken Trotsky's control of the Revolutionary War Council by introducing prominent new members, including Stalin. Incensed, Trotsky threatened to resign his offices and to go abroad to help the German Communists, then preparing a revolution of their own. Stalin offered a "compromise": he would withdraw his own name in favor of his old crony Voroshilov and that of Zinoviev's candidate, Mikhail Lashevich. The Central Committee confirmed the appointments, and Trotsky stormed out of the meeting, prepared to dramatize his displeasure by slamming the door. But the scene ended farcically when the massive barrier proved to much for him. "Thus, instead of witnessing a moving gesture, signifying a historic break," wrote an eyewitness, "we watched a sorry and helpless figure struggling in vain to close a door."[19]

The Politburo replied to Trotsky's letter of October 8 with a statement accusing him of dictatorial ambitions and recalling that he had "categorically declined the position of substitute for Lenin"—a position that "evidently he considers beneath his dignity." The statement continued: "He conducts himself according to the formula, 'All or nothing.' "[20] Trotsky's vehement response recited the various issues on which he and Lenin had collaborated during the previous year.

Confined to the upper reaches of the party, the dispute remained unknown to the lower echelon. But it had spread beyond the Central Committee, and on October 15 a declaration signed by forty-six prominent oppositionists challenged the official leadership with a searching critique of its deficiencies, particularly the failure of the economy and the growing "dictatorship within the party." Although the protesters acted independently of Trotsky, his letter had triggered their dissatisfaction, and they must have become frustrated and disillusioned when he declined to be associated with them. Aloof, hesitant, a master of poor timing, he again passed up his opportunity—not that the odds were now in his favor. By scattering his shots in ill-tempered complaints and by refusing to mount a full-scale assault, he at least averted the charge of factionalism and left ample ground for retreat.

Trotsky's immediate dilemma was solved for him by the "accident" of a prolonged illness. In late October he caught cold while duck hunting, and on November 5 the attending physicians diagnosed influenza. All his symptoms but one soon disappeared—a persistent fever or, to use Trotsky's words, "the constant sensation of running a temperature." Psychosomatic illness, contrary to widespread belief, is not "imaginary," but Trotsky's doctors could not find an organic basis for his "dogged, mysterious infection." The circumstances suggest a subconscious desire to avoid or to postpone a hostile confrontation. Bedridden for weeks at a time, he did keep his pen busy—his favored weapon for political skirmishing.

The troika, though shaken by the declaration of the forty-six, proceeded to condemn the opposition, including Trotsky, through the device of an enlarged Central Committee meeting. When this failed to check the ferment from below, Zinoviev announced a major concession on November 7: the party press would be thrown open to free debate. Since "party democracy" had become fashionable as a slogan—the reality lagged well behind—the leaders sought to conciliate Trotsky and to close ranks once more. He was unable to leave his Kremlin apartment, and the Politburo obligingly met there. A comprehensive resolution on party affairs was finally drafted that appeared to satisfy all concerned. It was published on

December 7 with appropriate publicity and the expectation on Trotsky's part that his opponents had mended their ways. But a paper agreement could not alter the prevailing balance of power, and the ambiguity of the document speedily led to "reinterpretation" and an even more serious split in the party.

The fresh rupture began with the publication in *Pravda* on December 11 of an open letter by Trotsky intended as an explication of the Politburo resolution on party reform. It was one of several brief essays written in December that later appeared in his pamphlet, *The New Course*. The theme was a familiar one—the bureaucratic degeneration of the party. The text, while laced with uncomplimentary phrases ("apparatus functionaries," "mummified bureaucrats"), mentioned no names and was not offered as a deliberate provocation. After what must have been several days of troubled debate, the troika chose to regard it as a willful violation of the agreement and launched a devastating offensive. Stalin, previously reluctant to discard his pose of cautious moderation, led the attack with an article in *Pravda* on December 15. His barbs were concealed by civility—Trotsky was still "comrade"—but he sarcastically refuted Trotsky's claim of being one of the "Bolshevik old guard." As for the degeneration of the party, there were indeed elements potentially dangerous in that respect: "I have in mind that section of the Mensheviks who joined our party *unwillingly* and have not yet rid themselves of their old opportunist habits." His allusion to Trotsky's "Menshevik" past, seemingly a harmless political ploy at the time, foreshadowed a vast "operation rewrite" that would one day distort party history beyond recognition.

In the frenzied controversy that followed in the press and at party meetings, the opposition was severely hampered by the organizational effectiveness of the general secretary's well-oiled "machine." The Secretariat controlled the party cells—and ultimately the voting procedure—while the press gradually ceased to function as a forum of open discussion. To party members, as to politically conscious outsiders, the quarrel seemed less a matter of principle—everyone gave lip service to "party democracy"—than of whether Trotsky or his rivals would seize the levers of power. The same man who had acquired a reputation for ruthless suppression of the trade unions was not a convincing spokesman for democracy, either within the party or in other areas of Soviet life. And to compound the opposition's difficulties, Trotsky retired from the field at the height of the battle. Depressed and apathetic, he refused public comment and prepared to leave for the warmer climate of the Black Sea.

Trotsky had not yet departed when a party conference met on January 16, 1924. There could only be one outcome, for the Secretariat had done its work well and only three oppositionists were present among the one hundred and twenty-eight voting delegates. Stalin set the tone in his report on "The Immediate Tasks of Party Affairs," largely devoted to a detailed analysis of Trotsky's "errors." Straightforward and matter of fact, his speech was devoid of personal abuse. Stalin did not link his adversary directly with the opposition, though he jabbed at Trotsky's equivocal conduct: "We are told that Trotsky is seriously ill. Let us assume he is; but during his illness he has written three articles and four new chapters of the pamphlet [*The New Course*] which appeared today. Is it not clear that Trotsky could perfectly well write a few lines in reply to the question put to him by various organizations and state whether he is *for* the opposition or *against* the opposition?"[21]

Stalin's patience had worn thin the next day after an opposition speaker reviewed the history of the dispute. Discarding his posture of objectivity, he denounced Trotsky for suddenly discovering "that the country and the party were going to rack and ruin and that . . . this patriarch of bureaucrats could not live without democracy. . . . He needs democracy as a hobby-horse, as a strategic maneuver. That's what all the clamor is about." He also dropped his polite pretense that Trotsky was not necessarily an oppositionist and accused him of slandering the Central Committee. "Only a man who has completely lost his head and is blinded by factionalism can . . . maintain that the October plenum [of the Central Committee] was the supreme expression of bureaucracy."[22]

The delegates obediently reaffirmed the Politburo's December resolution by a unanimous vote and overwhelmingly approved of censuring the Trotsky opposition for factionalism and for mounting a campaign "to revise Bolshevism, not only a direct departure from Leninism, but a plainly declared petty bourgeois deviation." Stalin emerged from the conference as the senior triumvir, and if not yet the master of the party, he now had the necessary organizational tools. The opposition was demoralized and politically impotent, and Trotsky himself, disabled by a paralysis of the will, was no longer the errant comrade of whom the party leaders need be solicitous. He had not been expelled as a heretic, though Stalin hinted at that possibility should he persist in his defiance. His political fate hung in the balance as he left Moscow by train on January 18 with outward indifference to the "conspiracy of the epigones," as he was to label his opponents at a later date.

CHAPTER 8

The Ascendancy of Stalin

TROTSKY and his wife reached Tiflis, the capital of Georgia, on January 21, 1924. There he received a telegram informing him of Lenin's death. The news came as a numbing shock, for Trotsky had never lost hope that the stricken leader might recover and that their abortive "bloc" could be revived. In his despair, he later recalled, "I knew only one urgent desire—and that was to be alone. I could not stretch my hand to lift my pen." Nevertheless, he managed to construct an emotional tribute on the theme of "Lenin is no more, but Leninism remains," and his message was transmitted to Moscow for public distribution. Many years later in the bitterness of exile he voiced his suspicion that Stalin might have hastened Lenin toward his end by furnishing or administering poison. But the medical evidence, including an autopsy, supports no other conclusion than that of an advanced case of arteriosclerosis and death by cerebral hemorrhage. Trotsky's hypothesis rests wholly upon speculation coupled with his recollection that near the end of February, 1923, Stalin informed his Politburo colleagues that Lenin had requested poison to end his suffering.

Trotsky considered returning for the funeral but maintained that a telegram from the "Kremlin" (or from Stalin according to a later version) deceived him about the date and advised him to proceed with his journey since he could not reach Moscow in time. That it was a deliberate conspiracy seems unlikely, but whatever the truth of the matter, he was not present for the speeches, the ceremonial ritual, and the final interment on January 27. His followers were distressed, and his older son, then nearly eighteen, wrote with bewilderment and reproach that he had not come at any price. But his presence on the scene could scarcely have raised his political stature even though it would have enhanced his public image. Nonetheless, the legend arose, fostered chiefly by Western jour-

nalists, that he lost out in the struggle for the succession because he
had not attended the funeral.

Lethargic and seemingly resigned to his fate, Trotsky sought refuge from the pressures of active politics in Sukhum, a Black Sea
resort with a mild winter climate. His morale was improved by a
cordial letter from Krupskaya, assuring him that her husband's attitude toward him had not changed from the time of their London
meeting in 1902. As his mental state grew better, his unpredictable
fever also subsided. But he made no attempt to end his self-imposed
isolation until May. This prolonged absence from the capital, as if to
demonstrate defiant contempt for his "inferiors," proved far more
damaging to his career than the episode of Lenin's funeral. It
amounted to a form of political masochism, and his opponents, if
perplexed by his behavior, were only too glad to indulge his eccen-
tricity.

Trotsky's control of the military establishment, already undercut
in September, was further impaired in March when his trusted
deputy, Sklyansky, was replaced by Mikhail Frunze. An able civil
war commander and a protégé of Zinoviev, Frunze carefully observed the proprieties by calling on Trotsky at Sukhum, together
with other representatives of the Central Committee, in order to
"coordinate" sweeping personnel changes in the War Commissariat.
To Trotsky it was "sheer farce," for the shakeup had been under way
for some time. Antonov-Ovseyenko had already been removed from
his key post, and Nikolai Muralov, also an ardent Trotskyist, was
dismissed as chief of the Moscow military district in favor of Voroshilov. (It was Muralov, so the story goes, who begged Trotsky for
the privilege of leading a detachment of soldiers into the Kremlin to
arrest his opponents.)[1] Another reorganization of the Revolutionary
War Council assured the troika of a commanding majority in that
body. Outflanked and isolated within his own domain, Trotsky remained war commissar but with little prospect of exercising the
authority that went with the title.

Stalin's command of the party was hastened by the so-called "Lenin enrollment" when some two hundred thousand recruits, chiefly
"workers from the bench," were admitted to the party in the four
months following Lenin's death. Hailed as a step that would regen-
erate the party—the innate virtue of the proletariat was a sentiment
that both Lenin and Trotsky shared—this infusion of new blood was
supervised by the Secretarial apparatus. Stalin had the effrontery to

claim that it was "evidence of the party's profound democracy." At the same time, a purge of oppositionists was quietly proceeding—disguised, however, as an attempt to rid the party of opportunists, careerists, and other undesirables.

Trotsky returned to Moscow in time to attend the Thirteenth Party Congress. Prior to the opening session, he was among those present at an enlarged Central Committee meeting which heard Lenin's "Testament." Krupskaya had sent the document to Kamenev with a note indicating Lenin's desire that its contents be divulged at the next party congress after his death. According to Trotsky, when Stalin first read it, his reaction was typically crude: "He shit on himself and he shit on us!"[2] Trotsky remained silent during the discussion that followed the formal reading while allegedly expressing his disdain of the whole procedure by gestures and grimaces. Once again he failed to act when presented with an opportunity that Lenin himself had provided from beyond the grave. Radek, who sat beside him, leaned over and commented, "Now they won't dare to go against you." "On the contrary," Trotsky replied, "now they will have to see it through to the bitter end, and moreover as quickly as possible."[3] With Stalin's career in jeopardy, his two partners, still convinced that Trotsky was the major enemy, came to the rescue of the general secretary by insisting that Lenin's fears about him had proved ill-founded. By a vote of thirty to ten, the Central Committee decided to preserve the confidentiality of the "Testament" by having it read aloud to delegation caucuses rather than allowing it to enter the official record of the congress. Trotsky later charged that the process was blatantly unfair: "The leaders of the delegations in their reading would swallow some words, emphasize others, and offer commentaries to the effect that the letter had been written by a man seriously ill under the influence of trickery and intrigue."[4] To cap the episode, Stalin offered to resign as general secretary, a token gesture under the circumstances, for the Central Committee (Trotsky included) returned a unanimous vote of confidence.

The party congress that met late in May, 1924, reconfirmed the verdict pronounced against the opposition at the January conference. Trotsky, a nonvoting delegate, spoke only once, a pallid defense of his views that repeated his warnings about party bureaucracy and reemphasized the virtues of a planned economy. Responding to Zinoviev's demand that the opposition confess its errors, he man-

aged an oblique recantation that may have been tinged with irony:
"Comrades, none of us wishes to be or can be right against his party.
The party in the last analysis is always right because the party is the
only historical instrument given to the proletariat for the solution of
its fundamental problems. . . . One can be right only with the party
and through the party, for history has created no other way for the
realization of what is right." Having retreated close to the point of
self-abasement—even Stalin found the notion of party infallibility
too much to swallow—he abruptly reversed his course and announced his disagreement with the decisions of the January conference as "in certain parts incorrect and unjust." But he concluded
lamely by reasserting his solidarity with the party: "I bear the consequences of its decision to the end."[5]

Trotsky's ambiguous performance could not have inspired his
friends (one pronounced it "blunderingly stupid"), but neither could
it alarm his enemies. Nevertheless, several party members of the
second rank rose to attack him, and Stalin soon joined the chorus on
the grounds that the "comrades of the opposition" had reopened old
wounds which had seemingly healed. He launched into a tedious
recapitulation of the controversy while avoiding the rancorous tone
of his rebuttal at the January conference. By reverting to his role of
the cautious moderate, he blocked the maneuvers of Zinoviev and
Kamenev to remove Trotsky from the Politburo, and Trotsky was
also reelected a member of the Central Committee.

Trotsky had salvaged his pride by refusing to admit his guilt; yet
he openly acknowledged his submission to party discipline. His
continued silence was an implicit recognition that if he had avoided
the status of a penitent, he had been reduced to that of a pro-
bationer, however eminent he remained in the eyes of his dwindling
band of followers. The ruling triad observed the political truce by
refraining from personal disparagement of their victim, but the
press hammered away at the opposition, including Trotsky's supposed deviation from true Leninism. Lingering anxiety about his
future intentions was instrumental in shoring up the deteriorating
alliance of the "epigones" for a while longer.

Invited to state his case at the fifth congress of the Comintern in
June, Trotsky declined because of the precariousness of his political
standing (though he claimed that the party had in effect muzzled
him). At previous congresses his name had epitomized the revolutionary mystique of Communism. His support abroad, particu-

larly strong in the German, French, and Polish Communist parties, had now largely dissipated, a tribute not only to Zinoviev's tireless energy but to the remorseless "Bolshevization" of the Comintern since the fourth congress. His more prominent sympathizers in the foreign parties had been intimidated or expelled, and none of the delegates ventured to question the wisdom of Soviet leadership by words of commendation for a fallen hero. Others, more vindictive, whether from motives of political expediency or of genuine conviction, echoed the charges already made in the Russian party. Yet such was the power of his reputation—and possibly the force of habit—that his usual concluding manifesto was solicited by the congress and promptly delivered. It was to be his last. He was not reelected to the Comintern Executive Committee and was replaced by Stalin, who had formerly been disinclined to play a major part in the affairs of the International.

Trotsky's summer quiescence was interrupted only once: in June he published a brief memoir about Lenin written during his stay at Sukhum.[6] The troika, though irritated by its tone of affectionate intimacy—it conveyed the impression that Lenin and Trotsky were equal partners on a higher plane than the other leaders—chose to regard it as a minor pinprick. Trotsky preferred to ignore his thirteen-year estrangement from Lenin, a decision of questionable intellectual honesty that proved embarrassing when his Leninist pose came under withering fire toward the close of the year.

Later in the summer Trotsky took a working vacation at the Caucasian resort of Kislovodsk. Perhaps encouraged because his Lenin memoir had not provoked serious retaliation, he again turned to the historical record for a more obvious measure of vindication and revenge. This time he focused on the more recent past, taking as his theme the blunders and faintheartedness of the Old Bolsheviks in 1917, principally Kamenev and Zinoviev. Their conduct, he wrote, was "not accidental," but it would be "too despicable to make use of what happened then in order to attack those who made mistakes" (a malicious thrust drawn from Lenin's "Testament"). Yet this was precisely the point of the article—to contrast their mistakes with the correct strategy of Lenin and Trotsky. It was not an accident, he further argued, that the Communist defeats in Germany and Bulgaria in 1923 had derived from the same kind of "Menshevik" timidity that Lenin had so strenuously denounced on the eve of the Bolshevik insurrection.

Trotsky completed his essay on September 15 and entitled it "The Lessons of October." His collected works began to be published earlier in the year, and the third volume, then being readied for the press, was a compilation of his articles and speeches of 1917. It therefore seemed appropriate that his polemic should serve as an introduction to the forthcoming volume. The official publication date was November 6, but copies reached key party members in October. Trotsky undoubtedly anticipated a counterattack; but he could not have foreseen the torrent of abuse that would descend upon him or the atrocities that would be perpetrated in revising party history so that it would conform to current political needs. When the furious recriminations had finally ceased—the episode became known under the genteel label of the "literary debate"—it seemed evident that he had not only made a serious tactical error but one of timing as well. For the triumvirs, instead of drifting apart, had been obliged to regroup against the renewed onslaught of Trotsky's pen. Yet Zinoviev later contended that the article was only a "pretext" and that different circumstances would have called for a different approach: "The trick was to string together old disagreements with new issues. For this purpose 'Trotskyism' was invented."[7]

Trotsky's biggest miscalculation, however, was probably in directing his shafts at the Zinoviev-Kamenev partnership, for they were his natural allies and, as incredible as it now appears, he had not yet fully grasped the political implications of the general secretary's party machine. "The Lessons of October" made only one unfavorable reference to Stalin, and that was achieved by allusion rather than by name. In attempting to demonstrate that he was a more orthodox Bolshevik than his rivals—that is, a better "Leninist"—he provoked an argument that he could not win. It gave them an opportunity to explore in depth the heresies he had committed long before the cult of Lenin was born.

Early in November, Bukharin, in an unsigned article in *Pravda* entitled "How Not to Write the History of October," opened the public debate on Trotsky's essay. Kamenev responded two weeks later with a lengthy speech that set the pattern of future hostilities. Trotsky was identified as an "agent of Menshevism", and his supposed unorthodoxy by Bolshevik standards was demonstrated by a veritable torrent of quotations from Lenin hinself. Stalin entered the contest with a speech of his own on the nineteenth, a better organized and more incisive attempt to undermine Trotsky's reputation. He expended considerable effort in belittling the "legend about Trotsky's special role in the October uprising" and declared that a five member "practical center" (including himself) had actually organized the insurrection. The "center," while not precisely a figment of Stalin's imagination, had never performed any functions and was not the only party organ created on the spur of the moment and promptly forgotten. Stalin conceded that "Trotsky did, indeed, fight well in October," but so had others, and in the period of Brest-Litovsk he lacked "courage and revolutionary steadfastness."

Stalin concluded that there were three basic features of "Trotskyism" that brought it into "irreconcilable contradiction with Leninism": (1) the theory of permanent (or uninterrupted) revolution, which Stalin deceptively coupled with Trotsky's alleged "underestimation of the peasantry" as a revolutionary force; (2) "distrust of the Bolshevik party principle, of the monolithic character of the party, of its hostility toward opportunist elements"; and (3) "distrust of the leaders of Bolshevism, an attempt to discredit, to defame them." Stalin ended on a note of restraint, a sentiment that Zinoviev and Kamenev did not share: "I am emphatically opposed" to "repressive measures. . . . What we need now is . . . an ideological struggle against revived Trotskyism."[8]

Zinoviev and a host of lesser party figures had their say—even Krupskaya delivered a mild rebuke. The local party organizations were also encouraged to express their indignation at Trotsky's nonconformity to the Bolshevik canon. Of the myriad charges hurled against him, none was more telling with the rank and file than his supposed anti-Leninism. Kamenev had been the first to use quotation mongering as a political ruse. He had quoted Lenin against Trotsky, and it was inevitable that the technique would be reversed. In 1913 Trotsky had made some particularly offensive remarks about Lenin in a letter to Menshevik leader Nikolai Chkheidze. Still incensed by the Bolshevik action in appropriating the name *Pravda* for the party newspaper, he labeled his tormentor "a professional exploiter of every kind of backwardness in the Russian working-class movement." And he characterized the "whole edifice of Leninism" as one "built on lying and falsification," bearing "within itself the poisoned element of its own disintegration."

Although the letter was not defamatory by the criteria of émigré politics, it was beyond the pale in the context of the burgeoning Lenin cult. It was discovered by party archivists in 1921, and

Trotsky was queried about his attitude toward publication. He replied in rather lofty tones that to publish it seemed inadvisable since readers would not "apply the necessary historical correctives." He was not disposed to revive old quarrels, nor did he consider that in his "disagreements with the Bolsheviks" he was "wrong on all points."[9] Stalin quoted briefly from the Chkheidze letter in his speech three years later, and the text of both letters was released to the press. This "exposé" was a devastating blow to Trotsky's credibility as a Leninist. It was with understandable resentment and pardonable exaggeration that he termed the "political forgery perpetrated by Stalin and his associates" one of the "greatest frauds in the world's history."[10]

Trotsky visibly wilted under the "volcanic eruption" that poured forth slander "in a cold lava stream." Again he took to his bed with a high temperature, trying to ignore the "campaign of ignorant lies." His wife described him as looking "pale and thin," with a cold and a "critical nervous condition." His decision to retreat into the dignity of silence was no more successful than it had been the year before. His admirers were dismayed, and the party wheelhorses, if mystified anew by his peculiar conduct, were relieved that he cooperated in his own destruction. His repetitive behavior pattern could not have been coincidental. It suggests a deep-rooted anxiety neurosis that sapped his will and inflamed his nerves when confronted with a personal crisis. For externalized crises—a revolution or a civil war—the process was reversed: his psychic juices, so to speak, flowed with abandon into the higher calling that History had placed before him. The inner doubts and insecurities vanished in such a setting, only to reemerge in a workaday world where practical politicians were in demand and revolutionary heroes were victims of technological unemployment.

That the state of Trotsky's health was not an insuperable obstacle to his continued literary activity is amply demonstrated by a lengthy defense of his position that he wrote in his Kremlin apartment during the latter part of November. It bore the working title "The Purpose of This Explanation: Our Differences" and presented a convincing if somewhat labored response to his critics. He refused to retract his previous words but denied any intention of substituting the "secret banner" of Trotskyism for the credo of Leninism. He ignored Stalin and concentrated his fire on Kamenev, whose mistakes in 1917 were reconfirmed and whose technique of quoting out of context was deemed reprehensible.[11] His essay remained unpublished, not because the press was closed to him or to his supporters, but because he sought to avoid fanning the flames of controversy. In short, he had capitulated, hoping to regain his place in the party by submitting to its will. He stubbornly declined to recant, however, and this ritual, soon to become mandatory for those seeking the party's absolution, proved a serious obstacle to his rehabilitation. Mere acts of contrition were no longer sufficient to demonstrate that he had purged himself of doctrinal error.

Ignoring for the time being his doctors' advice—they recommended another vacation in a warm climate—Trotsky decided to remain in Moscow. On January 15, 1925, he sent a letter to the Central Committee, his first official contact with the party leaders in many months. He tentatively defended himself from the "multitude of false and actually monstrous accusations" leveled against him by denying any taint of "Trotskyism" or any imputation that he had sought to revise "Leninism." He denied that he had flouted any party decisions since the Thirteenth Congress. But, as a token of his obedience to the party, he offered to undertake any work assigned to him and to relinquish his command—now purely nominal—of the Red Army: "The interests of the work demand that I be freed immediately from my duties as president of the Revolutionary War Council."[12]

The Central Committee, meeting shortly thereafter in joint session with the Central Control Commission, considered Trotsky's fate at some length. His ouster from the presidency of the Council and as commissar of war was foreordained, but he was allowed to "resign" from both offices. As to his future status in the party, opinion was sharply divided. Stalin, still formally respectful toward "Comrade Trotsky," again blocked Zinoviev and Kamenev in their desire for drastic punishment, and Trotsky retained his seat in both the Politburo and the Central Committee. But he was severely chastised in a lengthy resolution that reviewed his departure from the tenets of Bolshevism, noted that he had declined to acknowledge his mistakes, and warned of disciplinary action should he fail to abide by party decisions.

Trotsky, pleading ill health, had excused himself from the proceedings but indicated his availability should his testimony be required. He had not been called upon, and late in January he again journeyed to the Black Sea area to recuperate. "I yielded up the military post without a fight, even with a sense of relief." he confessed. "I was thereby wresting from my opponents' hands their weapon of insinuation concerning my military intentions." This reference to his alleged Bonapartist tendencies was an odd but revealing rationale: his ignominious retreat had been a partial victory after all because he had deprived his enemies of a stick to beat him with!

Trotsky returned to Moscow at the end of April and was almost immediately confronted with a minor but potentially serious crisis. One of his American sympathizers, Max Eastman, had recently published in New York a slender volume entitled *Since Lenin Died*. It related in some detail the power struggle in the party from a Trotskyist viewpoint and featured the first public account, including excerpts, of Lenin's suppressed "Testament." His major source had been Trotsky himself—Eastman had been in Russia in 1922–24—and he naturally expected that he was performing a political service for Trotsky and for the cause of historical truth. Normally Trotsky would have welcomed the book, but it placed him in an awkward and embarrassing dilemma. To repudiate it would further demoralize his followers, while the alternative of accepting it as an accurate version of the conflict would jeopardize his hope of regaining his position in the party. At first he tried to evade the issue by releasing a brief statement rejecting in advance and sight unseen any attacks that the book might have made on the party. But the Politburo demanded a forthright disavowal, and he chose the path of expediency by signing a declaration that was virtually dictated to him. Eastman's charge that certain documents written by Lenin in the last period of his life had been concealed from the party was, Trotsky claimed, "a slander on the Central Committee." As for the alleged "Testament," frequently cited in the "émigré and foreign bourgeois and Menshevik press," it was only a letter "containing advice of an organizational character." Assertions that it had been concealed or destroyed "represents a malicious invention."[13] His statement appeared in the Communist press abroad in July but was not published in the Soviet Union until September 1. He emerged from the affair humiliated and morally compromised. It signaled his political bankruptcy, and when he did finally decide to fight, his supporters were scattered, intimidated, and disheartened.

Without prior consultation Trotsky was appointed to the Supreme Council of the National Economy in May, 1925. Although not a

demeaning post, it seemed safely nonpolitical and an unlikely
sanctuary for fresh endeavors in empire building. Within the
sprawling Council he chaired three committees: Concessions, Elec-
trotechnical Development, and the Scientific-Technical Board for
industrial research. His new work was unfamiliar and not wholly
congenial; but if Trotsky plunged into it with something less than his
accustomed zest, he justly felt proud of his ability to master unusual
assignments. He reported later that he "made an honest attempt to
work in harmony with the new arrangements." He developed a
special interest in institutes of technology, most of them founded
since the revolution, and visited laboratories, picked the brains of
leading scientists, and studied textbooks on chemistry and industrial
technology. His ingenuity was not stultified by the technicalities of
his job, and he sought to relate his work to the problems of a socialist
economy. One result was a statistical comparison of industrial development and labor productivity between the Soviet Union and the
advanced capitalist countries, a study that revealed Russia's continued backwardness despite the economic gains registered under
the NEP. Trotsky felt that his bold reminder of the Soviet position
not only cast doubt on the "reactionary theory" of "socialism in one
country," a doctrine that Stalin was expounding as an answer to
Trotsky's "permanent revolution," but also implied that Russia
could not achieve socialism without a revolution in the West.

Trotsky's foray beyond the narrow confines of his assignment
aroused suspicion and fostered a "complicated intrigue behind the
scenes." "Much of the creative activity of Stalin and of his assistant
Molotov," he complained, "was devoted to organizing direct sabotage around me."[14] Concluding that his attempt to win a "political
holiday" for himself was "patently a failure," he insisted on resigning
his technical functions early in 1926 while retaining the Concessions
Committee (a less sensitive post since the Politburo decided on the
merits of each application).

With Trotsky in political limbo, the hue and cry over
"Trotskyism" gradually subsided. Without an enemy to hold their
alliance together, the troika fell into disarray. Kamenev had already
lost control of the Moscow party organization, and it was as
Zinoviev's auxiliary that the two confronted the general secretary.
Solidly entrenched at the head of the party in Leningrad (Petrograd
had been renamed) and still presiding over the Comintern, Zinoviev
remained a formidable antagonist. But his position was not impreg-

nable, and it crumbled at the Fourteenth Party Congress in December, 1925, where the Stalinist delegates swamped those of Zinoviev.

Trotsky's attitude toward the combatants was one of haughty contempt. He had deliberately avoided informing himself of the maneuvers and intrigues of the "epigones," taking a perverse satisfaction in his political isolation and in his ignorance of party affairs outside his own special province. The Stalin-Zinoviev split at the congress therefore caught him by surprise. He attended as a nonvoting delegate, maintaining an enigmatic silence while savoring the discomfiture of the Zinoviev opposition, which received the same kind of treatment that he and his followers had been subjected to at the Thirteenth Congress. Radek, a bitter opponent of Zinoviev, urged Trotsky to reach an understanding with Stalin, while Sergei Mrachkovsky opposed a bloc with anyone: "Stalin will deceive, and Zinoviev will sneak away." Yet the logic of the situation demanded that all the anti-Stalinist factions band together for mutual protection, and it was a gauge of Trotsky's deep-rooted hostility to Zinoviev that several months elapsed before a new coalition was forged.

The first indication that Trotsky had softened his stance toward Zinoviev occurred at a Central Committee meeting early in January, 1926, when Stalin proposed measures to dislodge Zinoviev from his Leningrad fiefdom. Trotsky objected, as did Kamenev. Bukharin, who had formed a partnership with Stalin, approved, and Kamenev reminded him that he had opposed similar reprisals against Trotsky in the past. Unable to resist a malicious quip, Trotsky interjected: "He has begun to relish it." Stung by the remark, Bukharin wrote Trotsky a few days later: "You think that I have 'begun to relish it,' but this 'relishing' makes me tremble from head to foot."[15] Trotsky replied, and a personal correspondence ensued on the basis of the friendship they once shared, but on political questions they soon reached a stalemate. Their exchange ended, as far as is known, in early March when Trotsky indignantly called his attention to ugly manifestations of anti-Semitism in the renewed campaign against the opposition.

In the interim, Stalin had crushed the Zinoviev organization in Leningrad. Molotov led an impressive delegation of party leaders to the northern metropolis, and by capitalizing on the verdict of the Fourteenth Congress, by engaging in vigorous missionary activity in the factories, and by transferring key party officials, they brought the local membership into line. A loyal Stalinist, Sergei Kirov, replaced Zinoviev as the Leningrad party boss. Kamenev was demoted to candidate membership in the Politburo, and other Zinovievists were replaced in the Central Committee. Stalin did not revive the attack on Trotsky, other than acts of petty harassment, because he hoped to postpone—or to circumvent—the formation of a united opposition. It also seems probable that Stalin had not yet closed his option of a rapprochement with Trotsky, for he is reported to have made overtures several months after the Fourteenth Congress.[16]

Not until April, 1926, did Trotsky bring himself to cement an alliance with his former enemies. Kamenev (his brother-in-law) acted as mediator. He had not spoken to Trotsky in private for over three years. "It is enough for you and Zinoviev to appear on the same platform," he told Trotsky at their first meeting, "and the party will find its true Central Committee." Trotsky reported that he laughed at such "bureaucratic optimism" and counseled his new partners to "prepare for a long and serious struggle." Yet even now they continued to underestimate their wily adversary: Stalin was "the outstanding mediocrity in the party" (Trotsky's phrase) whose success had been a triumph of intrigue and cunning. They failed to appreciate his tactical skills, for he had outmaneuvered them with practiced ease. It lay within his power to make a clean sweep of these troublesome malcontents, but as a master of political timing he preferred to strip them of their credibility and to deliver the coup de grace at his leisure. He accurately described their collaboration as a "direct, open, and unprincipled deal" and sneered at their "mutual amnesty" for the scurrilities with which they had once bombarded each other. Trotsky implicitly withdrew the aspersions he had cast upon Zinoviev and Kamenev in his "Lessons of October," and they in turn acknowledged that his strictures on party bureaucracy had been well taken.

The marriage of convenience had hardly been consummated when Trotsky, whose past conduct during political crises had been baffling enough, chose to leave Moscow in mid-April for medical treatment in Berlin. Under the psychological stress of a renewed confrontation with Stalin, his fever had flared up again. Zinoviev and Kamenev parted from him with "a show of real feeling," and he surmised that they did not relish "the prospect of remaining eye-to-eye with Stalin." He traveled incognito, though his identity, at least to the German authorities and the personnel at the private clinic where he became a patient, was an open secret. A throat specialist persuaded him that his tonsils might be the source of his trouble, and he underwent an operation without any discernible improvement in his condition.

Trotsky remained abroad for about six weeks. His absence delayed the formation of an effective and unified opposition, for the animosity between the Trotsky and Zinoviev factions could not be overcome by simple fiat. Although Trotsky was the key figure on the basis of his reputation and past popularity, he had carelessly squandered his assets, and his organized following was weak and dispirited. Zinoviev, despite his defeat in Leningrad, had a larger and more dedicated band of professionals under his command. Unprepared for open warfare on the Stalinist majority, the combined opposition resorted to semi-clandestine measures: secret meetings, coded messages, and underground couriers. But only a few thousand party members rallied to the cause. Further struggle seemed hopeless; yet the opposition leaders were sustained by the conviction of their moral and intellectual superiority and by their belief that a tiny but self-confident elite could eventually prevail over the flaccid mass of timeservers in the party. Had not Lenin built a powerful Bolshevik organization in equally unpromising circumstances?

Stalin shrewdly bided his time, content for the most part to isolate his prospective victims and to deal with them piecemeal through the authorized channels of the party. He was not above small-scale guerrilla warfare, however, and either prompted or condoned the investigations by the OGPU (the secret police) and other informers who reported the names and activities of the oppositionists. Reprisals, and eventually expulsion from the party, generally followed. The anti-Semitic whispering campaign of which Trotsky had previously complained also gained momentum. Since not only he but Zinoviev, Kamenev, Radek, and other leaders were of Jewish origin, in contrast to the Stalin-Bukharin stalwarts, it was perhaps inevitable that popular prejudice against Jews would infiltrate the party struggle. Stalin's own views are not definitely known, though his anti-Semitism became conspicuous in his later years. Trotsky asserts that Stalin's attitude toward this unsavory campaign was one of "friendly neutrality," a restrained judgment in the light of his charge made elsewhere that two of Stalin's henchmen, Kirov and Nikolai Uglanov, organized anti-Jewish propaganda "systematically and almost in the open."[17]

Zinoviev was subdued at a plenary session of the Central Committee in July, 1926. He lost his seat in the Politburo, and his presidency of the Comintern became largely an honorary title. Kamenev was further demoted—he was relegated to the politically harmless post of director of the Lenin Institute. Trotsky remained immune, though only temporarily, from retaliation. Stalin no longer needed him as an ally against Zinoviev; yet he realized that to dispose of his two major enemies at one stroke might grate upon the party's sensibilities.

The public—and even ordinary party members—remained ignorant of the split among the leaders. Desperate but unwilling to defy the party with an appeal to the masses over Stalin's head, the opposition decided by late summer to abandon secrecy and to carry its message directly to the rank and file party workers. At numerous cell meetings Trotsky and his colleagues sought to accomplish by oratory what they had failed to do by argument and intrigue in the upper reaches of the party. But they were received with indifference, if not hostility, and often found it impossible to make themselves heard. "Goon squads" beholden to the party apparatus interrupted the speakers with jeers and heckling remarks; lesser known oppositionists were threatened or assaulted; and meetings were sometimes broken up altogether. Trotsky himself was hooted off the platform at one Moscow factory meeting.

The opposition had come to a dead end. Trotsky and Zinoviev tacitly admitted as much when on October 4 they indicated to the Politburo their readiness for an armistice. Their bargaining power had been dissipated, and the peace terms were virtually those of unconditional surrender. About all that could be salvaged was freedom of conscience, for Stalin refrained from demanding a public disavowal of the opposition's arguments. On October 16 Trotsky and five of his leading associates signed an agreement to discontinue their factional activity. Admitting their violation of party discipline, they repudiated their followers abroad and abandoned the remnants of the Workers' Opposition with which they had recently formed an alliance. Again their obeisance was self-defeating. It gained them nothing but a temporary respite in their slide toward political oblivion, and it exposed their disciples to retaliation.

Stalin, perhaps angered by the publication on October 18 of the full text of Lenin's "Testament" in the West—it had been released by Max Eastman to *The New York Times*—chose to ignore the truce and called on his beaten opponents to confess their errors. Trotsky, bitterly resentful of Stalin's violation of the agreement, lost his temper at a Politburo meeting. Dramatically pointing at Stalin, he delivered the ultimate insult: "The First Secretary poses his candidature to the post of the grave digger of the revolution!"[18] Stalin turned pale, obviously upset, and hastily left the meeting. Trotsky's Politburo colleagues censured him, and his supporters were aghast at his audacity. Yuri Pyatakov, aware of Stalin's vindictive nature, warned prophetically, "He will never forgive you for this: neither you, nor your children, nor your grandchildren."[19]

On October 23 the Central Committee dropped Trotsky from the Politburo, removed Kamenev from his candidate status, and deprived Zinoviev of his Comintern leadership, though he was not formally replaced by Bukharin until later. The oppositionists were allowed to speak at the party conference that followed, and Trotsky's prowess as an orator remained undiminished as he made one of his last addresses to a party gathering. The delegates, though hostile and obstreperous, were impressed in spite of themselves. He was allowed to exceed the normal time limit, a token of respect that was not accorded Zinoviev, who was frequently interrupted and denied permission to continue.

Zinoviev, thoroughly demoralized, was ready to give up the struggle. Trotsky's mood was hardly better, but he was not prepared to abase himself. He professed to believe that the "breathing spell" during the winter of 1926–27, when Stalin, savoring his victory, moderated his campaign against the opposition, "allowed us to carry out a more thorough theoretical examination of many questions." Refusing to concede his incompetence as a politician, he persisted in rationalizing the debacle by farfetched social and ideological explanations. For example, if two of Stalin's supporters in the Politburo, Voroshilov and Mikhail Kalinin, were of peasant stock, then they must "objectively" represent the kulak strata of the population. If the masses, including ordinary party members, had remained indifferent or ill-disposed toward the opposition, then there had been a "shift to the Right" which, on the analogy of the French Revolution, brought the danger of a Soviet "Thermidor" and a betrayal of true Bolshevism.

In the spring of 1927 Trotsky seemed well on the road to political eclipse when "staggering events in China," brought on by the "criminal character of Stalin's policy" (Trotsky's appraisal), breathed new life into the opposition. The promise of a revolution in China—to be sure a "bourgeois nationalist" one rather than Communist—had been encouraged by Moscow as a means of thwarting capitalist imperialism. Soviet advisers and military supplies enabled the Kuomintang, the once impotent party of Dr. Sun Yat-sen, to attempt the formidable task of unifying China by challenging the war lords whose avaricious rule had split the country into semiautonomous principalities. The task of the Chinese Communists, Stalin had decided, was to do "coolie service for the Kuomintang." Under the military leadership of Chiang Kai-shek much of southern and central China was wrested from war lord control in the summer of 1926. But success (and Dr. Sun's death the previous year) widened the breach between the Left and Right factions, and Chiang, once fashionably "radical," became alarmed by the revolutionary ferment that had been unleashed by the campaign from Canton to the Yangtze. On April 12, 1927, he broke with his Communist "allies" and launched a bloody reign of terror in Shanghai. That Stalin was acutely embarrassed by his "fraternal" comrade—Chiang had been named an honorary member of the Comintern Executive Committee—is to understate the case. But he was understandably reluctant to confer credit on Trotsky by admitting that his policy in China had been mistaken.

Quick to denounce the strategy that led to the Shanghai massacre, Trotsky later maintained that he had opposed the Communist-Kuomintang alliance "from the very beginning."[20] The evidence, though not wholly conclusive, fails to support him. Until the eve of the Shanghai affair his comments on China were desultory, uninformed, and confined to the Politburo. He apparently expressed uneasiness about the trend of Soviet policy but was not sufficiently concerned (or knowledgeable) to take up the matter in the Central Committee or at Comintern meetings. Nor did he state his objections in public, either orally or in writing. Only on March 31, 1927, did he deliver a formal complaint in a letter to the Politburo in which he alluded to "fears of Chinese Bonapartism" and recommended the formation of Soviets in China.[21]

In his zeal to expose the fatuousness of Stalin's Chinese policy, Trotsky neglected to point out that he too was hesitant and uncertain about the proper course even after Chiang's coup. He did not advocate that the Chinese Communists break with the Kuomintang Left and was cautiously optimistic about revolutionary prospects during the summer and fall when disaster after disaster attended Communist efforts to seize power in various Chinese cities.

If the vagaries of politics in China proved a temporary boon to the opposition, events in England had the contrary effect. In the wake of a raid on the Soviet trade delegation in London on May 12, 1927, supposedly in search of a missing government document, Great Britain severed diplomatic relations with the Soviet Union. The break provoked a war scare in Russia that both Stalinists and oppositionists contrived to inflate for their own purposes. Official spokesmen lost no time in calling for unity, implying that those who failed to rally to the party and to the socialist fatherland in a time of danger were neither Communists nor patriots. Stalin himself spoke bluntly of "something like a united front from [British Foreign Secretary] Chamberlain to Trotsky." Trotsky rejected the charge as "insane infamy" but sought to couple the alleged threat of war with Stalin's blunders in China. Only new leadership, more responsive to the needs of the Russian proletariat and the international Communist movement, could avert fresh tragedy. His pronouncements remained unknown to the public, however, because the press erected a barrier of silence, and Stalin emerged from the episode with more credibility than Trotsky.

Stalin had now decided to remove his two irksome, if relatively powerless, antagonists from the Central Committee. He seized upon an indiscretion of Trotsky and Zinoviev as a sufficient cause for their expulsion: they had joined a public demonstration at a Moscow railway station that protested the honorable exile of a prominent oppositionist to a new post in the Soviet hinterlands. The Central Committee, after a number of turbulent sessions beginning in late July, finally passed the necessary resolution unanimously. But it was withdrawn when Gregory Ordzhonikidze intervened with Stalin, and another truce was arranged in which the opposition was given a "severe reprimand and warning."

As on previous occasions the agreement was flawed with ambiguities and proved only a temporary respite before hostilities resumed once more. The opposition leaders, maintaining that their views had a right to be heard, drew up a "platform" in September that amounted to a detailed indictment of Stalinist policy. The

Politburo denied a request for publication. Facing, at best, slow attrition through acts of harassment and intimidation, Trotsky and his associates resolved to go down fighting. The document was printed illegally, but the underground press was soon raided by the OGPU, and sixteen oppositionists said to be implicated were expelled from the party. As an act of desperation, Trotsky, Zinoviev, and Kamenev organized clandestine meetings in Moscow and Leningrad. But when they sought to proselytize party members, they were no more successful than they had been in 1926.

Trotsky's swan song as a party leader came on October 23 before an enlarged Central Committee, where his expulsion was again on the agenda. He spoke before a hostile audience, and its more extreme members subjected him to both verbal and physical abuse (books and at least one water glass were thrown at him). In a belated and futile effort to use Lenin's "Testament" as political ammunition against Stalin, he charged that the "rudeness and disloyalty of which Lenin wrote are no longer mere personal characteristics" and that they had "become the character of the ruling faction. . . . [because of] its belief in the omnipotence of methods of violence—even in dealing with its own party."[22] An astute prophet in this instance, he was less successful in predicting that Stalin's rule would be transitory and that his regime would collapse without warning. Stalin deftly blunted the force of Trotsky's appeal to Lenin's authority by quoting his beaten rival in 1925 when he had denied the authenticity of the "Testament." Besides, had he not offered to resign as general secretary and been urged to stay at his post by his colleagues, including Trotsky himself? And why should rudeness— Lenin had never complained of his mistakes—be considered a defect in his political position? The vote was a mere formality: Trotsky and Zinoviev were duly expelled from the Central Committee.

Against overpowering evidence that the Russian people were unacquainted with the opposition's arguments and unconcerned as to its fate, Trotsky retained a residual faith in the political instinct of "the masses." Properly informed and motivated—and with effective leadership—they might yet be aroused and turn on his oppressors. The tenth anniversary of the Bolshevik Revolution on November 7 seemed to offer something more than a medium for official self-congratulation and ceremonial ritual. A well-organized demonstration could provide the spark that sometimes transforms humble events into historic occasions. At any rate, Trotsky deemed that the opportunity was worth a try, and it did offer an honorable alternative to abject surrender.

Although beset by the familiar range of psychosomatic complaints—fever, insomnia, headaches, and dizziness—Trotsky resolutely prepared for what was to be the opposition's final confrontation with Stalinist authority. Placing himself, at least symbolically, at the head of the demonstrators in Moscow while Zinoviev performed a similar function in Leningrad, he toured the city with Kamenev and Muralov in an automobile. His appearance aroused no signs of popular enthusiasm, and those followers joining the official procession to Red Square with placards and slogans were roughly handled by party toughs whom Trotsky equated with "notoriously non-revolutionary and . . . Fascist elements." A dismal fiasco, the open protest deliberately flouted the spirit and letter of party regulations and subjected its perpetrators to speedy retaliation. Anticipating eviction from his Kremlin apartment, Trotsky moved that evening to a friend's residence. A week later he and Zinoviev were expelled from the party, the prelude to a sweeping but bloodless purge of the opposition.

Trotsky remained bold and undaunted. At least he strove to convey this impression, though he must have had private doubts and moments of personal depression. The suicide of his old associate, Adolf Yoffe, on November 16 affected him deeply. It was an act of political protest triggered by ill health. Trotsky spoke at the funeral, which he estimated drew some ten thousand mourners. This event was the last oppositionist demonstration as well as his last public appearance in the Soviet Union. Yoffe left an affectionate letter to Trotsky that ventured to chide him for his readiness in the past to abandon his convictions for the sake of compromise. "You are right," he wrote, "but . . . victory . . . lies in nothing but the extreme unwillingness to yield, the strictest straightforwardness, the absolute rejection of all compromise; in this very thing lay the secret of Lenin's victories." The advice came too late, but Trotsky, seldom given to introspection and self-doubt, certainly pondered the criticism, and his stubborn refusal to humble himself may have derived in part from Yoffe's letter.

Zinoviev and Kamenev, among lesser figures, were willing to plead for mercy, and in the end they were obliged not only to submit to the party but to confess their errors. Trotsky and his adherents, badly depleted by the end of the year, awaited their fate with stoical resignation. The Politburo decided in late December that the principal Trotskyists would be deported outside the Moscow area. In theory their banishment was to be under honorable conditions, with appropriate work assignments, for Stalin and his associates were concerned with their public image and sought to avoid martyring their beaten opponents. Trotsky negotiated through intermediaries and rejected Astrakhan, an old Tartar city on the Caspian Sea, as unsuitably hot and humid. But the bargaining was broken off when the OGPU, presumably at Stalin's instigation, requested his presence at its headquarters. He declined to appear and was peremptorily informed on January 12, 1928, that under the article of the criminal code dealing with counterrevolutionary activities he was being sent to Alma Ata, then a sleepy provincial city near the Chinese frontier.

CHAPTER 9

Exile and Assassination

THE date of Trotsky's deportation was set for January 16, 1928. It was postponed, however, when word of his departure leaked out and a large and unruly crowd of sympathizers gathered at the Kazan railroad station. Seeking to avoid a demonstration, OGPU agents unexpectedly called at his apartment on the seventeenth. They had to break down a door to confront him, and by an odd coincidence the official in charge had served on Trotsky's military train during the civil war. Embarrassed and deferential, he was urged to do his duty by the intended victim, who nevertheless considered it a matter of principle to offer passive resistance. Trotsky was literally carried away and put aboard a special railroad car at the deserted Yaroslav station, where a locomotive conveyed him to a junction outside the city and a rendezvous with a train to Tashkent. He was accompanied by his wife and older son; the other remained in Moscow.

Because Alma Ata had no rail service, the party, including an armed escort, left the train at Frunze and completed the last stage of the journey—about one hundred sixty miles—by bus and sleigh. Arriving on January 25, the Trotskys were assigned two rooms at a hotel and were treated with every consideration by the local police. Within three weeks they were permitted to move to a house of their own. Trotsky bombarded Moscow with telegrams of protest on matters both large and small, and within the confines of administrative exile he was given extraordinary leeway. No restrictions were placed on his correspondence (although the postal service was sometimes erratic), and in April he managed to arrange a clandestine message service with Moscow as well. He was allowed to go on lengthy hunting trips at a considerable distance from Alma Ata. His large library and personal papers were shipped to him. To augment his official allowance he worked as a translator, editor, and proof-

156

reader for the Marx-Engels Institute, whose director was his old associate David Ryazanov. One of his assignments was a translation of Marx's polemic, *Herr Vogt*, which undertook to demolish in two hundred pages of fine print the reputation of one of Marx's political enemies. "If we had begun to refute the Stalin slanders on the same scale," Trotsky wrote, "we should probably have to publish an encyclopedia of a thousand volumes."[1]

Trotsky's son Lyova took charge of his father's voluminous correspondence, acting not only as his secretary, research assistant, and bodyguard, but also as his negotiator with the local authorities and organizer of his hunting trips. Trotsky called him his "minister of foreign affairs," sometimes doubling as his "minister of posts and telegraph." Two of the assistants who had served him faithfully in Moscow tried to reach Alma Ata, and one managed to do so, but both were arrested and internally exiled. He employed a young girl as a typist, assuming that the OGPU would question her even though she could hardly be a politically knowledgeable informant.

Trotsky's moral authority was unquestioned among his followers; but as new quarrels broke out in the party—Stalin now confronted the so-called Right opposition led by Bukharin—and a "Leftward" course developed in 1928, there were grumblings about his political judgment. He welcomed Stalin's campaign against the kulaks as a vindication of the opposition, and he even allowed himself the luxury of a wish-fulfillment fantasy that Stalin, in the extremity of his fresh predicament, might yet rehabilitate his old adversaries to help do battle with the new ones. But feelers from the Bukharin camp posed an awkward dilemma and a conflict of principle: which of Trotsky's recent oppressors could he support in good conscience? Stalin had now seemingly "borrowed" portions of the Trotskyist platform except that the "bureaucratic degeneration" of the party was proceeding apace. Bukharin had not changed his "Rightist" views, yet he was prepared to admit, now that he was in the minority, that party democracy was inherently desirable and not simply a bourgeois affectation.

Recognizing that a strong stand in either direction would be divisive, Trotsky drew back from any endorsements, implied or otherwise, and dissociated himself from the brutal measures that accompanied Stalin's policy toward the peasantry. As for Bukharin, collaboration could extend only to the issue of restoring democracy in the party. Trotsky's cautious retreat irritated the "conciliationists,"

those who regarded the Bukharinists with contempt and argued that
Stalin's "Left turn" made an alliance with him politically desirable.

In the late summer Trotsky's health, never robust since his descent into political obscurity, grew worse. Persistent fever (which he
took to be malaria), headaches, gout, and colitis sapped his energy.
His friends grew alarmed and peppered party officials with complaints about his lack of medical treatment and prolonged banishment. His wife dispatched an indignant telegram to Uglanov, the
Moscow party secretary, who had spoken of his "fictitious" illness.
Some of the exiles were prepared to undertake a hunger strike on
his behalf, an action that he considered unwise since his health was
not precarious enough to prevent him from working.

In October the lax police supervision over the Trotskyist deportees was replaced by a stricter regimen. A number were actually
imprisoned, but the more prominent retained their "freedom." Stalin, aware of dissension among his opponents, had every expectation
of weaning them from their leader, and his intermediaries used both
blandishments and veiled threats to hasten the process. Trotsky,
who had never quite abandoned his naive vision of the dishonored
prophet suddenly restored to his rightful place in the party hierar-
chy, remained as defiant as ever. A "postal blockade" seriously curtailed his political activity, and in December an OGPU official sent
from Moscow delivered a verbal ultimatum to discontinue his leadership of the opposition or face a change of residence and isolation
from political life. Trotsky responded with a bitterly scornful letter
to the Cental Committee and the Comintern Executive Committee
in which he recited the indignities and persecution that he and his
sympathizers had been subjected to. To renounce his activities
would be to abjure his principles: "Only contemptible renegades
would be capable of giving such a promise." Again displaying his
fondness for the weak—and essentially misleading—comparison of
Stalin's Russia to the Thermidorean Reaction of the French Revolution, he placed his cause in destiny's keeping. "The greatest historical
strength of the opposition, in spite of its apparent weakness," he
declared, "lies in the fact that it keeps its fingers on the pulse of the
world historical process, that it sees the dynamics of the class forces
clearly, foresees the coming day and consciously prepares for it."[2]

Justifying his tactics and ideology by rhetorical appeals to the
"historical process" and to "class forces" was to Trotsky as congenial

and persistent an addiction as a theologian's reliance upon divine guidance. The psychological satisfaction he derived from being right in the long run may have helped to cloud his vision in the short run. Nothing but a major political upheaval could extract him from his predicament. His fate was decided in the Politburo, and Stalin had the necessary majority to do virtually as he pleased. Yet imprisonment—and certainly execution—would have flouted public sensibility and caused awkward repercussions in the party and in the international Communist movement. Expulsion from the country, on the other hand, would presumably strip him of political influence and seemed an expedient solution. Only Bukharin and his two supporters voted against it.

On January 20, 1929, the OGPU emissary, who had waited in Alma Ata for instructions, called on Trotsky and informed him of his banishment, though not his destination. He had provoked "anti-Soviet actions" and had prepared for "an armed struggle against the Soviet power." The accusation was ridiculous—"an insolent lie," as Trotsky put it—since the opposition had never contemplated the use of force. The next day was spent packing in feverish haste, as Trotsky's library and manuscript collection had grown ever larger. On the twenty-second the family, along with a solicitous escort (the OGPU agents were properly awed by their distinguished prisoner), set out by autobus for the railhead. The road over the Kurday mountain range was blocked by deep snowdrifts and had to be negotiated by sleigh, a painfully slow journey of more than seven hours. Once over the pass they transferred to a motor vehicle and reached Frunze without further incident.

A special train was provided, and the Trotskys, confined to a single coach, were obliged to endure a tedious odyssey of nearly three weeks. En route the officer in charge was informed by direct wire from Moscow that their ultimate destination was Constantinople (now Istanbul). Trotsky preferred exile in Germany, and the Soviet government appeared willing to grant his request, but the German authorities denied him a visa. While the negotiations were underway the train was sidetracked for twelve days near a lonely provincial station. With the temperature at one time fifty-three degrees below zero (Fahrenheit), the engine chugged up and down the track to keep from freezing. The journey resumed on February 8, and two days later the party arrived in Odessa, the familiar city of

Trotsky's school days. A steamer awaited their arrival, and with an icebreaker forcing a passage through the frozen waters of the Black Sea they set out for Turkish soil.

In Constantinople, Trotsky and his family stayed at the Soviet consulate, where they were hospitably received. The Turkish government had not been informed of his banishment, merely that he was there for reasons of health, but assured him when the situation became clear that he was a welcome guest. Apparently concerned about political reverberations, the Soviet government made no forthright announcement of his expulsion, and the public became aware of it only several weeks later when the press published a scornful article on "Mr. Trotsky in the Service of the Bourgeoisie." The title was occasioned by his initial contributions to the Western press, all of them trenchantly anti-Stalinist in tone and content.

Trotsky recognized the anomaly of his residence at the Soviet consulate. His hosts were not anxious to prolong it, although OGPU agents could easily keep him under surveillance, an arrangement that had a certain appeal when Stalin belatedly recognized that his ousted enemy might prove more than a minor irritant to the image, if not the stability, of his regime. After a diligent and anxious search, the Trotskys moved in early March to a spacious villa some distance from Constantinople. Located on one of the Prinkipo islands in the Sea of Marmara, their new abode offered privacy, scenic grandeur, and a kind of decadent elegance. But they remained largely indifferent to its aesthetic charm, and the natural austerity of their life style prevented any attempt to provide something more comfortable than what an American visitor has described as a "bare barrack."[3]

Trotsky had no expectation of dallying in this provincial backwater of Europe and sought refugee status in Germany, England, France, or Norway. The response was varied but always in the negative. His reputation as a revolutionary firebrand was such that domestic considerations prevailed over the supposed democratic right of political asylum. Frustrated by this "planet without a visa" (the title of the final chapter in his autobiography), he commented wryly, "When I ask to be given a brief object-lesson in democracy, there are no volunteers."

Without abandoning his struggle for a haven in the West, he plunged into political and literary endeavors with his customary zest and dedication. His correspondence alone would have consumed the working day of an ordinary man. One immediate objective was the launching of a modest periodical in the Russian language, the *Bulletin of the Opposition*, which would furnish a rallying point for his followers, both in the Soviet Union and abroad. The first issue appeared in Paris in July, and the *Bulletin* was published irregularly—sixty-five issues in all—until its demise in 1941. His chief work was his autobiography, which he had begun in Alma Ata and now rapidly pushed to completion. The German translation came out toward the end of the year, and the English edition was published in London early in 1930. It was well reviewed and displayed the consummate literary skill for which the author was so justly renowned. Like most autobiographers, Trotsky ignores or rationalizes defects of character and personality and his mistakes and blunders. His self-deception is notably conspicuous in the account of his political downfall. If Stalin was indeed a party hack and the epitome of mediocrity, how was he able to grasp the party machinery to crush his chief rival so easily? Trotsky never comes to grips with this glaring contradiction, if in fact he recognized its existence. For all its defects as a political testament and historical document, his autobiography must nevertheless be counted among the classics of its genre. It also provides a unique and indispensable record of the Russian revolutionary movement.

A world celebrity, Trotsky was inundated with requests for interviews and offers to write articles and books. Friends and admirers gathered at Prinkipo, and had time permitted the "Old Man" (as his younger adherents usually referred to him) could have presided over a political salon of considerable dimensions. He enjoyed playing the affable host—or at least assuming the role of oracle to a devoted band of disciples—but he seldom permitted social or other activities to interrupt his working regimen. The only major exception seems to have been fishing trips, some of them rather elaborate exercises on the order of his hunting expeditions at Alma Ata. These forays, often alone, presented excellent opportunities for assassination attempts had the OGPU (or anti-Communist Russian émigrés) been so minded. But Stalin had not yet declared a bloody vendetta against Trotsky and his followers, and Soviet agents acted with discretion, though at least one informer—and there may have been others—worked his way into Trotsky's entourage in the guise of a sympathizer. The Turkish government provided a police guard, and a number of supporters, chiefly young Americans, served as bodyguards and secretaries.

If Stalin refrained from the physical elimination of the opposition, he had no compunction about lesser measures of persecution. Those who remained steadfast Trotskyists were subjected to brutal penal conditions. Others, persuaded that Stalin's plans to industrialize the economy and to collectivize the farms had robbed them of ideological sustenance, edged toward capitulation. In July, 1929, after prolonged negotiations, some four hundred deportees, headed by Radek and Yevgeny Preobrazhensky, renounced their views and received, in effect, absolution from the party. Another group of several hundred, for whom Ivan Smirnov was the leading spokesman, surrendered in the fall under somewhat more honorable conditions: they were not obliged to abjure Trotsky in a public declaration. Trotsky could only observe from afar the steady attrition of his following. He was shocked and dismayed at their conduct, especially Radek's "betrayal," which was accompanied by unseemly recriminations directed toward him. Yet he recognized their plight and refrained from expressing in print the true extent of his feelings. Even Rakovsky, his oldest and closest political associate, showed signs of wavering, and by the end of the year the number of Trotskyists still in detention and apparently unrepentant had dwindled to a thousand or less.

Stalin had so far observed the letter, though hardly the spirit, of the Leninist tradition that the "sword of the revolution" might be turned against "class enemies" but never against fellow Bolsheviks. That precedent ended with the "Blumkin affair." Yakov Blumkin had achieved notoriety in 1918 when as a Left Socialist Revolutionary he participated in the assassination of the German ambassador in Moscow. Subsequently pardoned, he joined the Communist party and distinguished himself during the civil war, serving for a time on Trotsky's military staff. Later he became a senior official in the OGPU, and though his sentiments were openly Trotskyist he was allowed to continue work as a counter-intelligence specialist since he never became involved in the political activities of the opposition. He called on Trotsky during the summer of 1929 and offered to help arrange the smuggling of the *Bulletin* into the Soviet Union. Upon returning to Moscow he carried a rather innocuous set of written instructions from Trotsky, presumably designed to boost the morale of his adherents. Blumkin was promptly arrested, either because of his own frankness about his mission or because he was denounced by an informer. After a thorough interrogation he was secretly executed for treason. Stalin intended this brutal act as a stern lesson to others in the party who might emulate Blumkin. Paradoxically, those already beyond the pale—the declared Trotskyists in the jails and penal camps—continued to enjoy immunity from the death sentence.

By the early 1930's startling events in the Soviet Union and in the Western world brought an increasing sense of frustration to Trotsky, who had always conceived of himself as a man of action, however clumsy his performance in the arena of party politics. Stalin was pushing ahead on both the industrial and agrarian fronts with an awesome ferocity, while the Great Depression seemed to validate at last Marx's apocalyptic view of the fate of capitalism. And the incipient barbarism of Nazi Germany confronted Communists and "capitalists" alike with the frightening spectacle of a great nation run amuck. Trotsky's plaintive lament, "I am reduced to interpreting events and trying to foresee their future course,"[4] was written early in 1935, but it applies to most of his career in exile.

That Trotsky could no longer bask in History's limelight was psychologically debilitating. Yet he was not entirely dependent on "interpreting events," at least those of current interest. His *magnum opus*, a masterful three-volume *History of the Russian Revolution*, was written at his Prinkipo villa in less than three years. It would have been a lifetime achievement of rare distinction for a professional historian, but obviously he sought a mass audience not ordinarily available to scholars. Although the work was first serialized in the *Saturday Evening Post*, an impeccably "bourgeois" weekly (from which the author received the then princely sum of forty-five thousand dollars), its success with the critics far outstripped its popularity. The timing of the original publication (1932–33) was unfortunate because of the depressed economy, and the scope and seriousness of the work, despite its stylistic brilliance, did not commend itself to a large reading public.

Trotsky found in Max Eastman an exceptionally talented translator, and Eastman also became his unofficial literary agent from 1929 to 1933. With pardonable exuberance, he claimed too much for Trotsky's masterpiece: "This is the first time the scientific history of a great event has been written by a man who played a dominant part in it." It was indeed without precedent for a revolutionary of Trotsky's stature to write a classic account of events in which he had been intimately involved. And the research, if hardly definitive, was reasonably thorough and was conducted with a scrupulous regard for factual accuracy (he disdained reference notes and a bibliography). But no history—and certainly not Trotsky's—can be properly described as "scientific." The premises are obviously Marxist, and the bias is that of the victor judging the vanquished. There is, too, a pronounced tendency to project into the past the political struggles of the 1920's. Only Lenin and Trotsky emerge as revolutionary heroes. The other leading Bolsheviks, especially Stalin, Zinoviev, and Kamenev, are depicted as nonentities or worse. The enduring value of the *History* lies in the trenchant analysis, the dazzling insights, the ironic character sketches, and a narrative power of extraordinary vigor and pace. A magnificent panorama worthy of its subject, it has nevertheless been superseded as "scientific" history by various "bourgeois" specialists at work on particular aspects of 1917. One of the ironies of Trotsky's career is the estimable reputation that his *History* has enjoyed in the democratic West, while the author's homeland, sorely in need of a literary epic enshrining the party in its heroic year, continues to anathematize him as a turncoat and to proscribe his writings.[5]

A temporary respite in Trotsky's assiduous labors came in the fall of 1932 when the Danish government granted him a visa to accept an invitation to lecture in Copenhagen. Under an assumed identity and accompanied by his wife and three secretaries, he left Constantinople by steamship on November 14. His incognito was quickly penetrated, and it was under the glare of international publicity that he traveled via Athens and Naples to a landing near Marseilles, then by car and train across France to Dunkirk, and finally by ship to Denmark. He spoke in German before an audience of some two thousand in a Copenhagen stadium. The salient points of his topic, the Bolshevik Revolution, were drawn from his recently completed *History*. This lecture was to be his last public address of any consequence. He hoped that his Danish visa might be extended or that some other country—Sweden seemed a likely possibility—would prove hospitable. But his efforts were in vain, and he was obliged to leave on December 2. Returning through France and Italy, he and his party completed the last stage of their journey by sea.

A way out of the Turkish cul-de-sac appeared remote at the beginning of 1933. Yet Trotsky's persistence was finally to be rewarded later in the year. Meanwhile, he was beset by ill fortune, both personal and political. Of his two daughters by his first marriage, the younger had died of tuberculosis in Moscow during his banishment to Alma Ata. The older, Zinaida Volkhova, had been permitted to leave the Soviet Union after much delay and joined her father in Prinkipo. But her health was poor, and emotional problems threatened to overwhelm her. She was persuaded to go to Berlin for psychiatric treatment, but her condition grew worse and in January, 1933, she committed suicide. Her half-brother Lyova (Leon Sedov), who was acting as his father's political representative in Germany, telegraphed the tragic news to his parents. Trotsky was upset and abnormally depressed by her death, and he may have considered himself partly to blame. Never the epitome of tactfulness (except perhaps with strangers), he had been irritable with her at times, and his personality had inhibited the kind of emotional intimacy that his daughter sorely needed. Lyova, too, found it difficult to maintain a harmonious relationship with his father, and personal as well as political reasons may have dictated his move to Berlin. But his idealism, dedication, and hard work were never quite enough: Trotsky demanded perfection and more than once reprimanded him by letter for the slightest manifestation of carelessness or flagging energy.

Lyova left Germany for France after Adolf Hitler became Reich chancellor in January, 1933, and the *Bulletin of the Opposition*, which he had edited and published in Berlin, was reestablished in Paris. The Nazi triumph represented a staggering blow to international Communism, and within a few months the once powerful German Communist party had vanished with hardly a trace. The Comintern—that is to say, Stalin—contributed to the debacle with its "social fascist" line—a stubborn refusal to make a distinction between German Social Democracy and Hitler's National Socialism. Trotsky had repeatedly warned of the savage potential of the Nazi movement, and he predicted with unerring accuracy as early as 1931 that a fascist victory in Germany would lead to war against the Soviet Union. "Under the knout of the Stalinist clique," he lamented, "the terrorized and disoriented . . . German Communist Party . . . is delivering the working class up to Hitler and crucifixion."[6] His strictures on the idiocy of Comintern policy, indeed his incisive analysis of the Nazi phenomenon as a whole, constitute some of his finest political journalism. Yet it was all in vain. His alarms and admonitions went unheeded (and largely unnoticed) except for his loyal but minuscule following in the West, and his arguments were "rebutted" by means of a sneering cacophony in the international Communist press.

For all his prescience, Trotsky was caught by surprise when the German proletariat, with its proud tradition of trade union solidarity, collapsed without resistance. But he blamed its leaders, Social Democrats and Communists alike. One could expect cowardly behavior from the former: were they not petty bourgeois opportunists by any standard of revolutionary Marxism? The latter, on the other hand, were not constrained by faintheartedness or respect for parliamentary democracy. They had been corrupted by their Soviet masters, and Trotsky wondered rhetorically whether the blind folly of the Stalin dictatorship, "marching toward its own destruction with seven-league boots," would "drag the Soviet regime into the abyss along with it."[7]

The German disaster prompted Trotsky to sever his remaining ideological ties with the Comintern and to consider the founding of a new International. Having ventured thus far, the next logical step was a reevaluation of his attitude to the Soviet party and state. But he backed off from a fundamental revision, maintaining, as he did until his death, that the Soviet regime, having nationalized the means of production, was a "workers' state" which Marxists of whatever persuasion should be prepared to defend. Presumably the "ruling clique" should be overthrown, yet he was equivocal about its necessity and argued at one point that the slogan "Down with Stalin" was a mistake and that to cast out the bureaucracy "would surely serve counter-revolutionary forces."[8] He made a subtle but rather artificial distinction between a basically healthy "workers' state" and a corrupt bureaucracy that was said to be running it. His anti-Stalinist credo was a political tightrope act that attracted a few radical intellectuals to the ranks of Trotskyism; and it was to be a source of future quarrels and schisms. The working class constituency that he sought never materialized.

Stalin was not seriously weakened by his blunder in Germany, just as he had survived the China episode with only minimal damage to his prestige. His position had been shaken far more by domestic events, notably the severe trauma of forced collectivization and the subsequent famine. But he had recovered with a partial retreat: concessions to the peasantry, including a temporary turn to voluntary methods. And the breakneck tempo of the first Five Year Plan—"the mad gallop of industrialization," in Trotsky's words— had been slowed to accommodate more practical goals as the second began in 1933. Many ex-Trotskyists, such prominent figures as Preobrazhensky and Ivan Smirnov, were again imprisoned or deported, while Zinoviev and Kamenev were expelled from the party a second time and banished to the Urals. The last of the Trotsky stalwarts, Rakovsky, made his peace with Stalin in February, 1934, seemingly convinced that the Nazi threat to the Soviet Union justified his about-face. One may fully sympathize with the plight of the opposition. Certainly Trotsky's indignant protests at their treatment were wholly justified. Yet it is evident that his humanitarian sentiments were subordinate to his political stance. Other victims of Stalinist persecution, notably the millions of peasants who perished as a result of collectivization and famine, did not arouse his concern. Nor did he exhibit any compassion for the defendants who were accused of sabotage and conspiracy in the "Menshevik Trial" held in 1931, a foretaste of the notorious Moscow trials that occurred later in the decade. Indeed, he accepted the government's case, which was based chiefly on prearranged confessions, though he did have the grace to rectify his error some five years later.

In July, 1933, after weeks of anxious negotiation initiated by his French translator, Maurice Parijanine, Trotsky was permitted to emigrate to France. He was restricted to the provinces and obliged to live under an assumed identity, but he was delighted to find a haven in western Europe, whatever the conditions. The first months of his residence were spent at a rented villa near Royan on the Atlantic coast. He was bedridden much of the time, wracked by fever and suffering from headaches and insomnia. The adjustment to his new environment was psychologically difficult, and he recalled his youth in Paris with nostalgia and self-conscious awareness of his advancing years and recurrent ill health. A group of his supporters, chiefly French, gathered in Paris late in August to press forward with the idea of a Fourth International. No formal action was taken, but if the circumstances were inauspicious and the beginnings humble, the nucleus of an international Trotskyist organization had at least reached the planning stage. Although Trotsky professed optimism and his rhetoric became almost fatuous ("Tens of thousands,

hundreds of thousands of revolutionary workers will breathe with
relief upon learning that there is a way out from the revolutionary
impasse"),[9] his continued illness signified a spiritual malaise which
the Paris meeting—and his political prospects in general—failed to
alleviate.

In November, with the government's permission, Trotsky moved
to Barbizon near Paris. His health had improved, and he spent
much of his time preparing a biography of Lenin. The chance arrest
of one of his secretaries in April, 1934, disclosed his identity to the
local police, and the authorities, prodded into action by the sensational nature of the publicity that ensued, ordered him to move. He
would have been deported, but no country was willing to receive
him. Leaving his wife Natalia in Paris for the time being, he set out
with two companions by automobile to seek a new hideaway. But a
series of temporary accommodations, mostly in villages close to the
Swiss frontier, proved unsatisfactory. Finally, in July, a school
teacher of Trotskyist persuasion offered hospitality at his home in
Domesne near Grenoble. There, more isolated than he had been at
Prinkipo, Trotsky remained for approximately eleven months. "Our
life here differs very little from imprisonment," he wrote. "We are
shut up in our house and yard and meet people no more often than
we would at visiting hours at a prison."[10]

Trotsky wrote and published anonymously two pamphlets on
French politics during the Domesne period.[11] Still haunted by the
German tragedy, he applied its lessons too literally to the situation
in France and anticipated the rise of a powerful fascist movement.
To combat the danger he urged the formation of a workers' militia
and proposed the slogan, "Arm the proletariat and the revolutionary
peasants." The united front between French Communists and
Socialists, later expanded into a Popular Front against fascism, he
censured as a "program of passivity," not the "program of revolution" that he sought as the ultimate answer to the crisis of
capitalism. His prose, appropriately laced with pungent phrases,
did not conceal a shrill note of alarm and a tone of revolutionary
militance that was largely irrelevant to French politics in the mid-
thirties.

Trotsky sustained his anti-Stalinist literary barrage with regular
contributions to the *Bulletin* and other Trotskyist publications, often
unsigned or with the use of a pen name. But his firsthand knowledge
of Soviet affairs acquired through direct contacts had been cut off

well before his emigration from Turkey. Although Stalin's regime appeared to mellow somewhat in 1934, the assassination of Sergei Kirov, Zinoviev's successor in Leningrad, on December 1 of that year precipitated a mass purge of such savage ferocity that the persecution of the opposition seemed in comparison almost benign. Trotsky sought to unravel the mysterious affair with his accustomed skill and aplomb. Yet even he, second to none in his conviction of Stalin's ultimate depravity, never suspected that the threads of the assassination plot, insofar as they can be traced, led to the dictator himself. The official verdict, after the original version was disregarded, blamed Zinoviev and Kamenev, among others, and implicated Trotsky in a surprisingly perfunctory manner. The actual murderer, a disgruntled party member named Leonid Nikolayev, was executed along with supposed accomplices, and thousands of "conspirators," especially from the Leningrad party organization, were deported to concentration camps. Zinoviev and Kamenev were sentenced to long prison terms. Another interlude of political relaxation followed, a false spring that presaged new and more sinister developments in the scenario that Stalin was preparing.

Trotsky's younger son Sergei, who had scrupulously avoided politics and thus, he hoped, any imputation of Trotskyism, was arrested in the aftermath of the Kirov affair. Trotsky's first wife, Sokolovskaya, was deported, and his two sons-in-law were subjected to further persecution. These personal blows enervated him, and Trotsky complained in his diary in May, 1935, that his "attacks of illness" were more frequent, the symptoms more acute, and his resistance growing weaker: "I have a feeling that liquidation is approaching." Several weeks later—and for the only time in his career—he admitted that his numerous afflictions ("weakness, temperature, perspiration, inner physical emptiness") might be of emotional origin: "It is possible that it is my 'nerves' that give such a wide range to the external manifestations of the illness."[12]

Because of the French rapprochement with the Soviet Union in order to forestall the German danger, Trotsky recognized that his refuge in France was more insecure than ever. Deportation to colonial Africa loomed as a distinct possibility. Through contacts with the Norwegian Labor party, which took office in the spring of 1935, he finally secured a visa good for six months' residence in Norway. With Natalia and two secretaries he sailed from Antwerp in mid-June. He discovered that the restrictions on his personal freedom were scarcely more lenient than those he had encountered in France. The government insisted that he reside in the country away from Oslo, and he accepted the offer of Konrad Knudsen, a socialist editor, to live in his home, some thirty miles from the capital.

When his health permitted—it remained poor for some months after his arrival—Trotsky returned to his polemical journalism and to his one major work on Stalinist Russia, later published under the title *The Revolution Betrayed*. Temporarily abandoning his life of Lenin for lack of time, he never had the opportunity to complete it. A large fragment was published in France, but an English edition was delayed for thirty-six years.[13] Eastman had translated the first twelve chapters when the text unaccountably disappeared, "stolen and destroyed," Eastman concluded "by Trotsky's ingenious and implacable enemies." The manuscript mysteriously "surfaced" in the Houghton Library of Harvard University many years later. *The Young Lenin* is a reverent tribute to the Bolshevik chieftain, at times dogmatic in the worst tradition of Marxist scholasticism, and yet a charming and unpretentious chronicle that adds distinction to Trotsky's literary production.

The Revolution Betrayed is a much different kind of work—an elaborate anti-Stalinist manifesto combined, somewhat awkwardly, with a searching and often surprisingly objective critique of Soviet society and its institutions. The tone, while often scathing, is less embittered than the title implies. The major theme is familiar: the bureaucratic degeneration of the party—or more accurately, its ruling elite—and the betrayal of revolutionary Marxism. "The poverty and cultural backwardness of the masses has again become incarnate in the malignant figure of the ruler with a great club in his hand," he wrote. "The deposed and abused bureaucracy, from being a servant of society, has again become its lord." Despite his great concern about the corrosive impact of Stalinism on Russian society, Trotsky is curiously reticent about the totalitarian features of the Soviet regime. He is more troubled, for example, by the trend toward social inequality and the retreat from Marxist ideas on the family than he is by the ominous power of the secret police. Trotsky was admittedly writing before the Moscow trials and lacked the knowledge as well as the perspective that was later to focus on the political repressions of the Stalin era. Although concerned about both the lack of intellectual freedom ("The crude and ignorant command of science, literature and art") and the traditional "bourgeois" freedoms, he complains that the new "Stalin" constitution of 1936 is "juridically liquidating the dictatorship of the proletariat." Furthermore, instead of adhering to the Marxist task of fighting organized religion, the Stalinists are "gradually [establishing] a regime of ironical neutrality." Inevitably dated by the standards of later scholarship, *The Revolution Betrayed* is nevertheless an original and often penetrating analysis—it is *the* Trotskyist classic on Stalinist Russia.

Circumspect in avoiding the charge that he was interfering in Norwegian affairs, Trotsky nonetheless continued his political commentary on larger issues. The authorities gave their tacit consent even though a strict interpretation of the terms under which he was admitted forbade *any* political activity. Norway sought good relations with the Soviet Union, and Trotsky's unrelenting anti-Stalinist campaign was bound to create difficulties. The turning point came with the first of the notorious "show trials" in Moscow in August, 1936, when Zinoviev, Kamenev, and fourteen other Old Bolsheviks were charged with an assortment of treasonable acts. Trotsky himself was accused of being the chief plotter, aided by his son Leon Sedov, and four Trotskyists (Ivan Smirnov was the best known) were among the defendants. He promptly issued a ringing denial and called upon the Norwegian government to investigate his conduct, offering his full cooperation. "He was like a man in a delirium during those days," his wife wrote, "as if plunged into an insane nightmare."[14]

Soviet pressure on Norway to expel Trotsky became overpowering, and at a special cabinet meeting a majority voted to intern him, for no other country had offered him asylum. Ashamed to admit that they had yielded to the Soviet demand, the ministers took the official position that he had refused to abide by the terms of his residence permit. In September he and Natalia were moved to another location and placed under strict house arrest. He was denied visitors except for a lawyer, and his literary work as well as his personal correspondence were censored. Forbidden, in effect, from publicly refuting the elaborate testimony that portrayed him as the mastermind of an anti-Soviet "terrorist center," he was gratified that his son undertook that assignment for him by publishing in Paris a "red book" on the trial. The essence of the work was reported in the press, but its circulation was limited, even in France, and its impact on the general public was slight compared to the enormous publicity generated by the original charges. To those sympathetic to the Soviet Union on ideological grounds or because of its anti-fascist foreign policy, the official verdict seemed plausible if not wholly convincing.

Thoroughly disenchanted with the Norwegian government—the feeling was no doubt mutual—Trotsky again turned to his foreign supporters for a way out of his predicament. The noted Mexican painter Diego Rivera, among others, interceded with Lazaro Cardenas, the president of Mexico, and in December Trotsky was granted asylum. The Norwegian authorities, acting with almost indecent haste, placed their unwelcome guest and his wife, together with a police escort, aboard an oil tanker which set out for Mexico on the nineteenth. The voyage took about three weeks, and Trotsky used his enforced leisure to read books on Mexico and to write a journal, including his comments on the Zinoviev-Kamenev trial. His analysis became part of his book, *Stalin's Crimes*, published the next year in Paris and Zurich.

The tanker entered the harbor at Tampico on January 9, 1937. Made wary by his experience in France and in Norway, Trotsky was surprised by the cordial reception he received from Mexican officials, including a message of welcome from President Cardenas. The next day a special train took him inland "through sun-baked country, scattered with palm trees and cacti." At Coyoacan, a suburb of Mexico City, Rivera and his wife Frida Kahlo, an artist in her own right, provided spacious quarters for the Trotskys in their own lavishly furnished home. Rivera, whose politics were unpredictable, had once been a member of the Mexican Communist party. He now became Trotsky's friend, patron, and disciple, though it was the fame and revolutionary mystique of his guest that attracted him rather than doctrinal affinity.

Trotsky had scarcely acclimated himself to the Mexican scene when the second Moscow trial, another installment in Stalin's assault on the party's old guard, captured headlines in the world press. Of the seventeen defendants, three of the most prominent—Radek, Pyatakov, and Muralov—had been former Trotskyists. Again the testimony depicted Trotsky as a villainous traitor, this time working with Germany and Japan to bring about the defeat and dismemberment of the Soviet Union. "We felt," wrote Natalia, "that insanity, absurdity, outrage, fraud and blood were flooding us from all sides . . . . Leon Davidovich, over-tense, overworked, often feverish, yet tireless, made a note of all the forgeries and lies, much too numerous now to be refuted one by one. The vast Stalinist crime-manufacturing machine was working at full steam, and seemed to have grown completely indifferent to the credibility of its products."[15] As in the first trial, all the defendants made abject confessions and were pronounced guilty, but the precedent set previously—all sixteen "conspirators" had been shot—was slightly altered when Radek and Gregory Sokolnikov were spared and given ten-year prison sentences.

Evidence of treasonable conduct, other than the self-incrimination of the victims, was notably absent. In those few instances where Trotsky's activities abroad could be checked independently, it was demonstrated that the testimony against him was false. But there was no way of exonerating himself, for proving one's innocence when unfairly accused is a virtual impossibility. Nevertheless, his pride outraged and his reputation traduced, Trotsky strove to do just that. His adherents organized committees of defense, hoping to receive the moral support of the liberal and radical intelligentsia in the West. The response was not encouraging, but in March a Joint Commission of Inquiry of eleven members was established which proceeded to organize a "counter-trial." With the exception of Alfred Rosmer, none of the members were friends or supporters of Trotsky, although their political views, while varied, were overwhelmingly anti-Stalinist. The commission's reputation for integrity rested largely on the shoulders of its chairman, John Dewey, the distinguished American philosopher and educational theorist. He accepted the charge at considerable personal sacrifice, for it postponed his own work and subjected him to abuse and attempts at intimidation.[16] In preparing himself for the inquiry, Trotsky labored many weeks like a man possessed to assemble the necessary documents for his defense, and he expected the same energy and commitment from his immediate entourage and from his supporters abroad. The devoted Sedov, overworked and fatigued, did his best to carry out his assignments but was stung repeatedly by his father's angry rebukes and reproaches.

A five-member preliminary commission, headed by Dewey, held hearings on April 10–17, 1937, at Rivera's house in Coyoacan. Journalists and selected visitors—about fifty in all—were admitted after being searched for weapons, and a police guard stood watch outside.

Trotsky was questioned in detail, chiefly by his own counsel, Albert Goldman, a labor attorney from Chicago, and spoke in halting and sometimes ungrammatical English. The commissioners were courteous, even respectful, in their interrogation, and this seemingly deferential treatment irritated one of their number, Carleton Beals, a lecturer and writer on Latin American affairs. At the eleventh session he posed some embarrassing questions, one of which concerned Mikhail Borodin, who as Trotsky's supposed "emissary" was stated to have founded the Mexican Communist party in 1919–20. Trotsky suspected that the question was deliberately provocative, and in a statement to the commission he declared that Beals's information was false and had been used "to compromise my situation in Mexico." Beals resigned on the seventeenth, complaining in a letter to Dewey that he did not consider the proceedings "a truly serious investigation of the charges." Later he claimed that the "whole atmosphere of the trial had become that of a chummy clubroom, a pink-tea party with everyone uttering sweet platitudes." His criticism was to some extent justified—the interrogation could have been more rigorous—but the question was irrelevant to the purpose of the hearings, and the other commissioners agreed as to its "complete impropriety."[17]

Given the tenor of the deliberations, quite aside from the evidence presented, a guilty verdict was inconceivable. But the full commission had to be consulted and a formal report prepared. Its findings, released in September and published in book format a few months later, were therefore somewhat anticlimactic: that the Moscow trials were "frame-ups" and that Trotsky and Sedov were innocent.[18] Unfortunately for Trotsky, considering the enormity of his effort, his vindication made little impact upon public opinion, though the verdict was duly noted in the press.

In the Soviet Union, meanwhile, Stalin's great purge was proceeding with vindictive fury but without the fanfare of "show" trials. Even as knowledgeable an observer as Trotsky could not grasp the dimensions of the holocaust that the tyrant had unleashed. Indeed, beyond the Kremlin's inner circle no one could, and the grim and uncertain business of calculating the number of victims (to mention only the obvious legacy of the purge) goes on to our own time. The commonly accepted estimate of eight million arrests does not seem excessive. Lost in the avalanche of prisoners, the tiny remnant of Trotskyists—now perhaps no more than a few hundred—who had suffered long years of hardship and privation were shot in small groups during the spring of 1938 at the huge forced labor complex at Vorkuta in the Arctic region of Siberia. Presumably Trotsky's son Sergei was among them—he had been sent to Vorkuta—but no reliable information ever reached his parents as to his ultimate fate.

The NKVD (the OGPU had been administratively reorganized in 1934) did not limit its activities to the Soviet Union. Its agents were particularly active in Spain during the civil war, and the extirpation of Spanish "Trotskyists" proceeded with few legal restraints. Leon Sedov was naturally a high priority target for the Soviet intelligence network abroad, and he was kept under close surveillance. The task was particularly easy in Sedov's case because his closest friend and political associate was a talented Soviet agent, Mark Zborowski, who used the name Etienne in France. He collaborated in publishing the *Bulletin* and made himself indispensable to the French Trotskyist movement. Neither Sedov nor Trotsky ever suspected him, though both were alert in a general sense to the machinations of Stalinist agents. In February, 1938, Sedov, whose spirit was sorely troubled by personal problems, the frustrations of his political work, and the Moscow trials, suffered an attack of acute appendicitis which necessitated an immediate operation. He entered a small private hospital directed by a Russian émigré physician. The operation was successful, and he seemed to be recovering normally when he was suddenly stricken and died several days later. An inquest disclosed nothing sinister, but his widow suspected poison since Zborowski had made the hospital arrangements. Although there were a number of other circumstances that could be interpreted as peculiar, there is no direct evidence that Sedov's death was due to other than natural causes.

Upon hearing the news, Trotsky sank into a state of numb despair and remained secluded for over a week. His anguish was the more intense because of the harsh and unfair criticism that he had heaped on his son. He tried to make amends with a moving tribute published in the *Bulletin* and as a separate pamphlet.[19] Ironically, Zborowski took over the editorship of the *Bulletin* until its transfer to New York in 1939 and became Trotsky's most important political . confidant in Europe despite warnings from several sources that he was an *agent provocateur*.

In March, 1938, a little over two weeks after Sedov's death, Bukharin, Rakovsky, and others—twenty-one in all and officially known as the Anti-Soviet "Bloc of Rights and Trotskyites"—were arraigned in the last and most spectacular of the Moscow trials. Again, through confessions delivered on cue, the accused branded Trotsky as the evil genius who ordered them to commit an amazing variety of criminal acts. Rakovsky, his political associate since 1903, testified abjectly, for example, that beginning in 1924 he had been "a traitor to the Soviet Socialist fatherland" and that both he and Trotsky had worked for the British intelligence service. By daily statements to the press Trotsky attempted to expose the errors, fabrications, and distortions of the "buffoonish trial," one of the "last convulsions in the political crisis of the U.S.S.R." He predicted that the Soviet workers would remove Stalin and his "gangster collaborators from under the debris of the totalitarian abomination and make them give account for the crimes committed by them at a real court."[20] Stalin was to be condemned and Trotsky vindicated, not in a court of law but in the court of public opinion. Yet the verdict was a generation in the making, and in the interim the official version was given more credence than Trotsky could bring himself to admit (he insisted that "No one anywhere any more believes the accusers").

During the spring and summer of 1938 Trotsky kept at his political journalism and wrote a draft program and other material for the "founding" congress of the Fourth International held near Paris on September 3, 1938. His dream of an organization that would one day rival the Comintern never faltered, but the clandestine meeting of a small number of Trotskyist delegates (apparently twenty-two with voting rights) at the home of Alfred Rosmer did little to inspire confidence in its future. The single session was chaired by Max Shachtman, a leader of the Socialist Workers party in the United States, and the ubiquitous Zborowski represented the hypothetical "Russian section." The new International, formally established by a vote of nineteen to three, was in reality an exercise in political symbolism and a moral protest against Stalinism. Trotsky, in an inspirational message to a New York rally of his supporters, contrived to invest his artificial creation with a global mission: "During the next ten years the program of the Fourth International will become the guide of millions and these revolutionary millions will know how to storm earth and heaven."[21] A keen analyst of current events, he was, like ordinary mortals, not always gifted as a political prophet.

Not long after the Fourth International had been launched, the friendship between Trotsky and Rivera began to deteriorate. Temperamental differences and Rivera's "ideological crisis" (he had "abandoned Marxism for some eclectic hodgepodge," Trotsky strongly implied) were intertwined. Rivera supported a Right-wing general in the election campaign against President Cardenas, and in January, 1939, he resigned from the Mexican section of the Fourth International. Trotsky, while impressed with his host's "imagination" and "powerful creative spirit," considered him a political innocent and accused him of poisoning their relationship with "unprincipled intrigues and . . . behind-the-scenes insinuations, which are completely unfounded." No longer on speaking terms—he communicated with Rivera through intermediaries—he declared in mid-February that it was "morally and politically impossible . . . to accept the hospitality of a person who conducts himself not as a friend but as a venomous adversary."[22]

Trotsky's determination to make other living arrangements was frustrated by the difficulty of finding a suitable residence that also afforded proper security. Finally, early in May, he and Natalia moved to an old but comfortable house in an isolated section of Coyoacan. The property, initially rented and later purchased, included spacious grounds with a garden and handsome trees. A wall was constructed, and a solid iron gate barred the entrance to intruders. A number of disciples, chiefly young Americans, served as guards and performed secretarial and other chores as needed. Mexican police were also on continuous duty outside the gate.

Rivera's beneficence had provided a moderately affluent life style for over two years. Now it became necessary for Trotsky to augment his earnings at a time when the novelty of an article from his pen had worn off and when his publishers, who had been reasonably free with advances in the past, were disinclined to be generous without an actual manuscript in hand. Friends loaned him money for household expenses, and he set to work on the uncongenial task of writing a life of Stalin, for which he had signed a contract in 1938. He would have preferred to finish his Lenin biography, and the long intellectual partnership of Marx and Engels continued to fascinate him as a literary project. But the public taste—or so his publishers interpreted it—demanded topicality, and he needed the royalties that a salable book would bring.

Shut away in his study most of the time, Trotsky nevertheless departed from his monastic habits when the spirit moved him. He and Natalia took occasional motoring trips with a bodyguard. He fished in the gulf at Veracruz, and he savored the panoramic mountain scenery. Sometimes he would climb a rocky slope to collect a choice specimen of cactus for his garden. He also acquired rabbits and chickens, conscientiously caring for them himself. He saw a few old friends, but most of his visitors were sympathizers—or simply the curious—from the United States. Although his willingness to meet strangers was potentially dangerous, he sought the varied intellectual contact they provided.

In his analysis of current affairs, Trotsky took for granted the outbreak of another world war. His frame of reference was the first one—it could hardly be otherwise—and he accepted uncritically the Marxist premise about the nature of modern war: that it derived from the rival imperial interests of the great capitalist powers ("for the redivision of the world and colonial enslavement"). The war, he predicted, would lead to a proletarian revolution in the West, just as that of 1914 had led to the revolution in Russia. Yet the analogy was entirely too simplistic, and he implicitly acknowledged the limitations of his own faith by suggesting that History's inscrutable path might lie elsewhere, an indulgence that he had never before permitted himself in print: "If the world proletariat should actually prove incapable of fulfilling the mission placed upon it . . . nothing else would remain except . . . to recognize that the socialist program, based on the internal contradictions of capitalist society, ended as a Utopia."[23] Had he accepted the full implications of this statement, which he intended only as a hypothesis, he would have been repudiating his life's work. Obviously he had no such intention and went on to reaffirm the correctness of his views and to apply them specifically to the Soviet Union.

Under frequent criticism from some of his followers because of his refusal to amend his description of Stalin's Russia as a "workers' state" (albeit a "degenerated" one), Trotsky was placed in similar difficulties when he called for the "defense of the USSR" against its enemies. To be sure, his "defensive" slogan was unique—"For Socialism! For the World Revolution! Against Stalin!"—but the Nazi-Soviet Pact of August, 1939, the Soviet occupation of eastern

Poland in September, and the Winter War with Finland that followed aroused even greater unrest. The American Trotskyists, negligible in numbers and in political influence—the Socialist Workers
party had fewer than a thousand "hard core" members—were at
least a functioning sect, and its leadership of James P. Cannon, Max
Shachtman, and James Burnham was reasonably distinguished. The
party headed toward a schism in the early months of 1940, and
Trotsky, though he deplored the growing cleavage, helped to bring
it about. He supported Cannon because of his orthodoxy and abused
Shachtman and Burnham as "bankrupt" purveyors of "ideological
charlatanism," among other choice examples of his polemical art.
The Cannonites controlled a majority at a party convention in April,
where, ironically, the "Russian question" was not even debated.
However, the minority was "suspended," which was tantamount to
expulsion. The split, with echoes that reverberated in Trotskyist
circles outside the United States, doomed whatever slight chance
the Fourth International had of attracting a significant following.
The affair was inconsequential except to Marxist sectarians, but it
illustrated once more Trotsky's incompetence as a politician.

The last year or so of Trotsky's life was marred by interludes of
depression and hypochondria, not that these were new afflictions.
But he was haunted by the fate of his Soviet adherents (Natalia
wrote of his "inconsolable anguish") and discouraged by the impotence of the Fourth International. In March, 1940, he complained of
"high and rising blood pressure" and speculated that he would
probably die of a brain hemorrhage. That his death would come by
unnatural means—that is, by murder—he could not guess, but Stalin was determined to rid himself of his annoying if politically harmless enemy.

The NKVD assignment to liquidate Trotsky apparently came in
the wake of the Moscow trials. Since his dossier is said to have
occupied three floors of a Moscow office building, elaborate files
must have been accumulating from the time of his deportation to
Alma Ata or earlier. An experienced NKVD officer, Leonid Eitingon, was placed in charge of the operation, and he traveled to
Mexico in 1939 accompanied by two aides who had served as
Stalinist "hatchet men" in Spain. The Mexican Communist party
also became involved in the conspiracy. Its leaders had been vociferous in denouncing Trotsky but "soft" on the idea of political

assassination. They were therefore ousted in March, 1940, in a coup initiated by Soviet agents, supposedly representing the Comintern, and replaced by a more resolute clique, including the well-known painter David Alfaro Siqueiros.

Eitingon planned an armed assault on Trotsky's home and placed Siqueiros in charge of the raiding party. The preparations were elaborate. Some twenty men, Mexicans and Spanish refugees dressed in police or army uniforms, took part. Their arsenal included several submachine guns, an unknown number of smaller weapons, at least two dynamite bombs, and several incendiary bombs. About 4 A.M. on May 24 they approached Trotsky's residence on foot and surprised the police guard. A young New Yorker, Robert Sheldon Harte, was on duty at the gate and admitted the intruders with no evident resistance. Trotsky, who had worked late and taken a sleeping pill for his insomnia, was suddenly awakened by intense gunfire at close range. He and Natalia crouched on the floor under the bed as a hail of bullets swept over them for several minutes ("hundreds" of spent cartridge cases were found later). Two incendiary bombs were ignited but did little damage, and a dynamite bomb capable of leveling the whole structure proved defective. Assuming that they had accomplished their purpose, the raiders left and took Sheldon Harte with them. A month later his partly decomposed body was found in a shallow grave. Whether he was a martyr to the Trotskyist cause or had simply betrayed his trust, perhaps by direct collusion with the Stalinist enemy, could not be determined. Trotsky himself subscribed to the former view.

That Trotsky and his household could have survived the murderous attack without serious injury seemed incredible to the investigating officer, Colonel Sanchez Salazar. And Trotsky's extraordinary composure after his narrow escape also struck the colonel as suspicious. Convinced of a "put-up job," that the whole affair had been staged to gain sympathetic publicity and to discredit Stalinism, he arrested three members of the household staff and two secretaries for questioning. The pro-Communist press seconded this hypothesis with enthusiasm, and one daily called for Trotsky's expulsion from Mexico for his "provocation." Salazar soon abandoned the false scent, though his suspicion that the would-be assassins had access to inside information was well taken. Too many people had been involved in the attack for a curtain of silence to descend permanently, and on June 17 twenty-seven suspects were arrested, most of them Communists or sympathizers. The minor accomplices were released in return for information and nine others imprisoned. Siqueiros, who had been implicated, went into hiding, but Salazar tracked him down in a provincial village several months later. He denied that he and his men had tried to kill Trotsky—the shooting had been for "psychological effect." Released on bail in the spring of 1941, he managed to find a haven in Chile and then returned to Mexico three years later without further prosecution.

The controversy surrounding the bungled attempt on his life interrupted Trotsky's normal routine, including his biography of Stalin. Recognizing that he had received only a "reprieve" and that the NKVD would try again, he authorized further measures of "fortification"—higher walls, watch towers, and steel window shutters. But the next attempt was not to be a mass assault. Eitingon had left for New York after the Siqueiros fiasco to consult with his superior, Gaik Ovakimian, who now took charge of the Trotsky operation. Their conversation most certainly included the activities of an agent, Ramon Mercador, who had already made some progress toward ingratiating himself with Trotsky's entourage. A Spaniard who had fought on the Republican side during the civil war, Mercador became a protégé of Eitingon and allegedly received special training in Moscow in intelligence work and studied the voluminous Trotsky dossier. Handsome and sophisticated, he was assigned the task of seducing an American Trotskyist, Sylvia Ageloff, who was visiting in Paris in the summer of 1938. An introduction was arranged—Mercador used the name Jacques Mornard—and Ageloff, rather a plain girl, was flattered by the attention of the debonair and seemingly wealthy young man. The two became lovers, and their relationship continued until February, 1939, when she returned to the United States, with "Mornard" to follow later. He finally did so in September, traveling with a forged Canadian passport under the name Frank Jacson. Claiming to represent a Belgian firm, he went on to Mexico City for supposed business reasons.

Ageloff left her job in New York and joined her lover in Mexico in January, 1940. Her sister Ruth had worked briefly as a typist for Trotsky, and Sylvia visited the Trotsky household on more than one occasion. Her "husband" chauffeured her and became a familiar figure to the guards, but he never sought to venture beyond the gate. A few months later he was able to perform a number of services for Alfred and Marguerite Rosmer, who were guests of the Trotskys, and was invited into the house. He took special notice of the security arrangements, and it was this information (possibly supplemented by Sheldon Harte) that apparently enabled the Siqueiros party to penetrate the well-guarded compound with such surprising ease.

Not until May 28 did "Jacson" meet his future victim. It was a chance encounter as Trotsky was feeding his rabbits, and the visitor was invited to the breakfast table. Once the initial contact had been made, "Jacson" was discreet and did not presume upon their brief acquaintance. But he continued to make himself useful to members of the household, and at least once, possibly twice, he and his "wife" had tea with the Trotskys. He achieved the proper blend of deference and affability, posing as a sympathizer, though in the past he had maintained an attitude of political indifference. In June he went to New York for "business" reasons, but there seems little doubt that he reported to Ovakimian and Eitingon and received advice and instructions about the planned assassination. He returned to Mexico City late in July. Fully aware that his gruesome assignment was now irrevocable, he became nervous, irritable, and depressed, and one of Trotsky's aides later recalled that he had "prematurely aged, darkened as if some poison were working its way through his skin."[24]

On August 17 "Jacson" brought the draft of an article that Trotsky had promised to read and criticize. The visitor stayed only ten minutes, but his discourteous behavior—he sat on the edge of the writing table wearing a hat and carrying a raincoat—aroused Trotsky's apprehension. The interview had been a trial run, yet no one in the well-guarded compound, including the "Old Man" himself, considered "Jacson" anything more than eccentric.

On August 20 Trotsky consented to review the completed article despite his misgivings about the earlier version ("confused and full of banal phrases"). He went into his study with the intended murderer. Only a few minutes had elapsed when a prolonged and agonized cry, "half scream, half sob," alarmed the household. Natalia, who was in the adjoining room, rushed in and saw Trotsky in the doorway, his face covered with blood, his arms hanging limply. The assassin, using a short handled ice-ax concealed in his raincoat, had hit his victim a powerful blow in the expectation that death would be silent and instantaneous and that he could make his escape. But Trotsky had fought back, and "Jacson" had been unable to strike again before the guards seized him, beating him with their guns and fists.

Barely conscious and partially paralyzed, Trotsky was taken to a hospital by ambulance. An operation that evening disclosed a wound in his skull nearly three inches deep. with irreparable damage to the brain tissue. He never regained consciousness but struggled against death for another twenty-two hours. The end came peacefully at 7:25 P.M. on August 21, 1940, with Natalia at his bedside.

CHAPTER 10

Trotskyism and the Trotsky Legacy

THE Mexican government took charge of the funeral arrangements. Trotsky's body lay in state for five days, and one hundred thousand people were said to have filed past in silent homage. His body was cremated on August 27 and the ashes buried in the patio of the Trotsky residence in Coyoacan. A stone marker bearing the Communist insignia of the hammer and sickle marks his grave.

The bruised and bleeding assassin had been treated for his injuries and imprisoned. A letter written in French and found on his person stated that he was a disillusioned Trotskyist, but internal evidence indicated that the document was of NKVD origin. Under police questioning Mercador (his true identity did not become known for another decade) embellished his "confession" with a largely fictitious autobiography. Two court-appointed specialists, a psychologist and a criminologist, conducted elaborate tests and interviewed the defendant at great length. Mercador stuck to his original story despite numerous slips and contradictions. But at his trial, to avoid the harsh sentence that premeditated murder would likely bring, he claimed self-defense: he and Trotsky had quarreled violently, and he had struck the fatal blow before Trotsky could draw his revolver. It was a preposterous version, for it could not be reconciled with his previous statements, and the three judges who presided at the trial agreed. A sentence of twenty years was finally imposed in April, 1943 (Mexico had no death penalty for ordinary homicide).

Mercador refused all formal interviews, preserving an attitude of inscrutability throughout his prison term. Through his lawyer he was evidently provided with ample funds, presumably from Communist sources, which enabled him to maintain a privileged life style, including a mistress, unavailable to less affluent prisoners. His

184

conduct was exemplary, and he took an active interest in teaching fellow inmates how to read and write. He studied electrical engineering and was eventually placed in charge of the prison's electrical system. A petition for parole was denied in 1956 on the grounds that he had not expressed regret for his crime. On May 6, 1960, some three months before the expiration of his sentence, he was released from custody and taken to the airport. Two officials of the Czechoslovak embassy in Mexico City joined him there, and the three flew to Havana on a Cuban plane. He later traveled to Prague and then vanished from public notice, possibly in the Soviet Union. As Natalia Trotsky put it, "Mornard now goes to his reward—or elimination."

Natalia continued to live in the Coyoacan residence with Trotsky's grandson, the child of Zinaida Volkhova, who had committed suicide in Berlin. She sought to perpetuate her husband's memory by demonstrating an unswerving allegiance to his ideology (though she remained politically aloof after her resignation from the Fourth International in 1951), by writing memoirs which Victor Serge put into literary form, and by preserving Trotsky's study as it had been in his lifetime. She led a lonely and secluded life but resided in Paris for over a year in 1955–56. A trip to New York was aborted in 1957 when her visa was withdrawn because of her refusal to cooperate with the Committee on Un-American Activities of the House of Representatives. During the anti-Stalin campaigns led by Nikita Khrushchev in 1956 and 1961 she appealed to the Soviet authorities to vindicate her husband and son but received no reply. "De-Stalinization" in the Soviet Union did not include the rehabilitation of Trotsky. He remains, if not quite the traitor and archfiend of Stalinist legend, a heretic against whose false doctrines the party must be ever vigilant. Natalia returned to France in 1960 and died in a Paris suburb at the age of 79 in January, 1962. Her body was cremated and the ashes buried alongside her husband's.

Trotsky's archives had been sold to Harvard University for fifteen thousand dollars, and on the day of his death he received word that they had safely arrived. Among his other literary remains, the biography of Stalin was by far the most important. Several pages of the manuscript were spattered with his blood; others were destroyed in the struggle with the assassin. Seven chapters had been completed, and his translator and editor, Charles Malamuth, managed to piece together another five chapters (and supplementary material) from

Trotsky's notes and other fragmentary information. The book was
printed and advance copies had been sent to reviewers when Japan
attacked the United States. Since the Soviet Union had become a
wartime ally, the publishers, Harper & Brothers of New York, decided after consultation with government officials that in the interest
of Soviet-American harmony a hostile biography of "Uncle Joe"
might better be postponed. About ten thousand copies were sealed
in a warehouse despite the protests of Mrs. Trotsky's lawyer.[1] The
work was published in 1946 when the beginnings of the Cold War
had made the Western public more receptive to an anti-Stalinist
view.[2] Although Trotsky's literary craftsmanship and firsthand
knowledge lent distinction to the work, it is the least convincing of
his "scholarly" writings. The bias, while occasionally disguised, is
obvious enough, but the vitiating flaw is his inability to portray
Stalin as anything more than a party drudge who by duplicity and
good fortune became Lenin's heir (and probably the most powerful
individual who ever lived). Whatever else he was—and Trotsky's
venomous account is often on target—he was hardly a "mediocrity"
who lacked "initiative, originality, and daring" and the capacity for
"logical thinking."

The Trotskyist movement survived the leader's death, but it remained an exotic and somewhat artificial brand of Marxism, cut off
from the real political world and surviving as a cult dedicated to the
Trotsky mystique and to his ideological legacy. As events, particularly in the Soviet Union, rendered the prophetic value of the canon
increasingly obscure or obsolete, the devotees fell upon each other
with more ferocity than they normally displayed toward the
capitalist enemy. The bitterness of sectarian squabbles is usually in
inverse ratio to the authority and influence of the practitioners.
Thus, lacking political power or any prospect of obtaining it, the
Trotskyists turned inward to uphold orthodoxy and to suppress
heresy. But which individual and which organization championed
the true faith? Opinions differed, and if Trotsky had been unable to
achieve unity among his adherents in his lifetime, then a fading
image and an ambiguous credo would hardly suffice.

The American Trotskyists held the "company name" in the form
of the Socialist Workers party, and during World War II the "headquarters" of the Fourth International were shifted to New York. In
1948 an international congress met secretly in Paris but could not
even solve the dissension among French Trotskyists, where five

groups competed for "official" recognition. The only major point of agreement—and it took several years to develop a consensus—was a minority viewpoint expressed at the congress that the new Communist states in eastern Europe were "deformed" workers' states. A new controversy broke out in 1952 when Michel Pablo, the secretary-general of the International Executive Committee, urged Trotskyists to enter Communist and Socialist parties while retaining their own political cohesion. The doctrine of "entrism" was rejected by the Socialist Workers party, among others, and the movement was split for a decade. A "unity" congress met in an undisclosed location in 1963 with delegates and observers supposedly representing twenty-six countries. But fresh discord broke out, and by the mid–1960's four "international" organizations competed for members and ideological supremacy.

The Socialist Workers party and its affiliates of the so-called United Secretariat appeared to have the best claim to legitimacy. The largest of the four, it stood for "classical" Trotskyism in supporting all "workers' states" against their capitalist foes. It was officially neutral on the Sino-Soviet split but "leaned" to the Chinese and approved the Cuban regime of Fidel Castro. The Pablo group, with representation in Italy, Belgium, and Latin America, continued to uphold the doctrine of "entrism" as politically correct, and Pablo himself served the new revolutionary government of Algeria for a time. Still another sect was headed by Gerald Healy of the Socialist Labour League of Great Britain. Critical of the major Communist governments, the "Healyites" were faced with internal dissension when a rupture occurred between the British and French sections in 1971. The most extreme Trotskyists were the pro-Chinese faction wholly dominated by the Argentinian "J. Posadas" (Homero Cristali). He forecast a workers' revolution and socialism as the logical outcome of the "inevitable" atomic war. Ironically, the only Trotskyist party to attain any political importance, that of Ceylon, was virtually read out of the movement in the early 1960's by the four "major" organizations because it allowed its members to participate in the Ceylonese government.

To nonbelievers the arcane disputes and dogmatic fervor of the Trotskyists represented only aberrant political nonsense. Yet there were moments when their aspirations merged to some extent with larger mass movements, notably the wave of student unrest that climaxed in the Paris riots in 1968 and protests in the United States against the Vietnamese War in 1970. Although Trotsky's name, quite apart from his accomplishments, was scarcely known to the student rebels, a number of their leaders openly identified with the cause of revolutionary Marxism of which Trotsky became a militant symbol. Even terrorist groups sometimes invoked his image, a development that he would surely have found insulting. When Khrushchev's propagandists chose the epithet "Trotskyite" to describe the Communist "renegades" of Peking, they delivered a backhanded, although wholly inaccurate, compliment to the pervasive influence of the genuine Trotskyists. The Soviet view of Trotskyism in more recent times was unalterably hostile: Its "final defeat . . . will come all the . . . quicker the more energetically it is shown up to be the servant of imperialist reaction. However weak Trotskyism may be, it is an enemy which has to be fought decisively and without compromise."[3]

It would be sheer fantasy to suggest that Trotsky's legacy could by itself ever inspire a revolutionary wave of the future. Classical Trotskyism, if there is such an entity, has become almost wholly irrelevant as an analysis of contemporary society, whether of a conventionally capitalist variety or of a "workers' state." Part of the irrelevance stems from classical Marxism itself, of which Trotsky was an uncritical disciple, for it too has demonstrated its limitations. Marx's theories, intended for the industrial West, have proved more applicable to agrarian and pre-industrial societies. The class-conscious proletariat, always something of a Marxist abstraction, has not become the supreme instrument of historical change; nor have other premises once accepted by revolutionary socialists, including Trotsky, stood the test of time. An illustrative example is the Marxian view of human nature, which by the standards of later and more cynical generations seems remarkably naive in its expectation that the just and humane society to be created by socialism will somehow transform ordinary beings into paragons of virtue and intellect. Unlike Lenin, who quietly jettisoned the extravagant utopianism of his *State and Revolution,* Trotsky in 1924 waxed lyrical in his vision of the new society: "Man will become immeasurably stronger, wiser and subtler; his body will become more harmonized, his movements more rhythmic, his voice more musical. The forms of life will become dynamically dramatic. The average human type will rise to the heights of an Aristotle, a Goethe, or a Marx. And beyond this ridge new peaks will rise."[4] In this quixotic passage hyperbole and revolutionary romanticism clearly overrode common sense. One cannot imagine the pragmatic Stalin writing—or even thinking—in such impetuous and evangelical terms.

Rigid and inhospitable to any suggestion that his own (or Marx's) ideas might be in need of revision, Trotsky in exile became steadily more intolerant of divergent opinions, and one of his admirers frankly admitted that his "absolute conviction that he knew the truth made him impervious to argument towards the end and detracted from his scientific spirit."[5] On points of doctrine he would brook no contradiction. Eastman found him "over-sure of all his opinions," and "when that sureness is broken, he is dismayed—his functioning is broken—he does not know how to be in doubt."[6] Eastman's rejection of the Marxian dialectic was to Trotsky unforgivable: "Dialectic training of the mind [is] as necessary to a revolutionary fighter as finger exercises to a pianist." It not only furnished the key to Marxism, "the science of the workers' movement," but to any understanding of the "internal contradictions and dynamics" of the Soviet Union.[7]

Not without reason, Trotsky took pride in his analysis of Soviet affairs. But his last comments were frequently wide of the mark. "One of the main tasks of the Fourth International," he wrote in May, 1940, was to prepare for the "revolutionary overthrow of the Moscow ruling caste. . . . The epoch of great convulsions upon which mankind has entered will strike the Kremlin oligarchy with blow after blow, will break up its totalitarian apparatus, will raise the self-confidence of the working masses and thereby facilitate the formation of the Soviet section of the Fourth International."[8] That "Stalin's Bonapartist clique" would survive a terrible war and that Stalin's heirs, not the Soviet "working masses," would denounce the dead tyrant were developments alien to Trotsky's "dialectical" thinking. His critique of Stalinist Russia was nevertheless far more profound and searching than any that Khrushchev dared to attempt. The latter failed to probe behind the "cult of personality" and, as the Italian Communist, Palmiro Togliatti, complained, he evaded the problem of "why and how Soviet society could and did reach certain forms alien to the democratic way and to the legality which it had set for itself, even to the point of degeneration." But Trotsky too was a captive of his own assumptions and after 1917 invariably drew back from any basic examination of the Bolshevik tradition. He never questioned the dictatorship of the party in the name of the proletariat, and at one point he submitted a new proposition—the infallibility of the party—from which Lenin would have demurred and which even Stalin found unpalatable. Having accepted the October Revolution as History's justification of Bolshevik policy, he went on to co-sponsor the Lenin cult (though objecting to its cruder details), a commitment that made it impolitic to object to Lenin's handiwork—the monolithic party. Outvoted and outmaneuvered, he could only raise a fuss about shortcomings in the party itself. If he had captured a majority, it seems unlikely, given his autocratic temperament, that he would have found the party wanting in "democracy" or suffering under the iron heel of a bureaucratic "machine."

The defects of Trotsky's character and personality offer more convincing reasons for his political failure than ideological deficiencies, tactical blunders, or the resolution of social forces. There is insufficient data for a psychological case study, but his abrasive and pompous manner needs no further documentation. It erected a formidable barrier to the politics of personal persuasion, and his charismatic qualities, certainly a bridge to power in a democratic country, were less useful in a one-party state. Nor is it necessary to catalog the psychosomatic complaints which recurred with regularity in times of political and personal stress. There is ample testimony, especially Trotsky's own, about these ailments—with one exception. He is known to have had periodic fainting spells, but little information of a precise nature is available. He ascribed his "susceptibility" to a trait inherited from his mother, while a boyhood friend (later a physician) diagnosed epilepsy.[9] Neither theory is convincing in the context of his other symptoms. For one presumably well versed in psychoanalytic theory it is surprising that Trotsky had such limited insight into his own psyche, although self-diagnosis is admittedly a difficult feat. It would be possible to speculate endlessly about his drives and motivations, either in the classic Freudian mold or in the more recent derivations of the psychohistorians. The one conclusion that seems reasonably obvious is that he suffered from some kind of emotional insecurity whose origin is unknown. It may have been what is popularly called an inferiority complex masked by a compulsion to prove his superiority by intellectual precociousness and a flair for the dramatic. Whatever the etiology of his neurosis, it crippled him in moments of political crisis by warping his judgment and providing an array of physical afflictions to conceal his self-doubt and indecision.

Trotsky's personality structure was certainly influenced by his Jewish heritage, but how much it contributed to his behavior pattern is a matter of conjecture. He was ambivalent about his Jewishness and at times sought to conceal it. As a young man, when asked whether he considered himself a Jew or a Russian, he replied: "Neither! I am a Social-Democrat!"[10] He persistently disavowed any knowledge of Yiddish, yet it is clear that he could speak and read the language with reasonable facility. As a Marxist he regarded himself as an emancipated "internationalist" who rejected both Judaism and his ethnic identity. Since he expected that the problem of anti-Semitism would be solved automatically with the coming of socialism, he was unsympathetic to Zionism and to the creation of a Jewish homeland in Palestine. His attitude mellowed in middle age, at first because of his realization that anti-Semitism had been a significant factor in his political defeat, and later because of the Nazi persecution of German Jews. While still denying in 1937 that the "Jewish question" could be "resolved within the framework of rotting capitalism," he conceded that "assimilation" was perhaps not the proper answer, and he took a lively interest in Jewish affairs until the time of his death.

To dwell exclusively on Trotsky's shortcomings would do an injustice to a truly remarkable man, by any reckoning one of the great revolutionary heroes of the modern age. His brilliance and virtuosity, if overly flamboyant, tended to overshadow his fellow Bolsheviks, and even Lenin, clearly Trotsky's superior as a political tactician and party leader, could not match him as an orator or writer. A proud man, he was deeply humiliated by his fall from power and his vain attempt to rally his followers. Saddened also by the death of his four children, he bore it all with dignity and stoic resignation, though in his final years there were moments of despair and even self-pity. His martyrdom came too late to stir the conscience or to create a legend for the "toiling masses" in whose name he had theoretically devoted his life.

Trotsky's career after 1921 could be written off as an unfortunate example of the intellectual in politics—the man of ideas versus the man of action. Ideas, however, should be a guide to action, and it was this subtle interplay of theory and practice that Trotsky sought

to master. He was, it is true, overly enamored of the power of ideas
and in the long run tended to confuse Marxist dogma with historical
reality. But if he had died at the close of the civil war, he would be
universally acclaimed as the supreme exemplar of the statesman-
warrior-intellectual. His record is now compromised in the land of
his birth and his great triumphs, yet the ghost of Stalinism will not
be finally exorcised until the heirs of Brezhnev rehabilitate his
memory. Whatever his ultimate fate in the Soviet Union, Trotsky
achieved History's most prized accolade as he saw it: to be remem-
bered by mankind as a "genuine revolutionary leader."

Notes and References

Chapter One

1. Leon Trotsky, *My Life* (New York, 1960), p. 142; Nadezhda K. Krupskaya, *Memories of Lenin* (New York, 1930), 1: 85; Leon Trotsky, *Lenin: Notes for a Biographer* (New York, 1971), p. 33.
2. Anatoly Lunacharsky, *Revolutionary Silhouettes* (London, 1967), p. 68.
3. Trotsky, *My Life*, p. 40.
4. Ibid., p. 65.
5. Ibid., p. 72.
6. Ibid., p. 77.
7. Ibid., p. 99.
8. Max Eastman, *Leon Trotsky: Portrait of a Youth* (New York, 1970), p. 38.
9. Eastman, pp. 46, 67; G. A. Ziv, *Trotsky: Kharakteristika* (New York, 1921), p. 15.
10. Eastman, p. 58.
11. Ibid., p. 87.
12. Trotsky, *My Life*, p. 117.
13. Eastman, p. 117.
14. Trotsky, *My Life*, p. 134.

Chapter Two

1. Trotsky, *My Life*, p. 145.
2. Trotsky, *Lenin*, p. 48; Trotsky, *My Life*, p. 151.
3. *Vtoroi syezd RSDRP, iyul-avgust 1903 goda: protokoly* (Moscow, 1959), p. 275.
4. Trotsky, *My Life*, p. 162; N. Trotsky, *Vtoroi syezd ros. sots.-dem. rabochei partii: otchet sibirskoi delegatsii* (Geneva, 1903), p. 20.
5. N. Trotsky, *Nashi politicheskia zadachi* (Geneva, 1904), p. 54.
6. Nikolay Valentinov, *Encounters with Lenin* (London, 1968), p. 55.
7. L. Trotsky, *Sochinenia* (Moscow, 1925–27), 2 (Pt. 2): 20.
8. N. Trotsky, *Do devyatovo yanvarya* (Geneva, 1905).
9. Trotsky, *Sochinenia*, 2 (Pt. 1): 203–04.

10. Leon Trotsky, *1905* (New York, 1971), pp. 113–17.

11. Max Eastman in Julien Steinberg, ed., *Verdict of Three Decades* (New York, 1950), pp. 186–87.

12. Trotsky, *1905*, pp. 48, 277–78.

13. Ibid., pp. 231–32; D. Sverchkov, *Na zarye revolyutsii* (Leningrad, 1925), pp. 174–76.

14. Trotsky, *1905*, p. 263.

15. Ibid., pp. 353, 356.

16. Ibid., pp. 384–400.

17. Ibid., p. 424.

18. Leon Trotsky, *My Flight From Siberia* (New York, 1925).

Chapter Three

1. Trotsky, *My Life*, p. 203.

2. *Nasha revolyutsia* (St. Petersburg, 1906). The final chapter received the bland title "Itogi i perspektivy" (Results and Prospects). Some of this material, but not the essay in question, appeared in *Die Russische Revolution 1905* (Dresden, 1909). A Russian edition was published in 1919, and various editions in English have since appeared, of which the most comprehensive is entitled *1905* (New York, 1971).

3. Trotsky, *My Life*, pp. 212–14.

4. V. I. Lenin, *Polnoe sobranie sochineny* (5th ed., Moscow, 1958–65), 47: 137 (hereafter cited as PSS); Krupskaya, 2: 10.

5. *Nashe slovo*, No. 15, February 14, 1915.

6. Trotsky, *My Life*, pp. 205–08.

7. Trotsky to Axelrod, February 26, 1912, Nicolaevsky Collection, Hoover Institution, Stanford University.

8. *Pravda* (Vienna), No. 21, June 25/July 8, 1911.

9. Trotsky, *My Life*, p. 218.

10. Trotsky to Axelrod, April 29, 1912, Nicolaevsky Collection; *Pravda* (Vienna), No. 25, April 23/May 6, 1912.

11. Lenin, PSS, 48: 69.

12. Quoted in Abraham Ascher, *Pavel Axelrod and the Development of Menshevism* (Cambridge, Mass., 1972), p. 295.

13. Trotsky, *My Life*, p. 234.

14. Ibid., p. 246.

15. Lenin, PSS, 26: 197, 199.

16. *Nashe slovo*, No. 218, October 19, 1915.

17. For further details see Frederick C. Griffin, "Leon Trotsky in New York City," *New York History* 49 (October 1968): 391–403, and Bernard K. Hoffer, "Trotsky in the Bronx," *Esquire* 63 (April 1965): 156–57.

18. Trotsky, *My Life*, p. 278.

19. Ibid., p. 283; Sir George Buchanan, *My Mission to Russia* (London, 1923), 2: 120–21; *Pravda*, No. 34, April 16/29, 1917. See also William Rodney, "Broken Journey: Trotsky in Canada, 1917," *Queen's Quarterly* 74 (Winter 1967): 649–65.

Chapter Four

1. Leon Trotsky, *The History of the Russian Revolution* (New York, 1936), 1: 183 (hereafter cited as *History*); Trotsky, *My Life*, p. 289.

2. *Leninsky sbornik* (Moscow, 1924–70), 4: 303.

3. Trotsky, *History*, 1: 482; Nik[olai] Sukhanov, *Zapiski o revolyutsii* (Berlin, 1922–23), 4: 193.

4. Angelica Balabanoff, *Impressions of Lenin* (Ann Arbor, Mich., 1964), pp. 126–27; Angelica Balabanoff, *My Life as a Rebel* (New York, 1938), pp. 155–56.

5. Sukhanov, 4: 231; *Pervy vserossisky syezd Sovetov R. i S. D.* (Moscow, 1930–31), 1: 354.

6. Sukhanov, 4: 424–26; F. F. Raskolnikov, *Kronshstadt i Piter v 1917 godu* (Moscow, 1925), pp. 128–30; Victor Chernov, *The Great Russian Revolution* (New Haven, Conn., 1936), p. 424. Trotsky's version may be found in *My Life*, pp. 312–13, *History*, 2: 39–42, and *Sochinenia*, 3 (Pt. 1): 198–99.

7. Trotsky, *History*, 2: 233.

8. Ibid., p. 338.

9. Sukhanov, 6: 190.

10. Lenin, PSS, 34: 262.

11. Trotsky, *Sochinenia*, 3 (Pt. 1): 322–23; Sukhanov, 6: 248–51; Trotsky, *History*, 3: 67.

12. Trotsky, *History*, 3: 73.

13. Ibid., p. 151.

14. Sukhanov, 7: 76–77.

15. Trotsky, *Sochinenia*, 3 (Pt. 2): 15, 33; Robert Paul Browder and Alexander F. Kerensky, eds., *The Russian Provisional Government, 1917* (Stanford, Calif., 1961), 3: 1767.

16. Sukhanov, 7: 79–80.

17. Ibid., pp. 90–92.

18. Trotsky, *History*, 3: 121.

19. Ibid., pp. 207–08.

20. *Den* (Petrograd), October 25 (November 7), 1917.

21. Trotsky, *Sochinenia*, 3 (Pt. 2): 52–53.

22. John Reed, *Ten Days That Shook the World* (New York, 1960), pp. 99–100.

23. Trotsky, *Lenin*, p. 95; Trotsky, *My Life*, p. 324.

24. Sukhanov, 7: 174–75.

25. Quoted in Robert V. Daniels, *Red October* (New York, 1967), p. 175.

26. Sukhanov, 7: 203; Trotsky, *History*, 3: 311.

Chapter Five

1. Trotsky, *My Life*, pp. 337–38; Trotsky, *Lenin*, p. 119.

2. *Proletarskaya revolyutsia*, No. 10 (1922), p. 62.

3. *Secret diplomatic documents and treaties* (Petrograd, 1918), p. 3; James Bunyan and H. H. Fisher, *The Bolshevik Revolution, 1917–1918: Documents and Materials* (Stanford, Calif., 1934), pp. 243–44.

4. Bunyan and Fisher, p. 259.

5. Trotsky, *Sochinenia*, 3 (Pt. 2): 214–15.

6. Trotsky, *My Life*, p. 363.

7. Richard von Kühlmann, *Erinnerungen* (Heidelberg, 1948), p. 530.

8. *Mirnye peregovory v Brest-Litovske* (Moscow, 1920), p. 102; Trotsky, *My Life*, pp. 372–73.

9. John W. Wheeler-Bennett, *The Forgotten Peace: Brest-Litovsk* (New York, 1939), p. 186; Leon Trotsky, *Stalin* (New York, 1967), pp. 248–49.

10. Trotsky, *My Life*, p. 383.

11. Count Ottokar Czernin, *In the World War* (New York, 1920), p. 274.

12. L. Trotsky, *The History of the Russian Revolution to Brest-Litovsk* (London, 1919), p. 142.

13. R. H. Bruce Lockhart, *British Agent* (Garden City, N. Y., 1933), pp. 222, 224.

14. *Protokoly tsentralnovo komiteta RSDRP(b), avgust 1917–febral 1918* (Moscow, 1958), p. 214.

15. M. Philips Price, *My Reminiscences of the Russian Revolution* (London, 1921), p. 250.

16. *Sedmoi ekstrenny syezd RKP(b), mart 1918 goda: stenografichesky otchet* (Moscow, 1962), pp. 15, 59, 72.

Chapter Six

1. James Bunyan, *Intervention, Civil War, and Communism in Russia, April-December 1918: Documents and Materials* (Baltimore, 1936), p. 91.

2. L. Trotsky, *Kak vooruzhalas revolyutsia* (Moscow, 1923–25), 1: 310.

3. Jan M. Meijer, ed., *The Trotsky Papers* (The Hague, 1964–71), 1: 70–71; Trotsky, *My Life*, p. 438.

4. Trotsky, *Kak vooruzhalas revolyutsia*, 1: 235.

5. Trotsky, *My Life*, p. 442; Trotsky, *Stalin*, p. 289.

6. *Trotsky Papers*, 1: 248–51; Trotsky, *My Life*, p. 444; Trotsky, *Stalin*, pp. 295–96.

7. S. I. Gusev, quoted in G. V. Kuzmin, *Grazhdanskaya voina i voennaya interventsia v SSSR* (Moscow, 1958), p. 236.

8. *Trotsky Papers*, 1: 604–05.

9. Ibid., pp. 618–19, 646–47, 662–63.

10. F. Dan, *Dva goda skitany* (Berlin, 1922), p. 46.

11. Trotsky, *Sochinenia*, 15: 136.

12. Trotsky, *History*, 1: 5–6.

13. *Trotsky Papers*, 2: 348–49.

14. Trotsky, *My Life*, p. 458; Trotsky, *Stalin*, pp. 328–33.

15. Norman Davies, *White Eagle, Red Star: The Polish-Soviet War*,

1919–20 (New York, 1972), pp. 218–19; Thomas Fiddick, "The 'Miracle of the Vistula': Soviet Policy versus Red Army Strategy," *Journal of Modern History* 45 (December 1973): 639–43. See also Fiddick's Ph.D. dissertation, "Soviet Policy and the Battle of Warsaw, 1920" (Indiana University, 1974).

16. Lenin, PSS, 42: 202, 226.

17. *Desyaty syezd RKP(b), mart 1921 goda: stenografichesky otchet* (Moscow, 1963), p. 356.

18. Trotsky, *Kak vooruzhalas revolyutsia,* 3 (Pt. 1): 202.

19. Leon Trotsky, "More on the Suppression of Kronstadt," *New International* (August 1938), p. 249. See also Trotsky's article, "Hue and cry over Kronstadt," *New International,* April 1938.

Chapter Seven

1. Trotsky, *My Life,* p. 467. See also Trotsky, *Stalin,* p. 357, where the incident is correctly dated.

2. Paul N. Siegel, ed., *Leon Trotsky on Literature and Art* (New York, 1970), p. 58.

3. *Trotsky Papers,* 2: 440–43.

4. Louis Fischer, *The Soviets in World Affairs* (2nd ed.; Princeton, N. J., 1951), 1: 444.

5. Leon Trotsky, *The First 5 Years of the Communist International* (New York, 1972), 1: 132.

6. *Trotsky Papers,* 2: 462–63.

7. Victor Serge, *Memoirs of a Revolutionary, 1901–1941* (London, 1963), p. 141.

8. *Protokoll des III. Kongresses der Kommunistischen Internationale* (Hamburg, 1921), pp. 86, 90, 132.

9. Trotsky, *The First 5 Years,* 1: 281.

10. *Izvestia,* December 29, 1922.

11. *Trotsky Papers,* 2: 788.

12. Trotsky, *My Life,* pp. 478–79; Leon Trotsky, *The Stalin School of Falsification* (New York, 1972), pp. 73–74.

13. Lenin, PSS, 54: 329; Trotsky, *My Life,* p. 483.

14. Trotsky, *My Life,* p. 486.

15. Trotsky to Secretariat, March 28, 1923, Trotsky Archive T792, Houghton Library, Harvard University.

16. Trotsky to Stalin, April 18, 1923, ibid., T796; Trotsky, *Stalin,* p. 363.

17. Trotsky, *My Life,* pp. 481–82.

18. *Sotsialistichesky vestnik* (Berlin), No. 11 (81), May 28, 1924, pp. 9–10. The full text has never been revealed. Extracts appeared in Max Eastman, *Since Lenin Died* (London, 1925), pp. 142–43, and in Leon Trotsky, *The New Course* (New York, 1943), pp. 153–56.

19. Boris Bajanov, *Avec Staline dans de Kremlin* (Paris, 1930), p. 77.

20. Eastman, *Since Lenin Died,* p. 145.

21. J. V. Stalin, *Sochinenia* (Moscow, 1951–52), 6: 15.

22. Ibid., 29, 32.

Chapter Eight

1. Max Eastman, *Love and Revolution* (New York, 1964), p. 415.

2. Trotsky to Max Eastman, June 7, 1933, Trotsky Manuscripts, Lilly Library, Indiana University. A puritan in his personal habits, Trotsky could not bring himself to write the Russian expletive, and Eastman supplied the proper translation in an appended note.

3. Trotsky, *Stalin*, p. 376.

4. Leon Trotsky, *The Suppressed Testament of Lenin* (New York, 1935), p. 17.

5. *Trinadtsaty syezd RKP(b), mai 1924 goda: stenografichesky otchet* (Moscow, 1963), pp. 158–59.

6. Leon Trotsky, *Lenin: Notes for a Biographer* (New York, 1971), with an Introduction by Bertram D. Wolfe.

7. Leon Trotsky, *The Stalin School of Falsification* (New York, 1962), p. 92.

8. Text of the speech in J. V. Stalin, *Sochinenia*, 6: 324–57.

9. *Pravda*, December 9, 1924.

10. Trotsky, *My Life*, p. 516.

11. "Tsel etovo obyasnenia: nash raznoglasia," Trotsky Archive T2969.

12. *Pravda*, January 20, 1925.

13. *Bolshevik*, No. 16, September 1, 1925.

14. Trotsky, *My Life*, pp. 519–20.

15. Quoted in Trotsky to Bukharin, January 9, 1926, Trotsky Archive T2976.

16. Victor Serge and Natalia Sedova Trotsky, *The Life and Death of Leon Trotsky* (New York, 1975), p. 136.

17. Trotsky, *Stalin*, p. 399; Trotsky, "Termidor i antisemitizm," February 22, 1937, Trotsky Archive T4106.

18. The quotation is from Isaac Deutscher, *The Prophet Unarmed: Trotsky, 1921–1929* (New York, 1959), p. 296, who may have embroidered the account of Serge and N. S. Trotsky, p. 149. See also *Trotsky's Diary in Exile* (New York, 1963), p. 69.

19. *Trotsky's Diary in Exile*, p. 69.

20. Leon Trotsky, *Problems of the Chinese Revolution* (New York, 1932), p. 19.

21. Trotsky Archive T3036.

22. Leon Trotsky, *The Real Situation in Russia* (New York, 1928), p. 7.

Chapter Nine

1. Trotsky, *My Life*, p. 550.

2. Ibid., pp. 560–61.

3. Eastman, *Love and Revolution*, p. 562.

4. *Trotsky's Diary in Exile*, p. 3.

5. On Trotsky's *History*, see also Robert D. Warth, "Leon Trotsky: Writer and Historian," *Journal of Modern History* 20 (March 1948): 27–41 Robert D. Warth, "On the Historiography of the Russian Revolution,' *Slavic Review* 26 (June 1967): 254–55; and Bertram D. Wolfe, "Leon Trotsky as Historian," *Slavic Review* 20 (October 1961): 495–502.

6. Serge and N. S. Trotsky, *Life and Death of Leon Trotsky*, p. 185.

7. *Writings of Leon Trotsky* [1932–33] (New York, 1972), p. 142

8. *Byulleten oppozitsii*, No. 33 (1933).

9. *Writings of Leon Trotsky* [1933–34] (New York, 1972), p. 68.

10. *Trotsky's Diary in Exile*, p. 22.

11. *Où va la France?* and *Encore une fois, où va la France?*, both published in English as *Whither France?* (New York, 1936).

12. *Trotsky's Diary in Exile*, pp. 119, 145.

13. *Vie de Lenine; Jeunesse* (Paris, 1936); *The Young Lenin* (Garden City, N.Y., 1972).

14. Serge and N. S. Trotsky, p. 202.

15. Ibid., p. 212.

16. See James T. Farrell, "Dewey in Mexico," in Sidney Hook, ed., *John Dewey* (New York, 1950).

17. *The Case of Leon Trotsky: Report of Hearings on the Charges Made Against Him in the Moscow Trials* (New York, 1968), pp. 415–16. For Beals' view of the proceedings, see his article "The Fewer Outsiders the Better," *Saturday Evening Post*, June 12, 1937.

18. *Not Guilty: Report of Commission of Inquiry into the Charges Made Against Leon Trotsky in the Moscow Trials* (New York, 1938). Reprinted with a new introduction in 1972.

19. *Leon Sedoff: Son, Friend, Fighter* (New York, 1938). The text is also available in *Writings of Leon Trotsky* [1938–39] (New York, 1969), pp. 68–73.

20. *Writings of Leon Trotsky* [1937–38] (New York, 1970), pp. 147–48.

21. *Writings of Leon Trotsky* [1938–39] (2nd ed.; New York, 1974), p. 87.

22. Ibid., pp. 272, 274, 281–82.

23. Leon Trotsky, *In Defense of Marxism* (2nd ed.; New York, 1973), p. 9.

24. Joseph Hansen, "With Trotsky to the End," in Hansen et al., *Leon Trotsky: The Man and His Work* (New York, 1969), p. 22.

Chapter Ten

1. "The Reminiscences of Cass Canfield" (1967), pp. 269–70, Oral History Project, Columbia University.

2. *Stalin: An Appraisal of the Man and His Influence* (New York, 1946). Another publisher (Stein and Day) brought out a new edition in 1967 with an Introduction by Bertram D. Wolfe.

3. M. Basmanov, *Contemporary Trotskyism: Its Anti-Revolutionary Nature* (Moscow, 1972), p. 213.

4. Leon Trotsky, *Literature and Revolution* (Ann Arbor, Mich., 1960), p. 256.

5. Serge and N. S. Trotsky, *Life and Death of Leon Trotsky*, p. 3.

6. Eastman memorandum, July 10, 1932, Trotsky Manuscripts, Indiana University.

7. Trotsky, *In Defense of Marxism*, pp. 54, 83. See also John P. Diggins, "Getting Hegel out of History: Max Eastman's Quarrel with Marxism," *American Historical Review* 79 (February 1974): esp. 65–71.

8. *Writings of Leon Trotsky [1939–40]* (New York, 1969), p. 38.

9. Trotsky, *My Life*, p. 325; Ziv, p. 33.

10. Quoted in Joseph Nedava, *Trotsky and the Jews* (Philadelphia, 1972), p. 116.

Selected Bibliography

PRIMARY SOURCES

A comprehensive bibliography of Trotsky's published writings and speeches, arranged chronologically, has been compiled by Louis Sinclair: *Leon Trotsky: A Bibliography* (Stanford, Calif., 1972). The main repository for Trotsky's unpublished work (1918–1940) is the Trotsky Archive at the Houghton Library, Harvard University. The section dealing with his exile (1929–1940) is closed until 1980. Trotsky's correspondence with Max Eastman and related material is available at the Lilly Library, Indiana University. The Nicolaevsky Collection at the Hoover Institution, Stanford University, contains a number of Trotsky manuscripts.

Trotsky's published writings are too numerous to mention individually. His *My Life* (New York, 1930) is a brilliant and indispensable autobiography despite self-serving distortions not unusual in a work of this genre. There are various editions, the most recent of which has an Introduction ("With Trotsky in Coyoacan") by Joseph Hansen (New York, 1970). His *Sochinenia* [Works] (Moscow, 1925–27), planned as a complete edition of his writings and speeches, was suspended following his expulsion from the party. Twelve volumes were published of a projected twenty-one (Vols. II and III each appeared in two parts). Another basic collection deals chiefly with the civil war period: *The Trotsky Papers, 1917–1922*, 2 vols. (The Hague, 1964–1971). Both volumes were edited and annotated by Jan M. Meijer with admirable care and expertise. The work may be supplemented by *Kak vooruzhalas revolyutsia* [How the Revolution Armed Itself], 3 vols. (Moscow, 1923–25), a collection of his military writings, speeches, and other material. See also his *Military Writings* (New York, 1969). A new edition of his work on the Revolution of 1905, including his essay on the theory of permanent revolution, may be found in *1905* (New York, 1971). The events of 1917 are the subject of his most famous work, *The Russian Revolution*, 3 vols. (New York, 1932–33). There is an abridged paperback version edited and selected by F. W. Dupee (Garden City, N.Y., 1959). His unfinished *Stalin* (New York, 1946) is a badly flawed biography but conveys the essence of Trotsky's anti-Stalinism. His *The Revolution Betrayed* (New York, 1937), a thoughtful if negative appraisal of Stalin's Russia, is less bitter than the title implies. *The Writings of Leon Trotsky* (New York, 1969–75) is a useful twelve-volume edition of his more ephemeral works (largely journalistic) covering the period from 1929 to 1940. The chief editor was George Breitman, and the volumes were published under Trotskyist auspices.

Anthologies of Trotsky's work include Irving Howe (ed.), *The Basic Writings of Trotsky* (New York, 1963), and Isaac Deutscher (ed.), *The Age of Permanent Revolution* (New York, 1964). See also Irving H. Smith (ed.), *Trotsky* (Englewood Cliffs, N.J., 1973), which contains extracts from Trotsky's work and selections about him.

SECONDARY SOURCES

1. Works about Trotsky

Surprisingly, in view of Trotsky's historical importance, there are only two serious biographies. The "definitive" work for our time is the monumental trilogy of Isaac Deutscher, *The Prophet Armed, The Prophet Unarmed,* and *The Prophet Outcast* (New York, 1954–63). Although a scholarly and literary achievement of rare distinction, the author was an independent Marxist whose admiration for his protagonist, while by no means uncritical, seldom confronted the Trotsky mystique. In some respects an anti-Marxist "answer" to Deutscher (but using much of his research), Joel Carmichael's *Trotsky: An Appreciation of His Life* (New York, 1975) is intended for the educated public rather than a scholarly audience. Its censorious tone belies its subtitle, and the generally unflattering portrayal is a useful reminder of Trotsky's defects as an individual and as a politician. The same author's two-part article, "Trotsky's Agony," in *Encounter* magazine (May and June, 1972) is more sharply focused. Victor Serge and Natalia Sedova Trotsky's *The Life and Death of Leon Trotsky* (New York, 1975) is a pietistic biography stressing the post-1929 period and helpful for personal details. Joseph Hansen and others, *Leon Trotsky: The Man and His Work* (New York, 1969), is a collection of articles by devoted Trotskyists. E. Victor Wolfenstein's *The Revolutionary Personality: Lenin, Trotsky, Gandhi* (Princeton, N.J., 1967) is a fascinating exercise in psychological biography but rather stereotyped in its orthodox psychoanalytical approach. In his *Trotsky and the Jews* (Philadelphia, 1972), Joseph Nedava emphasizes the importance of Trotsky's Jewish heritage. See also the relevant chapter in Robert S. Wistrich, *Revolutionary Jews From Marx to Trotsky* (New York, 1976). Two older works, classics of their kind, portray the prerevolutionary Trotsky: Edmund Wilson, *To the Finland Station* (New York, 1940; new ed., 1972), and Bertram D. Wolfe, *Three Who Made a Revolution* (Boston, 1955). *Trotsky: A Documentary* (London, 1972) by Francis Wyndham and David King is an excellent pictorial study in large paperback format. The accompanying text is drawn largely from Deutscher's biography.

2. Russian Marxism and the Bolshevik Revolution

Lenin and the Bolsheviks dominate, at least retrospectively, the history of Russian Social Democracy. As an independent figure Trotsky has therefore been somewhat neglected in most general accounts of Russian Marxism. However, Leonard Schapiro's *The Communist Party of the Soviet Union* (2nd ed.; New York, 1971), the standard scholarly history, devotes appropriate attention to him, as does J. L. H. Keep's *The Rise of Social Democracy in Russia* (Oxford, 1963), which carries the story to about 1907. Trotsky's relations with Lenin may be followed in Adam B. Ulam's *The Bolsheviks* (New York, 1965), the most satisfactory biography of the Bolshevik leader. See also Louis Fischer's *The Life of Lenin* (New York, 1964), an ample if somewhat sprawling work, and Robert D. Warth's *Lenin* (New York, 1973), a concise treatment. Trotsky appears, with varying degrees of prominence, in other biographies of leading Marxists: *Plekhanov* (Stanford, Calif., 1963) by Samuel H. Baron; *Martov* (London, 1967) by Israel Getzler; *Pavel Axelrod and the Development of Menshevism* (Cambridge, Mass., 1972) by Abraham Ascher; *The Merchant of Revolution* (London, 1965) on Helphand-Parvus by Z. A. B. Zeman and W. B. Scharlau; and *Rosa Luxemburg*, 2 vols. (London, 1966) by J. P. Nettl.

Trotsky's own history of the revolution is a literary masterpiece, but as objective scholarship it has been superseded by less tendentious works. William Henry Chamberlain's *The Russian Revolution*, 2 vols. (New York, 1935; new ed., 1965) is the standard general account of the revolution and civil war. Narrower in scope but an impressive new synthesis is Alexander Rabinowitch's *The Bolsheviks Come to Power: The Revolution of 1917 in Petrograd* (New York, 1976). Robert V. Daniels's *Red October* (New York, 1967) presents a "revisionist" view of the Bolshevik seizure of power. Marcel Liebman's *The Russian Revolution* (New York, 1972) is an excellent Leninist interpretation. Joel Carmichael's *A Short History of the Russian Revolution* (New York, 1964) relies heavily on Nikolai Sukhanov's firsthand account (7 vols. in the original Russian edition; abridged and translated as *The Russian Revolution* [London, 1955]). The official Stalinist history of the revolution is contained in the first two volumes of M. Gorky and others (eds.), *The History of the Civil War in the U.S.S.R.* (originally published in Moscow in 1936–42, reprinted with introductory essays by Robert D. Warth in Gulf Breeze, Fla., 1974–75). Post-Stalin histories continue to denigrate Trotsky. See, for example, P. N. Sobelev (ed.), *History of the October Revolution* (Moscow, 1966).

3. Soviet Russia: The First Decade

Trotsky's diplomatic activity as commissar for foreign affairs is covered in John W. Wheeler-Bennett, *The Forgotten Peace: Brest-Litovsk, March 1918* (New York, 1939), Robert D. Warth, *The Allies and the Russian*

Revolution (Durham, N.C., 1954; reprinted, New York, 1973), and George
F. Kennan, *Russia Leaves the War* (Princeton, N.J., 1956). There is no
specific study of Trotsky's role in the civil war. E. H. Carr's monumental *A
History of Soviet Russia* (1917–1929) (New York, 1951–   ), of which elev-
en volumes have thus far appeared, devotes much attention to Trotsky,
usually within the broader context of Soviet policy. On Trotsky's relations
with Lenin and Stalin in the early 1920's, see Moshe Lewin, *Lenin's Last
Struggle* (New York, 1968), and Adam B. Ulam's essay in his *Ideologies and
Illusions* (Cambridge, Mass., 1976). The standard biographies of Stalin
should also be consulted since they provide full accounts of the struggle for
power: Ronald Hingley, *Joseph Stalin* (New York, 1974), a skillful depiction
of the man and the ruler; Adam B. Ulam, *Stalin* (New York, 1973), a
comprehensive "life and times"; Robert C. Tucker, *Stalin As Revolutionary*
(New York, 1973), an unconventional treatment (to 1929) that stresses his
personality; and Robert D. Warth, *Joseph Stalin* (New York, 1969), a concise account. Other biographies that relate to Trotsky's activities include
Stephen F. Cohen's *Bukharin and the Bolshevik Revolution* (New York,
1973) and Warren Lerner's *Karl Radek* (Stanford, Calif., 1970). On the
political opposition and intraparty struggles, see Leonard Schapiro, *The
Origin of the Communist Autocracy* (Cambridge, Mass., 1956) and Robert
V. Daniels, *The Conscience of the Revolution* (Cambridge, Mass., 1960).
Paul Avrich's *Kronstadt 1921* (Princeton, N.J., 1970) is the best study of the
Kronstadt revolt. Richard B. Day's *Leon Trotsky and the Politics of
Economic Isolation* (Cambridge, Eng., 1973) is a closely reasoned "re-
visionist" view of Trotsky's economic policies.

There is an extensive secondary literature on Soviet foreign policy. Trots-
ky's role diminished as the decade wore on, but it may be followed in such
general works as Adam B. Ulam, *Expansion and Coexistence* (2nd ed.; New
York, 1974), and Robert D. Warth, *Soviet Russia in World Politics* (New
York, 1963). See also the valuable pioneering study on the 1917–1929
period by Louis Fischer: *The Soviets in World Affairs*, 2 vols. (new ed.,
Princeton, N.J., 1951). On the Stalin-Trotsky controversy concerning
China, Conrad Brandt, *Stalin's Failure in China, 1924–1927* (Cambridge,
Mass., 1958), is skeptical of Trotsky's claims, while a Trotskyist viewpoint is
presented in Harold R. Isaacs, *The Tragedy of the Chinese Revolution* (3rd
ed.; Stanford, Calif., 1961). The original edition (London, 1938) contains a
Preface by Trotsky. There is no specialized work on Trotsky and the Communist International, but his role is partially recorded in F. Borkenau,
World Communism (Ann Arbor, Mich., 1962), an anti-Communist interpretation, and Günther Nollau, *International Communism and World Revolution* (London, 1961), a more objective but less engaging work. See also on
the early years: James W. Hulse, *The Forming of the Communist International* (Stanford, Calif., 1964), and Albert S. Lindemann, *The 'Red Years':
European Socialism versus Bolshevism* (Berkeley, Calif., 1974). On Trotsky

and the two most important European Communist parties, consult Ruth Fischer, *Stalin and German Communism* (Cambridge, Mass., 1948); Werner Angress, *Stillborn Revolution* (Princeton, N.J., 1963); and Robert Wohl, *French Communism in the Making, 1914–1924* (Stanford, Calif., 1966).

4. Exile, Assassination, and Legacy
Other than the Deutscher and Carmichael biographies there is no extended work on the exile period. Trotsky's *Diary in Exile* (Cambridge, Mass., 1958) is revealing on his residence in France and Norway in 1935. The Soviet government published the proceedings of the three Moscow trials in English. For the most spectacular of the three, the "Bukharin trial" in 1938, see Robert C. Tucker and Stephen Cohen (eds.), *The Great Purge Trial* (New York, 1965). Robert Conquest, *The Great Terror* (2nd ed.; New York, 1973), is the most complete study of the Stalinist purge. Trotsky's testimony before the Dewey Commission is preserved in *The Case of Leon Trotsky* (New York, 1937; new ed., 1968), and the full report of the Commission was published under the title *Not Guilty* (New York, 1938; new ed., 1972). Alexander Solzhenitsyn's contemporary classic on the forced labor camps, *The Gulag Archipelago*, 2 vols. (New York, 1974–75), includes the fate of the Russian Troskyists.

On Trotsky's assassination the most useful work is that of a journalist: Isaac Don Levine, *The Mind of an Assassin* (New York, 1959). See also his *Eyewitness to History* (New York, 1973). The Mexican officer who investigated the murder, Leandro A. Sanchez Salazar (with his co-author Julian Gorkin), furnish firsthand information in *Murder in Mexico* (London, 1950). Nicholas Mosley, *The Assassination of Trotsky* (London, 1972), is a brief and well written popular account but misleadingly titled since it concerns Trotsky's whole career.

There has been little serious investigation of Trotskyist political movements. No overall survey exists, but Robert J. Alexander, *Trotskyism in Latin America* (Stanford, Calif., 1973), is a model of its kind. Frank N. Trager, *Marxism in Southeast Asia* (Stanford, Calif., 1959), contains summary information on Trotskyism in Indonesia and Indochina. Constance A. Myers, *The Prophet's Army: Trotskyists in America, 1928–1941* (Chicago, 1977), is a valuable synthesis and may be supplemented on ideological matters by John P. Diggins, *Up from Communism* (New York, 1975). Trotsky's followers have published little of consequence in book format, but Nicolas Krassó (ed.), *Trotsky: The Great Debate Renewed* (St. Louis, 1972), is a relatively high-level discussion. At the other extreme, the tedious minutiae of internecine dispute may be sampled in C. Slaughter (ed.), *Trotskyism versus Revisionism: A Documentary History*, 4 vols. (London, 1974).

Communist literature on Trotskyism seldom rises above the level of polemics. See, for example, Leo Figuères, *Le Trotskisme, cet antiléninisme* (Paris, 1969). The Soviet view is even more rigid, although the absurd charges made against Trotsky during the Stalin era have been implicitly withdrawn. V. A. Grinko and others, *The Bolshevik Party's Struggle Against Trotskyism* (Moscow, 1969), covers the period 1903–1917, and is continued in a volume with the same title by V. L. Ignatyev and others (Moscow, n.d.). *Against Trotskyism* (Moscow, 1972) is a documentary collection (1903–1927), including Lenin's writings and various party pronouncements. The burden of M. Basmanov's *Contemporary Trotskyism: Its Anti-Revolutionary Nature* (Moscow, 1972) is self-explanatory.

Index